Learner-Focused Feedback

For every educator who continuously strives to grow and positively impact learners every day—you never cease to inspire us.

Praise for *Learner-Focused Feedback*

"A leader's most important job is to help teachers understand their impact on student learning. Collecting evidence of learning through observation is a difficult skill to master, but Tepper and Flynn have given us the tools we need in this essential new resource."

John Hattie
Graduate School of Education,
University of Melbourne, Australia

"Learning is incredibly complex. Observing classrooms in order to help teachers grow deserves careful and informed consideration of many integrated parts. I'm grateful to have this excellent book as a cornerstone resource in my work to support teachers."

Julie Stern
Author of *Tools for Teaching Conceptual Understanding*

"*Learner-Focused Feedback*, Tepper and Flynn's companion book to *Feedback to Feed Forward*, delves deeply into student learning, how to observe, which questions to ask, and strategies that lead to next steps. The book is a treasure of resources. Children, teachers, and coaches are the winners here. I have never read such a thorough discourse on learning. After 26 years outside of the classroom, it makes me want to go back."

Claudia Frandsen
Director, Leadership Support Services
Ventura County Office of Education

"Tepper and Flynn's *Learner-Focused Feedback* delivers the educational framework necessary to develop a school culture that fosters and embraces teaching and learning for impact. Evidence-based feedback that focuses on the learner is the ultimate approach to not only empower educators to be intentional with every detail of their instruction. It also guides the observer to provide feedback from a growth mindset perspective. I believe *Learner-Focused Feedback* will create the structures to build a school culture based on trust to allow room for promoting educational equity and student achievement."

Miladys Cepero-Perez
Professional Learning Designer and Educational Consultant working on her PhD at
Florida Atlantic University in Educational Leadership

"*Learner-Focused Feedback: 19 Strategies to Observe for Impact* is a must-read for all administrators and instructional leaders. What a gem! I have quoted, cited, and used this book for my own growth as a school leader observing teachers. The knowledge, experience, and research contained in the pages guides my walk-throughs, from the foundational understanding that "a culture of observation and feedback drives a culture of learning" to the essential second strategy, to define "learning," and beyond to the strategies on how to adapt evidence collection during an observation. There are not many books that are as practical as *Learner-Focused Feedback*. It is an indispensable book if you want to observe for impact."

Kjell Fenn
Headmaster, New Covenant Academy and author of
Engage: Motivational Strategies for a Dynamic Classroom

"*Learner-Focused Feedback: 19 Strategies to Observe for Impact* is an essential how-to guide for educators seeking professional growth in the area of observation and feedback. Amy Tepper and Patrick Flynn flawlessly weave classroom examples with strategies for evidence collection that serves as a learning tool and sets the tone for an effective, meaningful conversation. They remind us that observation is not always about evaluation. Using observation and evidence-based feedback for professional growth builds a culture of learning. This book will show you how!

Whether you're a teacher, instructional coach, or administrator, Tepper and Flynn guide you through strategies to plan for and adapt to student interactions during an observation in order to improve the quality of feedback for the teacher. Simply put, this book is delicious. Try it in digestible bites through the chapters or all at once for the big picture."

April Strong
District Instructional Coach
Martin County School District, Stuart, FL

"Every school and district have processes in place for classroom observations that can range from peer coaching, informal observations, learning walks, and formal evaluations. These processes are most meaningful when the observer(s) can truly gather information on how instruction, strategies, practices, environment, curricula, and goals *impact student learning*. In *Learner-Focused Feedback,* Tepper and Flynn mix the right balance of research, practice, and experience in thousands of classrooms to help observers focus and adapt to what is happening in the classroom to truly understand what students are actually learning. The feedback that can emerge from these adaptive and effective observation practices can most certainly help teachers move their practice forward and in turn improve student learning!"

Kevin J. Hanlon
K–8 Curriculum Coordinator, Cheshire Public Schools, CT

"*Learner-Focused Feedback: 19 Strategies to Observe for Impact* serves as an essential field guide for supporting teaching and learning in all classrooms. This book highlights why observation and feedback of classroom practice serve as key levers for improving student outcomes and cultivating a culture of learning. This is the first book that provides the context of adapting evidence collection strategies *during* a classroom visit making it a must read for anyone supporting teachers through observation and feedback. Tepper and Flynn make their own learning (metacognitive processing) visible and show readers how to advance evidence-collection practices. The inclusion of examples of collected evidence followed by *stop and think* prompts provides opportunities for reflection and development of observation practices for administrators, coaches and classroom teachers alike."

Robert Testa
Assistant Superintendent, Vernon Public Schools, CT

"Every leader knows that educators need high quality feedback. *Learner-Focused Feedback: 19 Strategies to Observe for Impact* is the practical guide that gives exemplary examples and tools to actually give feedback to move teachers to better instruction."

Mollie Sullivan Raab
Associate Administrator
Independent School District 622
North St. Paul, Maplewood, and Oakdale, MN

Learner-Focused Feedback

19 Strategies to Observe for Impact

Amy Tepper and Patrick Flynn

FOR INFORMATION:

Corwin
A SAGE Company
2455 Teller Road
Thousand Oaks, California 91320
(800) 233-9936
www.corwin.com

SAGE Publications Ltd.
1 Oliver's Yard
55 City Road
London EC1Y 1SP
United Kingdom

SAGE Publications India Pvt. Ltd.
B 1/I 1 Mohan Cooperative Industrial Area
Mathura Road, New Delhi 110 044
India

SAGE Publications Asia-Pacific Pte. Ltd.
18 Cross Street #10-10/11/12
China Square Central
Singapore 048423

Publisher: Arnis Burvikovs
Development Editor: Desirée A. Bartlett
Senior Editorial Assistant: Eliza Erickson
Production Editor: Tori Mirsadjadi
Copy Editor: Jared Leighton
Typesetter: C&M Digitals (P) Ltd.
Proofreader: Lawrence W. Baker
Indexer: Maria Sosnowski
Cover Designer: Scott Van Atta
Marketing Manager: Sharon Pendergast

Printed in the United States of America

Library of Congress Cataloging-in-Publication Data

Names: Tepper, Amy, author. | Flynn, Patrick (Patrick W.), author.

Title: Learner-focused feedback : 19 strategies to observe for impact / Amy Tepper, Patrick Flynn.

Description: Thousand Oaks, California : Corwin, a SAGE company, [2020] | Includes bibliographical references and index.

Identifiers: LCCN 2019038870 | ISBN 9781544368269 (paperback) | ISBN 9781544368276 (epub) | ISBN 9781544368283 (epub) | ISBN 9781544368290 (pdf)

Subjects: LCSH: Teachers—Rating of—United States. | Teacher effectiveness—United States. | Teaching—United States—Evaluation. | Effective teaching—United States. | Observation (Educational method) | Feedback (Psychology)

Classification: LCC LB2838 .T46 2020 | DDC 371.14/4—dc23
LC record available at https://lccn.loc.gov/2019038870

This book is printed on acid-free paper.

20 21 22 23 24 10 9 8 7 6 5 4 3 2 1

Contents

List of Online Resources xi

Feedback to Feed Forward Strategies xiii

Preface xv

Acknowledgments xix

About the Authors xxi

Chapter 1: Why Observe for Impact? 1

Building a Culture of Learning 3
Building a Culture of Observation and Feedback 8
The Skills of Observation 13
Teachers as Learners 18
Leaders Leading Learning 20
Strategy 1: Mindfully plan for effective observation and feedback 21
What's Ahead 26

Chapter 2: What Do You Need to Understand About Learning? 29

Understanding the Concept of Learning 32
Strategy 2: Define *learning* 34
Overarching Goals for All Learners 35
Strategy 3: Create goals for all learners 36
Our Three Goals 37
Cautions for Observers 41
How the Brain Works 48
Strategy 4: Understand how learners learn 48
Identifying Learning in Action 53
Strategy 5: Understand how teachers create outcomes 54
Recognizing Impact on Learning 54
Determining Causal Attribution 61
Give It a Try 64
What's Ahead 66

Chapter 3: How Can You Prepare for Evidence Collection? 67
Preobservation Planning 69
Planning Your Tools 70
Planning by Using Expectations 72
Strategy 6: Plan evidence collection based on your framework 73
Planning to Interact With Learners 75
Planning Using Learning Goals 81
Planning Based on Disciplines 82
Strategy 7: Plan evidence collection based on discipline-specific expectations 84
Planning Based on Standards 90
Give It a Try 92
What's Ahead 93

Chapter 4: How Can You Adapt Evidence Collection Upon Arrival? 95
Your Goals as an Observer 96
Adapting 101: The Basics 99
Metacognition in Motion 102
Strategy 8: Purposefully choose your evidence collection methods 103
Making It Count 107
Strategy 9: Engage in conversations through questions 108
Strategy 10: Set high expectations for responses 109
Timing Is Everything 111
Strategy 11: Use what you know about the timing of your arrival 111
Using the Learning Goals 117
Foundational Understandings 120
Strategy 12: Interact to determine prior learning 120
Strategy 13: Interact to determine relevance and context 124
Strategy 14: Interact to determine understanding of essential vocabulary 128
Student Ability to Meet Expectations 130
Give It a Try 131
What's Ahead 132

Chapter 5: How Can You Adapt Evidence Collection as a Lesson Unfolds? 133
Observing for Learning 138
Observing for Causal Attribution and Impact 145
Observing for Good Struggle 149
Adapting During an Observation 152

Adapting Based on Active Engagement 153
Strategy 15: Adapt based on what students are doing 153
Strategy 16: Adapt based on what students are writing 159
Student Notes 159
Mid-Lesson or End-of-Task/End-of-Lesson Reflections 161
Adapting Based on Tools and Resources 165
Strategy 17: Adapt based on what students are using (or not using) 165
Adapting Based on Discourse 172
Strategy 18: Adapt based on student conversations and group work 172
Strategy 19: Adapt based on teacher–student interactions 174
Give It a Try 176
What's Ahead 177

Chapter 6: How Do You Cultivate a Culture of Learning? 179

Building a Culture of Learning 180
Developing Feedback About Impact 182
Building Trust 191
Making a Culture Shift 194
The Six Steps 198
Final Thoughts 209

Strategies List 211

List of Figures 213

References 217

Index 223

Visit the companion website at
resources.corwin.com/learnerfocusedfeedback
for downloadable resources.

Note From the Publisher: The authors have provided web content for this book that is available to you through a QR (quick response) code. To read a QR code, you must have a smartphone or tablet with a camera. We recommend that you download a QR code reader app that is made specifically for your phone or tablet brand.

List of Online Resources

Learner-Focused Feedback Book Study

Chapter 1

Resource 1.1: ReVISION Learning Supervisory Continuum

Resource 1.2: The Big Picture for Evidence Collection

Chapter 2

Resource 2.1: Learner-Focused Feedback Sample

Chapter 3

Resource 3.1: Focus Area Questions

Chapter 4

Resource 4.1: Adapting 101

Resource 4.2: Potential First Assumptions

Resource 4.3: Focus Area Evidence Collection

Chapter 5

Resource 5.1: Observation Example: Pulling Strategies Together

Chapter 6

Resource 6.1: Observation and Feedback Self-Assessment and Resource Alignment

Resource 6.2: Feedback Provider and Receiver Dispositions

Resource 6.3: Feedback on Feedback Survey

Visit the companion website at
resources.corwin.com/learnerfocusedfeedback
for downloadable resources.

Feedback to Feed Forward Strategies

Strategy 1 • Understand the structure

Strategy 2 • Understand the connections

Strategy 3 • Understand the research

Strategy 4 • Identify challenging phrases

Strategy 5 • Identify key levers

Strategy 6 • Engage in the *behavioralization* process

Strategy 7 • Develop an awareness

Strategy 8 • Observe with a wide lens

Strategy 9 • Collect a balance of evidence with purpose

Strategy 10 • Place yourself where the learning is occurring

Strategy 11 • Do what it takes to collect evidence

Strategy 12 • Be comprehensive in your collection of evidence

Strategy 13 • Maximize the use of your notepad or tablet

Strategy 14 • Listen to teaching and learning

Strategy 15 • View learning in action

Strategy 16 • Interact with learners

Strategy 17 • Organize your evidence

Strategy 18 • Ask questions about what you observed

Strategy 19 • Determine causes of outcomes

Strategy 20 • Focus on the overall observed impact on student learning and engagement

Strategy 21 • Use the instructional framework to recognize expectations

Strategy 22 • Use what you know about research-based strategies
Strategy 23 • Use framework language to develop claims about practice
Strategy 24 • Cite quantitative and qualitative data
Strategy 25 • Incorporate the impact on the learners
Strategy 26 • Move away from summarizing or listing
Strategy 27 • Incorporate evidence-based areas of growth and strength
Strategy 28 • Determine an accurate root cause
Strategy 29 • Use key levers for next steps
Strategy 30 • Use logic
Strategy 31 • Build on teachers' needs and strengths

Preface

When we finished writing *Feedback to Feed Forward* in January of 2019, we were already well into the draft of this book. We realized our work in supporting those who support teachers through observation and feedback was not done.

We asked ourselves if we were overcomplicating things. Friends and colleagues asked us why the first book was so long, seeking guides that were shorter, quicker reads. Well-respected thought leaders, long in the field, told us that this work is simple: Observers should just seek to answer whether students are learning.

Yet we have spent day after day (and year after year) with observers—intelligent, well read, advanced-degreed teachers, coaches, and administrators—who are not sure how to answer this question. It is not a simple question, and therefore, it is not simple to answer. Observing to determine how and if students are learning is complex because the concept of learning is complex. Observing for *why* this is occurring or not or how the teacher is impacting learners is even more complex. *Feedback to Feed Forward* (2019) and this book, *Learner-Focused Feedback* (2020), are written for all observers who recognize that this is complex and important work—that feedback must support teachers as learners with a focus on impact.

We know the quality of evidence collected while observing is directly related to the quality of the feedback. Observers we support through embedded sessions and collaborative classroom visits have begged for the "magic list of questions" that we ask learners. (*Spoiler:* We adapt our list every time we step into a classroom, but Chapter 3 will get you started with a comprehensive list of possible questions.) We watch as observers run through a litany of questions, move quickly around a room to maximize time, and leave a classroom with pages of notes yet are still unable to clearly determine if students were engaged and learning, to what level, and why.

Building on our foundational standards of effective observation and feedback and twenty-one core skills introduced in *Feedback to Feed Forward*,

Learner-Focused Feedback offers new strategies for engaging with learners in a variety of ways within different instructional structures. This book is meant to serve as a companion or extension to our first book and to welcome a new audience—teachers as observers—both of their own classrooms and those of their colleagues. Whereas our first book addressed the roles of observers and administrators, we've made extensive efforts in this book to address the additional needs of teachers as their own observers and as observers and mentors to their peers.

If you are holding this book, we expect that you have been reflecting on the actions you take during an observation and the quality of your feedback. Whether you are a veteran or just beginning as an observer, you might find yourself facing challenges, such as the following:

- You have the sense that you are not collecting enough data from students.
- You are missing evidence.
- Your feedback statements lack specificity.
- You are unable to clearly determine a teacher's effectiveness and impact on engagement and learning.

These challenges are common and most likely due to how you are collecting evidence of the *learning* occurring during a lesson. If those challenges resonate, then this book is for you. This book will serve as an explicit "how to" for collecting evidence during a classroom visit and for video observations.

Regardless of your experience level or role, we suggest reading the chapters in order, though we know this will require time, patience, and dedication to the process. As a result of reading this book, we expect you will improve your ability to effectively observe for impact to support teachers with learner-focused feedback. More specifically, you will be able to do the following:

1. Identify outcomes we are seeking for our students as global citizens (Chapter 1)
2. Recognize what *learning* means and how students learn (Chapter 2)
3. Plan evidence collection in order to observe for learning (Chapter 3)
4. Modify and adjust evidence collection approaches at the beginning and as the lesson progresses or learning unfolds (Chapters 4 and 5)
5. Conduct an analysis to develop feedback that supports teachers in understanding their impact based on evidence (Chapter 6)
6. Set a plan in motion to build a culture of observation and feedback to drive a culture of learning (Chapter 6)

Each chapter begins with an essential question, and throughout each chapter, you will find authentic classroom examples, observer think alouds, and detailed graphics and tables, in addition to stop-and-think questions that will allow you to reflect on your own practices. We also provide supplemental online resources for support found at **resources.corwin.com/learnerfocusedfeedback**. In Chapters 2 through 5, we begin with a field story and end with suggestions found under the section titled "Give It a Try," for specific next steps based on your role. All of these tools will set you up for success and will open the door for rich discussion within your team.

Your practice as an observer will improve by reading this book, but you may find you benefit from taking the time to build the foundations from the first book at some point. If you are jumping in with us without having read *Feedback to Feed Forward*, we provide a list of the original thirty-one strategies in the front matter of this book and an overview of essential understandings in Chapter 1.

Ultimately, the strategies offered in this book are bigger than just observation. Readers who implement these strategies will become stronger members of a learning community (students, teachers, coaches, and administrators) focused on impact as they learn to own their own learning.

Clearly, we did not succeed at creating a short guide because that is not what you needed. You needed us to recognize the complexity of the work of an observer and to help you break it down into manageable pieces. This book was not written to be read in one sitting. It will take time to master the strategies included. Put the book down (not back on the shelf!) every so often to try out the strategies in real classrooms or while watching video lessons. Ask yourself as an observer, "How did that go?" Call or e-mail us with questions—we live for talking about instruction (www.tepperandflynn.com)! We are hoping you work through each chapter placing stickies, writing in margin notes, and highlighting text for rereads. We hope you revisit sections as you practice new strategies, share your learning with your team . . . and, most importantly, that you come to rely on this book as a valuable resource for understanding the teaching and learning occurring in your classrooms and how to support teachers with learner-focused feedback.

Acknowledgments

We would like to express our gratitude to Corwin and must especially thank Desirée Bartlett, Ariel Curry, and Eliza Erickson on the editing team and Tori Mirsadjadi, Jared Leighton, and the entire production team. We know we required a great deal of patience, support, and guidance along the way. We also continue to be grateful for our senior editor, Arnis Burvikovs, for believing in us, always telling us like it is, and giving us the opportunity to meet many other authors in the Corwin family (and beyond). All the best as you start your new adventures in retirement as this goes to print. We will miss you. Our writing and work have grown as a result of all of you through your encouragement and counsel.

We are thankful for friends and colleagues who tirelessly read our drafts and support our vision, especially Bob Testa, who upon reading said, "This one is better than the first one!" and our loudest cheerleader and behind-the-scenes organizer, Amanda Van Blaricom, who has read and reread draft after draft. You never let us forget what we are offering to the world! We would still be living in our drafts if it were not for Maureen Armstrong, our scrupulous copy editor and comma cop. We were highly disappointed to find we still have not mastered an em dash and failed miserably at knowing when to use *that* or *which*. We are thrilled to know we still have you to catch our mistakes.

We are grateful for our families and friends who just spent another year wondering where we were and why we weren't returning calls. Thank you for your continued love and support.

Patrick would like to acknowledge his son, Galen. This book will arrive on the shelves as you are preparing to leave for college. Thank you for always reminding me of what it takes to achieve a goal through dedication and commitment. I hope this can be a reminder to you that anything is possible.

Amy would like to remember Bobbi, who would have been thrilled to see a second book of ours on her shelf. Thank you for inspiring excellence and a love of reading and writing.

Lastly, we would like to recognize the leaders, coaches, and teachers we meet each day who strive to improve teaching and learning in their schools, regions, and districts. These educators recognize the need not only to create supportive and productive learning environments for students but also to live by the idea that we are better together. Thank you for all you do. You are the reason we get up every day.

Publisher's Acknowledgments

Corwin gratefully acknowledges the contributions of the following reviewers:

Shelly Allen
Field Supervisor, Clinical Instructor
Beaumont, TX

Ray Boyd
Principal
Western Australia

Sister Camille Anne Campbell
President, Academy
New Orleans, LA

David G. Daniels
High School Principal
Conklin, NY

Donna Fong
Clinical Instructor, Graduate Studies, Educational Leadership
Beaumont, TX

Judith Hayn
Professor of Teacher Education
Little Rock, AR

Nicky Kemp
Assistant Superintendent
Auxvasse, MO

Lena Marie Rockwood
Assistant Principal
Revere, MA

About the Authors

Amy Tepper has served as a teacher, administrator, and program director in various K–12 settings and start-ups that include virtual, home school, blended, and public schools. She held the position of executive director of a Sylvan Learning Center; opened an alternative sixth- through twelfth-grade school in Okaloosa County, Florida; and later was actively engaged in Florida high school redesign and career education reform, providing technical assistance across the state. Amy had the opportunity to collaborate with a team of parents to develop the Ohana Institute, an innovative blended school, focused on global citizenship and discovery learning, serving as director in its first year. As a consultant, she provided instructional and administrative coaching at an international school in Panama until 2013 when she returned to support schools in the U.S. Amy has since completed countless classroom observations through work as a peer validator, evaluating practices in Newark and New Haven schools, and in providing embedded, ongoing support for instructional leaders and teachers in the areas of high-quality observation, feedback, and teaching and learning. She is the coauthor of *Feedback to Feed Forward: 31 Strategies to Lead Learning* (Corwin, 2019).

Patrick Flynn has worked as a teacher, teacher leader, curriculum director, coach, and executive program director in K–12 settings in over eleven different states. As the executive director of high schools for Edison Schools and the chief academic officer for Great Schools Workshop in Sacramento, California, Patrick worked with building and district administrations in nine states to implement systemic high school reform. In his coaching and as a professional development director for a Regional Service Center in CT, he provided professional learning in the areas of transformational leadership, performance management systems, standards-driven instruction, and data-driven decision making. Patrick is founder and executive director of ReVISION Learning Partnership, providing professional development and support to districts and educational organizations in Connecticut, New York, New Jersey, and Louisiana since 2010. He has led several school improvement initiatives in rural and urban settings and supported school reform internationally in the United Arab Emirates with the Abu Dhabi Education Council. He has presented nationally and internationally, including as a keynote speaker at the Forum on Big Data at the Tianjin University of Technology, in Tianjin, China. Patrick is highly sought after for his leadership in providing the highest-quality professional-learning opportunities for teachers, administrators, and district personnel. He is the coauthor of *Feedback to Feed Forward: 31 Strategies to Lead Learning* (Corwin, 2019).

1 Why Observe for Impact?

"Education is the kindling of a flame, not the filling of a vessel."

—Socrates

Educators are a unique breed. We get up at the crack of dawn every day to make a difference, to kindle flames, to inspire, not just our students but our colleagues, our leaders, and teachers around us. If you are an educator reading this, you are seeking answers for how to make a greater difference in the lives of the learners around you, including yourself. You are working to drive change and promote growth, and we welcome you to this journey.

We wrote *Feedback to Feed Forward* (2019) with a sense of urgency in order to ensure that teachers everywhere received the high-quality feedback they needed and deserved and that their instructional leaders could develop the skills to provide that feedback. Readers of that book are now *feeding forward*, meaning their observation and feedback

- go beyond summarizing events to providing an analysis of effectiveness,

- allow teachers to accurately and clearly see how they are impacting learners, and
- lead to improved reflection, instructional practices, and student outcomes.

But we knew we had much more we could share. We wrote this new book to extend the skills of instructional leaders and concentrated on what we were noticing about continued skill gaps and challenge areas, responding to what those leaders were requesting of us—new strategies to build on their capacity, especially for the interaction with students during classroom visits. In addition, we are inviting a new reader—teachers who attend to student learning every day and who ideally support each other through peer-to-peer observations.

Frequent classroom observation and feedback—whether conducted by a supervisor, coach, department chair, or peer—that is learner centered (focused on our students) and learning focused (focused on the teacher as a learner) can drive change and growth in our schools. The skill set required for collecting evidence from students is a difficult one to master. We wrote this book to provide guidance for that work.

Here you will find nineteen strategies that will allow you to determine

- to what degree learning is occurring during lessons and, most importantly,
- why or how the teacher is impacting observed outcomes.

We expect whether you are a leader, coach, or teacher, you will find this book to be a highly accessible how-to guide. In several of our districts, teachers are participating in the same rigorous observation and feedback training as their leaders to ensure they too can serve as highly impactful supports. Beyond this, teachers who learn the skills of observation, evidence collection, and feedback and observe for learning in each other's classrooms can refine practices for their own ongoing checks for understanding and develop a newfound awareness with their own students. You will begin to analyze student learning in action more extensively and recognize the instructional practices and environments that serve to increase levels of student engagement and deeper learning. These are the first steps toward the creation of a culture of learning in a school that drives the actions and beliefs of all who impact students' lives each day.

Building a Culture of Learning

How can we ensure that teachers, coaches, leaders, and students are interacting within and supported by an environment of learning, ensuring a collective mission, purpose, and implementation towards student success?

We have been inspired by the educators who ensure that every experience (from the classroom and building to the district level) is focused on learning and what is best for learners. In order to understand and cultivate this type of culture of learning, we must first define school culture. Great Schools Partnership (2013), a leading school reform organization in the northeast United States, defines it as the beliefs, perceptions, relationships, attitudes, and written and unwritten rules that shape and influence every aspect of how a school functions.

In a school with a strong **culture of learning**

- ✓ There is a firmly rooted *collective belief* that everyone has the ability to learn (Hattie & Zierer, 2018)
- ✓ A *growth mindset* (Dweck, 2006) permeates the school halls and walls
- ✓ Staff's *perception of their current performance and understanding of their impact* is accurate
- ✓ Staff and student *relationships* are based on a collaborative approach to learning
- ✓ *Policies and procedures* are designed through the lens of supporting systems and structures that ensure learning for all

A **culture of observation and feedback** drives a culture of learning. The strategies in this book directly support the first three items by building the capacity of all observers to provide accurate assessments of teacher effectiveness through observation and feedback. This collective ability, in turn, serves to promote the development of the fourth and fifth bulleted attributes. In Chapter 6, we leave you with specific suggestions related to all five attributes so that limitations in relationships, collaboration, or systems do not go unaddressed as these can surely impact the growth of a culture of learning.

Impacting Self-Belief

Fundamental to the establishment of a culture of learning, leaders and teachers must possess a belief in their own abilities related to student success.

Albert Bandura (1994) defined self-efficacy as *the belief in one's capacity to execute the courses of action that will lead to attainment of an outcome or some achieved success*. We know from Hattie (2017) (and our own time in classrooms) that the practice of building student self-efficacy leads to positive outcomes, with a significant effect size (.92). Through high-quality observation and feedback, we have found we can directly address and provide opportunities to promote what Bandura (1994) identifies as the four sources of self-efficacy. Let's break down the relationships demonstrated in Figure 1.1.

FIGURE 1.1: PATHWAYS TO PROFESSIONAL GROWTH

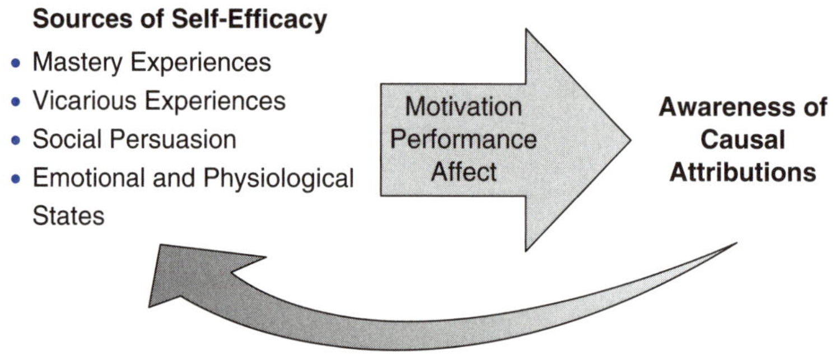

According to Bandura (1994), one's self-efficacy is determined by the following:

> **Mastery experiences:** Opportunities to engage in actions with success. When we do something well, we continue to build our confidence and capacity.
>
> **Vicarious experiences:** Opportunities to witness others engaged in actions who are successful, especially those people we consider similar to ourselves.
>
> **Social persuasion:** Opportunities to receive boosts of verbal encouragement about our capacity to succeed.
>
> **Emotional and physiological states:** Opportunities to reduce the stress associated with potential failure and to improve physical and emotional states of mind and being.

As individuals experience or interact within each of these contexts, they experience increases in motivation and performance, along with a positive affect.

As we are seeking to support teachers' self-efficacy through our approaches to observation and feedback, we must seek to draw conclusions with teachers about the causal attributions—or how they are causing or impacting observed student outcomes. These moments, over time, can act as efficacy boosters. For example, an observer may help a teacher understand how her use of a small-group intervention during a math workshop increased the number of students able to successfully complete independent work. This provides her with a new level of understanding as she engages in that strategy again and an increased level of efficacy from the mastery experience. If she is provided with an opportunity to see others engage in that same teaching strategy vicariously, she is now seeing it with a new level of understanding and so on. New learning becomes cyclical in its influence on efficacy. Teachers become more aware of and empowered by an understanding of causal attributions (impact). They recognize what is within their control, and self-efficacy increases.

Unfortunately, many teachers receive often cursory, general, or nonactionable feedback in the form of a summary of teaching that does not promote reflection or analysis of impact as a result of observations, and this can set them up for failure. They may be given action steps or be told to *differentiate*—an enormous endeavor for most—without being provided with the necessary data to reflect on or discuss which students require differentiation and why, nor any support or resources as to how to meet those students' needs. *To differentiate* is not a bite-sized and attainable next step (nor is "develop clear and rigorous learning targets" or "turn learning over to students").

Though never an observer's intent, you can actually decrease efficacy through feedback. This will occur when teachers who seek to grow do not know how to move forward or recognize why they need to make a specific change. Additionally, you can diminish belief in ability when teachers lack a clear understanding of necessary building blocks or long-term steps to achieve desired outcomes. The real diminisher can lie in a lack of understanding *in how long it might take* for new instructional practices to become refined to fully influence student outcomes.

> It is more difficult to instill high beliefs of personal efficacy by social persuasion alone than to undermine it. Unrealistic boosts in efficacy are quickly disconfirmed by disappointing results of one's efforts. But people who have been persuaded that they lack capabilities tend to avoid challenging activities that cultivate potentialities and give up quickly in the face of difficulties. By constricting activities and undermining motivation, disbelief in one's capabilities creates its own behavioral validation. Successful efficacy builders do more than convey positive appraisals. In addition to raising people's beliefs in their capabilities, they [observers/feedback providers] structure situations for them in ways that bring success and avoid placing people in situations prematurely where they are likely to fail often (Bandura, 1994).

Two important lessons should be derived from this research as you begin your journey toward creating a culture of learning through observation and feedback. We can increase teachers' levels of self-efficacy if we do the following:

- ✓ Devote energy and resources toward building the skill set of the observer to ensure high-quality observations are rooted in specific evidence and lead to honest, specific, and practical feedback. Up to this point, we are consistently failing observers by inserting them into a feedback cycle without proper training and ongoing support—hence the urgency for both *Feedback to Feed Forward* (2019) and this book.
- ✓ Recognize and convey to all stakeholders that the consistent execution of high-quality observations and feedback within a cycle will take time to establish and that no shift in culture within a school occurs simply or without challenge.

Impacting Collective Belief

We know that we are more powerful together. We also know from Goddard, Hoy, and Hoy (2004) and John Hattie (2017) that **collective teacher efficacy**—a collective belief of teachers in their ability to positively affect students—has a significant effect size (1.57) and is, in fact, the greatest influence on student achievement as of this date. It is important to note that simply having an individual on a team with a high level of self-efficacy does not necessarily translate to a collective belief in that group or in collective teacher efficacy. But leaders can support teachers who collaborate from a place of high self-efficacy who are equipped with an understanding of *why* they are being successful or not. Imagine the potential of, say, PLCs and data teams when the group is focused on the causal relationships being identified routinely in classrooms through observation and feedback, building a more accurate picture of effective teaching and learning. The consistent identification of these relationships begins to form a basis of belief in one's capacity as well as the group's ability to impact students.

Hattie and Zierer (2018) identify a set of beliefs or "10 Mindframes for Visible Learning" that serve to influence collective teacher efficacy. These should drive every decision and every action taken within a school. Five mindframes for visible learning that propel our thinking and work every day include the following:

Your teachers believe . . .

1. their fundamental task is to **evaluate the effect of their teaching** on student learning and achievement

2. success and failure in student learning **is about what they did or did not do because they are change agents**
3. it is important to **talk more about the learning** than teaching
4. assessment is about **impact**, and
5. they can have a positive impact on **all learners**.

These mindframes are rooted in a system in which everyone in the school is a collaborator in improving teaching and learning and are, in fact, "responsible for its success" (Hattie, 2012, p. 170).

These mindframes begin with a belief, prevalent in every action taken by adult and student alike, that not only *can every student and adult learn* but that *they indeed have the ability to do so*. Albert Bandura's (1994) work has helped us to recognize the difference between the simple belief of "I can learn" and the concept of self-efficacy: "I have the ability to execute the courses of action that will allow me to successfully navigate that learning." We often speak about the fact that we need to believe all have the capacity to learn, but what about the ability to learn? "This is built on skill, and students need to be taught how to think about their own thinking and how to act upon their learning" (Fisher & Frey, 2013, p. 98). Ability is based on application of the necessary skills, taking action toward new learning. While Fisher and Frey were speaking of students, the same applies to adults within our schools.

However, in our thinking about observation and what teachers have experienced through evaluation and supervision, we know observers, at times, default to the negative or nonimpact of the teacher (like a "gotcha"), citing only practices that produced less-than-effective outcomes. In fact, we see—and it is essential to highlight routinely—the positive impact of a teacher's actions on students. Teachers need to build on their strengths, reflect on how choices and strategies are creating positive outcomes, and continue effective practices. Either positive or negative, effective or ineffective, significant or insignificant, these are the causal attributions we seek by asking "Why?" when considering outcomes and learners. These are at the center of what helps a teacher learn and grow. (We devoted two full chapters in *Feedback to Feed Forward* to the skills related to the practice of building on strengths, if this is an area of need for you.)

Stop and Think: How has feedback you have received about your performance helped you to change practice and impacted your level of self-efficacy? Were you able to understand cause–effect relationships and shift your practice as a result of the feedback? Why, or why not?

Building a Culture of Observation and Feedback

Quality observation of classroom practice with resultant feedback is a key driver in the shift toward a culture of learning if—and only if—the focus of the evidence collected is on student learning and teacher impact and it occurs frequently. Marshall and Marshall (2017, pp. 26, 27) recommend frequent "10- to 15-minute classroom visits" (miniobservations) in order to ensure we, as observers, understand "what is really happening in classrooms," building coaching points and "spreading suggestions over 10 or so visits throughout the school year."

Administrators, instructional coaches, and teachers who become fluent in strategies of evidence collection, especially when evidence is generated through interactions with students, will develop a clear understanding of what is happening for learners in the classroom. These observers will then be able to use that evidence to make connections between teaching and learning for the observed teacher, building a deeper understanding over time of the courses of action that lead to success.

However, though we continue to see the goal for observation simplified as whether students are learning or not, the driving question behind this book, which arises time and again, reminds us of the complexity of this task:

How can teachers, coaches, and leaders alike observe learning in action and provide feedback that supports understanding of causal attributions?

To answer this question, this book highlights nineteen strategies (and recalls the thirty-one strategies from our previous book). Furthermore, the importance of core dispositions and key cultural attributes cannot be understated. In order for a culture of observation and feedback to collectively permeate a school, teachers must willingly open their classroom doors to any observer and be willing to receive written and verbal feedback. Observers need to organize their time to ensure observations occur frequently and strive to improve their evidence collection and analysis skills to ensure that these observations lead to accurate and actionable feedback.

In Chapter 2, in order to observe teachers' impact on learners, we dive into how learners learn. This will help inform and drive your evidence collection practices. Chapters 3 through 5 provide the steps and strategies to plan for and then adapt your evidence collection as learning unfolds. Chapter 6 pulls all of your work together into the development of feedback and provides guidance as you begin to apply these strategies toward the establishment of a culture of learning.

Observing for Impact

We often take larger groups into a classroom (leaders, coaches, or teachers) to observe a lesson and watch as some will choose to stay against a wall while others move quickly to see what students are doing. Not too long ago, we visited a second-grade reader's workshop lesson with a team of observers. Observers lined the back of the room, though students were gathered on the carpet. Within minutes, all students began talking to partners, yet not one observer moved to determine what was being said. Had the observers chosen to remain removed from the learning, their feedback to the teacher would likely have been something like this:

```
10:10 Teacher showed students the new strategy through modeling in a mentor text.

10:15 Teacher led a turn-and-talk where students shared with a partner when they would use the new strategy in their own story.

10:20 Teacher had students go back to their seats to try on their own.
```

However, because we utilize our sessions and group classroom visits as learning opportunities for observers, we waved them closer to the learners so that they would be able to answer the following questions:

- What were the students saying to each other?
- What was the depth of the responses? How many partners gave only one-word answers or didn't share?
- How many were way off track (off topic or not accurate/misunderstanding)?
- How many were engaged in a high-level conversation, demonstrating they understood the new strategy?

Without evidence to answer these questions, observers would not be able to provide meaningful feedback regarding this teacher's impact on the students.

Why didn't those observers move in closer to students? Consistently, observers share that they worry they are bothering students or disrupting the lesson. We think that perhaps

- they do not know what to look for or collect, so they are missing the value or need, or

- they do not know how to collect evidence of engagement and learning.

For years, evaluation, observation, and the support of teachers through feedback only focused on the *teaching* occurring in the classroom. Much of the feedback consisted of summaries, narratives, or lists of evidence. As a result, feedback was not conveying information about how teachers' practices were leading (or not leading) to learning or how teachers were creating outcomes through their choices, strategies, and tasks. We have come to find that many observers still do not have the skills to collect evidence to support this type of thinking or understanding or to observe for impact. Nor have states, regions, professional-learning providers, or thought leaders offered solutions or provided the specific and comprehensive training and support required to do this work well—until now!

Observing for Learning

> *"If you want to understand teaching, you need to understand how children learn."* —Nuthall, 2007, p. 154

Consider this:

> The standard view of the classroom is that the teacher provides students with a set of activities. Some students do the activities well and learn more. Others do not complete the activities or do not do them as well, and consequently do not learn as much. The assumption seems to be that all students experience essentially the same activities, and perform them according to their motivation or ability. It is assumed that learning is more or less the automatic result of engaging classroom activities. Research shows that almost none of that is true. (Nuthall, 2007, p. 103)

One day, early on in their transition from observing just teaching to teaching and learning, one of our groups was observing a sixth-grade writing lesson. The instructional leaders were thinking about the learners and were thrilled to see students working on a rigorous standard inside Google Classroom as the teacher had been making great efforts to integrate technology. Students were reading an argumentative piece of writing and were required to highlight in different colors the claim, supporting evidence, and introduction to the evidence. Let's look at feedback samples from each observer based on what was collected and determined about the lesson. Notice how these excerpts show varying degrees of attention to the learners in the room.

Here is a quick note about our samples: If you read *Feedback to Feed Forward*, you will remember that we begin the journey in our training of observers with the development of directive feedback. Taking the time to analyze and process the evidence and create impact statements also allows an observer to prepare for conversations, craft highly effective reflection questions, and be ready when it is time to shift stances and provide evidence, or more observer-directed statements, in feedback meetings.

Observer 1: The teacher modeled an example of how to complete the task and gave clear directions. All screens were visible, and nearly all students were actively talking to a neighbor and highlighting in different colors.

Observer 2: The observer asked students, "What are you doing?" and they listed the directions and color coding correctly. Clearly, students knew what to do, were engaged using technology, and were working in partnerships.

Observer 3: Nearly all students were attempting to complete the task correctly. The observer noticed three groups had multiple yellow highlights (claim) and questioned the students, "Can you have more than one claim?" and students were unsure. In two groups, when the observer grew closer, it was clear one partner was telling the other what to highlight, the partner complied, but it was incorrect. When following the teacher, the observer heard him reteaching what a claim was to different groups, as they had not gotten started after ten minutes. Based on this, clearly half of the class was not ready to begin the independent task, as they were missing foundational understandings.

Notice how Observer 3's attention to student understanding influenced the quality of the feedback. Observer 3 didn't want to stop there. She asked herself why students were struggling. The depth of her evidence allowed her to analyze cause-and-effect relationships and identify causal attribution for the outcomes.

Though the teacher started the class with a five-minute introduction about claim and evidence and highlighted a document as an example, he did not take the time to assess prior learning or ensure everyone had the basic understandings of each to begin the task. (The teacher polled three random students.)

The other group members admitted that it had not even occurred to them to determine if the students were highlighting correctly! Though, on this day, the training group was composed of administrators, this is a frequent occurrence, even when teachers are observers. Listening to Observer 3 share her findings allowed for great discovery learning for the other observers. As you read through our classroom examples and recommended strategies for effective evidence collection throughout the book and the questions we ask students, you will experience your own discoveries about how to engage with learners.

> **Stop and Think:** When you consider the three feedback samples, which one represents one you have received? Why do you think that is? Is there one that aligns to your previous training?

Making the Shift

The examples from Observer 1 and 2 clearly lack evidence, resulting in feedback that lacks depth. This is directly tied to the observers' choices and actions in the classroom during the lesson. This book offers guidance on how to make more productive choices and actions that will result in richer evidence collection. But to understand what to collect and how to collect it, it is critical for you, as an observer, to truly understand *why* you are collecting evidence from learners.

Your goal as an observer is to develop feedback that helps a teacher understand three key things through *relevant* evidence, regardless of whether you are a peer, coach, or supervisor:

1. How and why you are making a claim about overall effectiveness of instructional practices (which could include clear and objective support of a performance level rating)
2. How the teacher is impacting student engagement and learning
3. How the teacher is progressing toward overarching goals—district/region, school, or professional

Through feedback, we can develop these understandings, build reflective practice, help teachers determine actionable next steps for growth, and continually improve outcomes for students, all of which lead to a culture of observation and feedback that drives a culture of learning.

The Skills of Observation

The process of observing is not as simple as gathering a clipboard or laptop, setting foot into a room (or hitting play on a video), and watching a lesson unfold. Instead, it is a complex process that requires high levels of cognitive and metacognitive processing executed in real time, when done effectively. To engage in this level of work and to develop high-quality feedback that promotes growth, observers must master a set of twenty-one core skills (Figure 1.2) and move toward proficiency in three core competencies:

1. Effective **observation and evidence collection**
2. Explicit **analysis of effectiveness** of instruction evidence
3. Development of **high-quality feedback**

FIGURE 1.2: ReVISION LEARNING CORE SKILLS OVERVIEW

3 Core Competencies	Observe and Collect Evidence	Analyze Effectiveness	Provide Written/ Verbal Feedback
21 Core Skills	Unpack a rubric	Analyze objectively	Recognize research-based strategies
	Describe look-fors	Analyze evidence	Build on instructional strengths
	Identify types of data	Determine student engagement levels	Scaffold next steps
	Collect qualitative evidence	Determine impact on engagement	Review for objectivity
	Collect quantitative evidence	Determine impact on learning	Compose feedback
	Collect evidence of student engagement	Determine performance levels	Create clear connections
	Observe objectively	Craft a claim	Develop reflective questions

Source: Tepper and Flynn (2019).

To support an observer's development of these competencies and corresponding skills, our organization, ReVISION Learning Partnership (RVL), developed six standards of effective observation and feedback housed within Domain 1 of the ReVISION Learning Supervisory Continuum. These standards outline expected practice for observation and *written* feedback, or the collection and processing of evidence that serves to prepare for an effective conversation. (We created Domain 2, which addresses expectations for verbal feedback, as well). "Though our ultimate goal as observers is to promote teacher reflection about these areas, many times the teachers we coach require directive or guided feedback, as they are not ready or are unable to arrive at their own conclusions about the effectiveness of their lessons" (Tepper & Flynn, 2019, p. 127). The standards serve as the backbone of our learning designs for observers, and through these, we are able to measure the quality of feedback while also leveraging growth, supporting the development of those skills necessary to ensure observers can develop and deliver feedback that feeds forward.

The standards are as follows:

> **RVL 1.A:** Evidence cited is directly aligned to the appropriate indicators of practice on an instructional framework (evaluative or non-evaluative) and claims are clearly supported.
>
> **RVL 1.B:** Qualitative and quantitative evidence cited in feedback is aligned, appropriate, and facilitates targeted growth and improvement.
>
> **RVL 1.C:** Evidence cited in feedback connects teacher action with student engagement and intended learning outcomes.
>
> **RVL 1.D:** Feedback contains areas of strengths and areas of growth explicitly connected to the framework indicator and observed practices/evidence and are developed based on indicator language and the key levers between ratings.
>
> **RVL 1.E:** Evidence cited is objectively stated and without opinion.
>
> **RVL 1.F:** Feedback report serves as a comprehensive learning tool containing clearly articulated evidence-based statements and explicit connections, with pre-planned reflective questions.
>
> (For the full RVL Supervisory Continuum Domain 1, see Resource 1.1 in the Resource Center **resources.corwin.com/learnerfocusedfeedback)**

Feedback to Feed Forward was dedicated to building the capacity of instructional leaders (administrators, coaches, and department chairs) in all six standards. Standards RVL 1.A, RVL 1.B, and RVL 1.C are the primary focus of this book for *all observers* regardless of your role. However, each of the standards plays a critical role as they form the foundation of observer practice and high-quality feedback. In this book, we focus on the capacity of observers to enter a classroom and recognize learning in action, to make decisions and take steps needed to collect both quantitative and qualitative evidence of how students are learning (RVL 1.B), and to analyze and help teachers to see how they are causing those outcomes (RVL 1.C). This allows for the observer to generate, either in a directive or reflective/collaborative manner, feedback that

- conveys claims (RVL 1.A) about the causal attributions (helping a teacher to recognize impact), ideally aligned to the district/region's expectations for teaching and learning,
- represents accurate assessments of teaching and learning, and
- generates honest dialogue about teaching and learning focused on next steps.

As a school seeks to build a culture of observation and feedback as a key driver of a culture of learning, training observers to become proficient in these standards of practice becomes crucial.

Essentials of Evidence Collection

Whether you are a teacher observing a peer, a coach, or a leader observing those you support, determining specifically *what* to collect may be challenging. Perhaps you are reading this book to improve *how* you are currently collecting evidence. The *what* will be directly related to your understanding of how students learn, which will drive *how* you collect evidence. We have come to understand that students need repetition, are influenced by peers, arrive with different background knowledge and experiences, and require monitoring. This means that "over time students achieve different learning outcomes even in the same classroom and from the same activities . . . learning does not come directly from classroom activities; learning comes from the way students experience these activities. What matters is what students extract from experiences—the sense they make of them" (Nuthall, 2007, p. 154, 155). Again, this validates the idea that observing for learning is complex!

It is this very idea—what students extract—that should drive all your evidence collection during a lesson, to better understand how students are making sense of the learning experiences. In Chapter 3 of *Feedback to Feed Forward*, we introduced ten strategies solely dedicated to evidence collection. As the chapters ahead will serve as an extension of those strategies, we thought it important to review the foundational strategies before we dig in. If you feel overwhelmed at any point, stop and return to the first book (but notice we provide those thirty-one strategies in the front of this book). Those foundational strategies from our first book will be cited with an "FF" as you read on. The use of FF Strategies 7–9, shown in Figure 1.3, will enable you to become a more accurate and objective observer, whether you are observing live classrooms or watching videos of recorded lessons.

FIGURE 1.3: FOUNDATIONAL STRATEGIES FF 7–9

Strategy	Description
FF Strategy 7: Develop an awareness	Recognize the biases you bring into a classroom or might develop as a lesson unfolds
FF Strategy 8: Observe with a wide lens	Keep a broad perspective of overall teaching and learning during an observation (See Figure 1.4)
FF Strategy 9: Collect a balance of evidence with purpose	Be mindful of what you are collecting and why during an observation versus blindly scripting

Source: Tepper and Flynn (2019).

Your goal as an observer is to ensure you are measuring effectiveness in terms of how a teacher is impacting student engagement and learning. Even if you visit the same classroom multiple times or have been working with a teacher all year on a particular practice, such as refining a minilesson or checking for understanding at critical points, "it is still important to consider how that one particular practice fits into the context of what we consider to be the 'big picture' (Figure 1.4). Remember, this provides a framework for your evidence collection, development of feedback, and conversations with teachers" (Tepper & Flynn, 2019, p. 67).

FIGURE 1.4: BIG-PICTURE GOAL

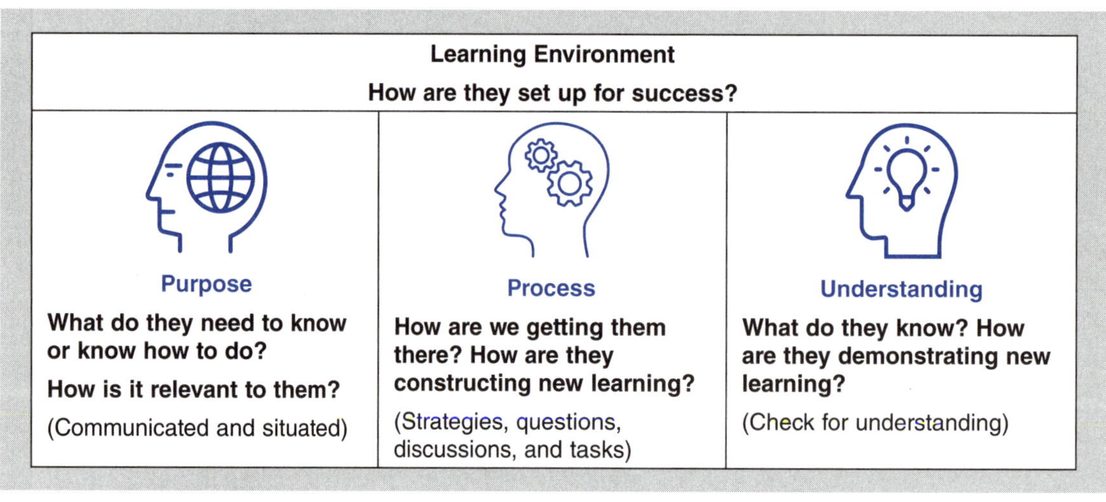

Source: Tepper and Flynn, LLC.

(See Resource 1.2 in the Resource Center, **resources.corwin.com/learnerfocusedfeedback**, for a printable version of more big-picture questions.)

The FF Strategies shown in Figure 1.5 and Figure 1.6 should be part of your everyday toolbox. Regardless of your goals for an observation or the content areas, grade levels, or time spent in a classroom, you should use these strategies for each observation. This will ensure you depart a classroom with the necessary evidence to analyze effectiveness and develop impactful feedback. FF Strategy 12 is one of the most important. If you are only collecting evidence from a handful of students, your claims about practice (or ratings as an evaluator), your analysis of effectiveness, and/or your coaching points will be inaccurate.

FIGURE 1.5: FOUNDATIONAL STRATEGIES FF 10–13

Strategy	Description
FF Strategy 10: Place yourself where the learning is occurring	Follow the learning during an observation, as it may be occurring in multiple places
FF Strategy 11: Do what it takes to collect evidence	Use all of your senses, moving and attending to opportunities to maximize your time in a classroom
FF Strategy 12: Be comprehensive in your collection of evidence	Ensure you engage with a high number of learners
FF Strategy 13: Maximize the use of your notepad or tablet	Refine your use of your evidence collection tools for efficiency and effectiveness

Source: Tepper and Flynn (2019).

FIGURE 1.6: FOUNDATIONAL STRATEGIES FF 14–16

Strategy	Description
FF Strategy 14: Listen to teaching and learning	Pay close attention not just to teacher statements, conversations, and questions but also any time learners are speaking
FF Strategy 15: View learning in action	Watch learners and look at what is in front of them or what they are using. Watch the teacher's and learners' actions and movements
FF Strategy 16: Interact with learners	Engage with learners directly in authentic conversations about their learning and to make their thinking visible

Source: Tepper and Flynn (2019).

FF Strategies 14–16 form the basis for the chapters ahead, with a focus on how to comprehensively collect evidence from students (Figure 1.6).

FF Strategy 14 is powerful in that "the language we use when we think is closely connected to the way we talk socially." You can listen to conversations to "confirm the kinds of processes most likely going on in students' working memories. These processes are sort of implied when we say students are 'making sense' of experience, or 'constructing' their own meaning" (Nuthall, 2007, p. 75).

Though you cannot interact with students if watching a video, you can identify how the teacher was interacting and consider questions you might have asked during the lesson.

Teachers as Learners

In Chapter 2, we will explore the concept of students as learners—what they should be learning and how you will know if this is occurring. To begin our swim into the deep end, let's wade into the concept of students leading their own learning—the goal in our classrooms every day, which will form the foundation of your evidence collection. Keep in mind too that teachers can lead their own learning as well. Frey, Hattie, and Fisher (2018) use the term *assessment-capable visible learner*, or a student who can answer three key questions at any given time.

- Where am I going?
- How am I going?
- What is next?

Assessment-capable teachers are those who can foster assessment-capable learning in a classroom, but in our work in schools, we have pushed this one step further. We see in a culture of learning that teachers can become assessment-capable learners themselves. Observation and feedback can drive their ability to answer the same three questions. Teachers can answer "Where am I going?" through the teacher performance standards or instructional rubrics that define teaching and learning in their school. They recognize "How am I going?" more clearly when they receive accurate assessments of their practice from an observer or conduct accurate reflections, especially when these are related to causal attribution. And when they are receiving feedback from an observer, the two are working together to answer "What's next?" resulting in improved self-reflection along the way.

Teachers need to become collaborators as they engage in their own learning—with each other and with their students. They need to think critically and remain cognitively flexible in their decision making inside the classroom. They need to cross curricular lines, breaking from their silos that often limit thinking about classroom environments and student interaction with learning. Teachers can build these skills and work toward becoming assessment-capable teachers and learners through professional learning, guided professional-learning communities, observation and feedback, and self-reflection.

What is important for an observer (and teachers themselves) to recognize is that certain skills, dispositions, and tools are at the heart of developing assessment-capable learning in the classroom that stem from common understandings and knowledge, (explored ahead in Chapter 2 and also in Feedback to Feed Forward Chapter 2). This continues to reinforce the evidence that needs to be collected to support teacher growth. We provide some examples of each in Figure 1.7, and we encourage you and your team to create a more extensive list together.

FIGURE 1.7: SKILLS, DISPOSITIONS, AND TOOLS FOR TEACHERS

	Teachers
Skills Need to know how to . . .	• Build student capacity to work independently • Use appropriate scaffolding • Model self-monitoring, using criteria, making adjustments, and utilizing resources and evaluating effectiveness of resources • Plan/facilitate learning vs. delivering content • Give feedback to drive student-owned learning
Dispositions Need to be willing to . . .	• Turn learning over to students • Allow good struggle • Have high expectations/belief that students can achieve and think at high levels
Tools Need to have available . . .	• Clear and specific daily learning goals • Clear and specific learning criteria • Time throughout each lesson for reflection • Time in each lesson to unpack goals and criteria

Stop and Think: As you look at the list in Figure 1.7, consider what may already be in place in your building or classroom.

Many of the practices teachers have employed in the past still remain relevant, and it is not necessary to change everything we do (something many fear). Remember, our observation and feedback should identify causal attributions or instructional choices that help teachers see "How am I going?" in terms of *effective* outcomes—those practices that are allowing students to reach goals—along with any of those practices that can be or need to be altered, slightly or significantly.

Leaders Leading Learning

Through no fault of their own, teachers often are not in a position to develop or utilize these necessary skills consistently, accurately, and with the passion that called them to the work in the first place. The skills of a leader to model and effectively monitor progress toward a compelling vision and mission for teaching and learning and to demonstrate capacity to provide relevant feedback along the way are essential to teacher and school success. In the simplest terms, leaders are the cultivators of the environment in a culture of learning, yet they often lack the skills and support from their own leaders necessary to embody this role. Leading learning for all is no easy task, and the solutions—and therefore, the skills—are not one-dimensional and cannot be oversimplified. Leaders must be prepared to

- increase teacher involvement/engagement,
- decrease teacher isolation,
- develop teacher skill sets for effective collaboration,
- create goal consensus among staff,
- determine the learning needs (at all levels—students, teachers, leadership, and organization), and, most importantly,
- **build capacity in their own practice and among their staff to observe for and collect evidence of the causal attributions that impact student learning.**

In this sense, leaders need to be able to cultivate teacher ownership of learning as they develop their own capacity as leaders. We often highlight this when working in a new district or region by saying that assessment-capable students are developed by assessment-capable teachers who are supported by assessment-capable leaders. None of this can occur without purposeful planning and deepening an understanding of research about teaching and learning.

We know there is plenty of research about the importance and impact of planning and executing effective formative assessments in the learning process. We build on this thinking to help you take proactive steps to support teachers, to determine areas of strength and growth, and, finally, to build your teachers' understanding of the research through your feedback.

Generally, when research-based strategies or expected outcomes are observed in a classroom, they will be considered teacher strengths, as they result in desired actions, behaviors or dispositions, new learning, and/or high levels of engagement (or a teacher is moving in that direction). Think back to the second-grade English language arts example. The observer is aware of the structure of the workshop model and saw elements of the research-based strategies, even though the teacher was not 100 percent successful.

When we think about a lesson in terms of what the research says—what we know students need and what we do or do not see related to this—we begin to form the foundation of our feedback and next steps for the teacher. When you are developing feedback for growth, building a teacher's understanding of the related supporting research is critical because this serves to increase the objectivity of your feedback and validate your conclusions while also promoting more purposeful planning and future reflection on the teacher's part.

This leads us to our first strategy, purposeful planning in support of teachers. This should serve as the foundational step for leaders who should involve teachers in each part of the process.

Strategy 1: Mindfully plan for effective observation and feedback

There are many elements that can be prepared ahead of time as you begin your journey toward a culture of learning driven by a culture of observation and feedback, and Chapter 3 is focused entirely on planning for an observation. Chapter 6 is dedicated to the establishment of a culture of learning. However, regardless of your role, we wanted to briefly mention the steps leaders and leadership teams should take, either simultaneously as you shift to more learning-focused observation and feedback or before involving teachers in peer observations. These steps are critical and should not be skipped, as you may be engaging in dramatically different observation practices from previous years and/or your feedback (and, if you are an evaluator, your ratings) might be radically different from what teachers in your building have seen or experienced. There's no "Gotcha!" in this formula!

Schools are forewarned that jumping into the observation and feedback strategies we are proposing without adequately preparing the staff can set you up for failure. Leaders may improve their own skills in their own roles and responsibilities, but without supporting the culture in all aspects, the pathway to a cohesive vision and a sense of collective efficacy will be met with challenges too daunting to overcome. We offer a few suggestions at this point (and many of these are reinforced throughout the book). Let's explore three initial steps.

1. Build a shared understanding and knowledge of effective teaching and learning.

Building a shared understanding begins with building a common definition of learning; this will then require that all members of the school understand how to recognize it in action (more on this in Chapter 2). As schools begin with the definition, they must remember they have access to a tool that helps to guide this process—their instructional framework or teacher performance standards. Teachers and leaders should work as teams toward understanding the outcomes associated with the standards and unpack the expectations in their instructional frameworks, ultimately building a common understanding of all aspects of effective teaching and learning. (And sometimes, this work results in the discovery that the standards do not outline the desired teaching and learning!)

2. Become transparent as observers.

Teachers should know what is being observed, what evidence is being collected, and how observations will be carried out. It is also imperative to

> talk to your teachers about observations. They are often intimidated, unsure, or unhappy about an observer's movement in their classrooms and interaction with their students. For many who have been teaching for over five years, there is a significant change in an observer's behaviors. Be transparent and share with them how an observer's actions and interactions with students increase support for growth. They should in turn let students know visitors may stop and chat, listen, or read over shoulders, and why. (Tepper & Flynn, 2019, p. 74)

This should not be based on a broad communication such as, "We are observing Domain 1 of the Marzano Learning Map" (LSI, 2017). Teachers should understand that observers will interact with students (without disrupting the normal learning cycle). And they need to be clear that you will focus your attention on identifying causal attributions for observed outcomes. Without understanding specifically how you will be collecting evidence inside the classroom, teachers may often see your interactions in the classroom as disruptive or view them through a lens of uncertainty or mistrust. This leads to Step 3.

3. Set protocols and expectations for your classroom visits.

Ultimately, when an observer visits a classroom, we want to ensure it is a positive experience and that a minimal footprint is left on the classroom and students. Whether you are a leader, coach, or peer, it is important for teachers to know that you are not in their rooms to complete a checklist or to catch them doing something wrong. But your actions will speak volumes. You need to follow through and demonstrate that your visits are about growth. All observations should result in some form of feedback and, ideally, a conversation.

Because of past messaging, previous experiences, or fear, teachers often feel pressure to put on a special show or create what they think you want to see. Who can blame them? Some become highly stressed anticipating peers' visits. Prepping for these experiences takes up too much of their valuable time and ultimately may not allow a visitor to give feedback that is applicable or useful. It takes time to build trust and for the one being observed to truly see that what we want them to do is to just keep teaching. We say this because of a few scenarios we have encountered.

Scenario 1: A group of observers entered a fifth-grade classroom, and the teacher stopped her instruction for four to five minutes and spoke directly to us: "Welcome! Class, can everyone say 'Welcome' to our visitors? Today, we are working on preparing for our interviews with someone from the previous generation. . . . Earlier we. . . . We are about to. . . ."

Though absolutely well meaning, the teacher was nervous (not at all strange with six of us arriving and because observations were highly infrequent in her building!), but she didn't need to interrupt her flow. In Edison Schools, Patrick recalled a student who was assigned to quietly greet visitors without disrupting the class and would orient the observer to the day's learning. Beyond this, when a teacher restates the directions or expectations for the entire class, it makes it difficult for us to discern if students understand the purpose and are making connections on their own.

(Continued)

(Continued)

Scenario 2: On a number of occasions when we have interacted with learners, a teacher or paraprofessional followed us, uneasy about what we were doing and what the students were saying. After a student said he wasn't sure how to complete his task, the para emphatically corrected the student: "You know this; we just did this!" "It's in your notes!" We have even had paras or teachers answer for students. They are often afraid that the student is providing "wrong" answers. Our big lessons learned was this: Make sure everyone knows that it is okay if a student is unsure or struggling when there is a visitor, and include paras in your vision building.

It can be stressful to open your door to visitors, but we ask observed teachers to remain as authentic as possible. Strive to build a culture where stepping out of comfort zones is part of everyday thinking as opportunities for growth (Figure 1.8).

FIGURE 1.8: THE MAGIC

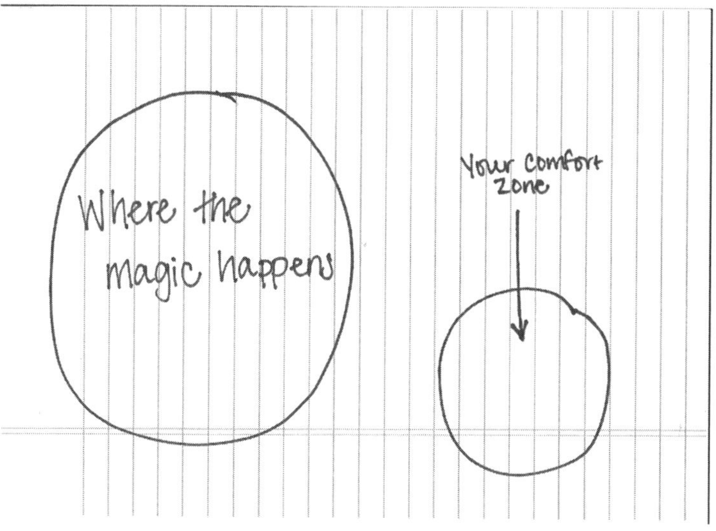

We have seen some positive ways to integrate or acknowledge visitors, such as in the following scenarios.

Scenario 1: We have entered a classroom of kindergartners learning math on the carpet, and right away, the teacher integrated counting the visitors (as five adults staring down at them might have been very intimidating). We have also been in classrooms where we participated as respondents to student surveys in the moment. These are great quick events when frequent observation is a new experience.

Scenario 2: Often, teachers try to calm students when visitors arrive, "Oh, they are here watching me." However, Patrick recently encountered a situation where the second-grade teacher was very transparent with the students that the visitor was interested in knowing more about the *learning*.

Student to Patrick:	Are you the researcher?
Patrick:	The researcher?
Student:	You are here to watch us.
Patrick:	I am! I am here to watch and talk with you about your learning.
Teacher to Students:	Remember, as researchers we are always looking to understand what new learning is happening.

This resulted in an eagerness to tell Patrick what they were doing and learning throughout his whole visit.

Who and How Often

Additionally, as you look to apply observation and feedback beyond evaluation, begin to consider some questions to help you (and the teachers) mindfully prepare for an observation. To get the ball rolling, for leaders and coaches, look at a list of the teachers you support and think about the following:

- Who would benefit from more frequent observations? Why?
- What specifically is the teacher's areas of growth, need, or focus? On what are you basing this?
- Is the teacher meeting expectations?
- When during a lesson or day is the best time to visit? Why?
- How could video be used in the process?

For teachers,

- Who would like peer support and classroom visitors?
- When can you go and visit your peers' classrooms?

Stop and Think: Examine our three suggestions. What is your school/district level of readiness for each? Which are already in motion?

What's Ahead

While we are not suggesting that observation and feedback alone are the sole pathway or panacea to school improvement for teachers and leaders, what we have come to see—district after district, school after school—is that when you make feedback a key driver, focusing on the learning occurring within our classrooms and observing for impact, you can create change.

Feedback is the driver in perfecting our systems of talent development and professional learning with teachers and leaders, helping to create a culture of openness to ongoing, never-ending growth and excellence and environments of clarity, trust, and support (Dewitt, 2017; Hattie, 2012; Park, Takahashi, & White, 2014; Tepper & Flynn, 2019).

This will only occur when the feedback we provide supports a teacher's understanding of

- how/why you are making a claim about the overall effectiveness of instructional practices,
- how the teacher is impacting student engagement and learning, and
- how the teacher is progressing toward overarching goals (district/region, school, or professional goals).

And there is a focus on building self- and collective teacher efficacy.

As you progress through the chapters of this book, you will find the strategies you need as an observer to ensure you are able to focus on the learning occurring in the classroom. This is what will allow us, as teachers and leaders, to build deeper levels of understanding about how teachers impact students in our classrooms. As you turn to Chapter 2, you will dive into the core knowledge needed and definitions of student learning to help identify look-fors and to set the foundation for your initial strategies for evidence collection.

Chapters 2 through 5 offer strategies for observers to utilize, providing you with proven methods to apply before and during an observation. These will ensure you have the capacity to effectively plan for and adapt your evidence collection relative to the learning in the classroom. Each chapter ahead ends with role-specific suggestions, so whether you are a teacher, administrator, or coach, you can personalize your application of the strategies to meet your needs. Chapter 6 will further support all educators in preparing to engage in the work through feedback samples and next steps in culture building.

As Socrates reminded us, you have the power to kindle the flames of growth and learning; how will you become the spark?

Turn the page to find out!

2 What Do You Need to Understand About Learning?

From the field . . .

The work has transformed how I interact with students and teachers on a daily basis and continues to transform me as an observer—more importantly, as a leader of learning. The new strategies have completely changed my role—from my mindset, to the evidence I collect, to the feedback I provide. Previously, during observations, I would focus on scripting the "things" that were going on in the classroom. Now, I enter the classroom with a focus on students and what they are ***learning****, rather than what they are* ***doing****. I spend time talking to students about what they are learning—the purpose—how they are learning—the process—and their perspective on what they have learned—the understanding. When the focus is centered on the thinking and learning, listening to students express what they need, and viewing them as partners in the learning process, it changes the way you view classroom observations.*

When I stopped focusing on the words and things and I began to collect specific evidence about the learning, my feedback to teachers became more

(Continued)

(Continued)

direct and supportive. This approach has allowed me to make a very specific claim, connect it to a specific example from the observation, promote reflection, and then help a teacher arrive at a reasonable, actionable next step. I was not prepared for how well teachers received this style of feedback! Surprisingly, teachers became more open to suggestions, began implementing next steps, and now initiate conversations solely around the learning in the classroom.

—Gina Olearczyk, Assistant Principal

"The most necessary task of civilization is to teach people how to think. It should be the primary purpose of our public schools. The mind of a child is naturally active, it develops through exercise. Give a child plenty of exercise for body and brain. The trouble with our way of educating is that it does not give elasticity to the mind. It casts the brain into a mold. It insists that the child must accept. It does not encourage original thought or reasoning, and it lays more stress on memory than observation."

—Thomas A. Edison

You just need a few minutes in a classroom to figure out that teaching people how to think (adults or children) is no easy task. In a culture of learning, each one of us has a role in helping others on our team and in our school to *think*. Any observer highly attentive to student engagement and learning during a lesson has the opportunity to develop feedback that feeds forward—helping teachers to think more deeply about their practices and how they are impacting their students' ability to think and learn. In a culture of learning through observation and feedback, not only do we all have the opportunity to learn, but also, we are driven by the mindset and desire to continuously improve.

For those of you excited about getting right into our evidence collection strategies, be patient. This is a research-heavy chapter meant to provide foundational knowledge that will enable you to conduct more purposeful observations and develop more impactful feedback. Remember, we are not scientists, neurologists, or psychologists, so we are just wading into complex concepts about learning in this chapter. We would never attempt to tackle the vastness of the idea of *learning* here in one chapter, as volumes have been written by experts. However, with twenty-five years each in education and thousands of classroom visits, we wanted to present you with information and key takeaways that have made a significant difference in our own practice as observers and teachers of observers. We encourage you to seek out additional resources at any point you think, "Hey, that was interesting. I want or need to know more." We'll also provide recommendations as we go.

For you to comprehensively and accurately collect evidence of not just the teaching but also the learning occurring (or not occurring) during a lesson and to accurately determine why this is the case, there are some critical understandings an observer ideally should possess; we've identified five of these in Figure 2.1. Use the Fist to 5 Rating Scale to check your level of understanding.

FIGURE 2.1: LEARNING PREASSESSMENT

Critical Understandings	Self-Assessment of Each Critical Understanding
1. What *learning* means and how learners learn	
2. What we want students to achieve or what type of learner we want to develop in our classrooms	
3. Those factors that increase or decrease engagement and learning	
4. What effective teaching and learning look and sound like in terms of teacher actions and student outcomes	
5. How effective teaching and learning are defined in your instructional framework	
Rating Scale	
Fist	I don't understand at all.
1	I need help. I just have a very basic understanding.
2	I could use more practice, reading, and learning.
3	I understand pretty well and can communicate somewhat what I know.
4	I mostly understand and can communicate what I know easily.
5	I completely understand and can teach someone else.

Stop and Think: Do a quick self-assessment of the critical understandings listed in Figure 2.1. Make note of the areas you want to know more about, and look up the additional resources related to those areas. (You will find recommendations throughout this chapter.)

Ideally, Elements 1–4 are aligned or integrated into your district's performance expectations.

In this chapter, the fourth critical understanding, "What does learning look and sound like?", should become more evident as you build an understanding of the first three and practice using the strategies outlined in the upcoming chapters. We give you opportunities and reminders to stop and align the teaching and learning described to your own instructional framework (the fifth understanding).

If you are struggling with any of the previous questions, that is understandable. However, it is important to continue to build your core knowledge to ensure you accurately observe for or provide feedback about whether learning is occurring, to what level, and why.

Understanding the Concept of Learning

We came across this great line from the opening of Paul Ramsden's (2003) *Learning to Teach in Higher Education* that encapsulated our sentiments: "The basic idea of this book is that we can improve our teaching by studying our students' learning—by listening to and learning from our students . . . improving teaching involves the same process that informs excellent student learning. Good teaching involves striving continually to learn about students' understanding and the effects of teaching on it" (pp. 6–8).

In our training sessions, we ask participants to brainstorm about the concept and definition of *learning*. Figure 2.2 shows the thinking from one of these sessions. We are always amazed at how both varied and thought-provoking responses are, from session to session or even participant to participant.

FIGURE 2.2: LEARNING BRAINSTORM

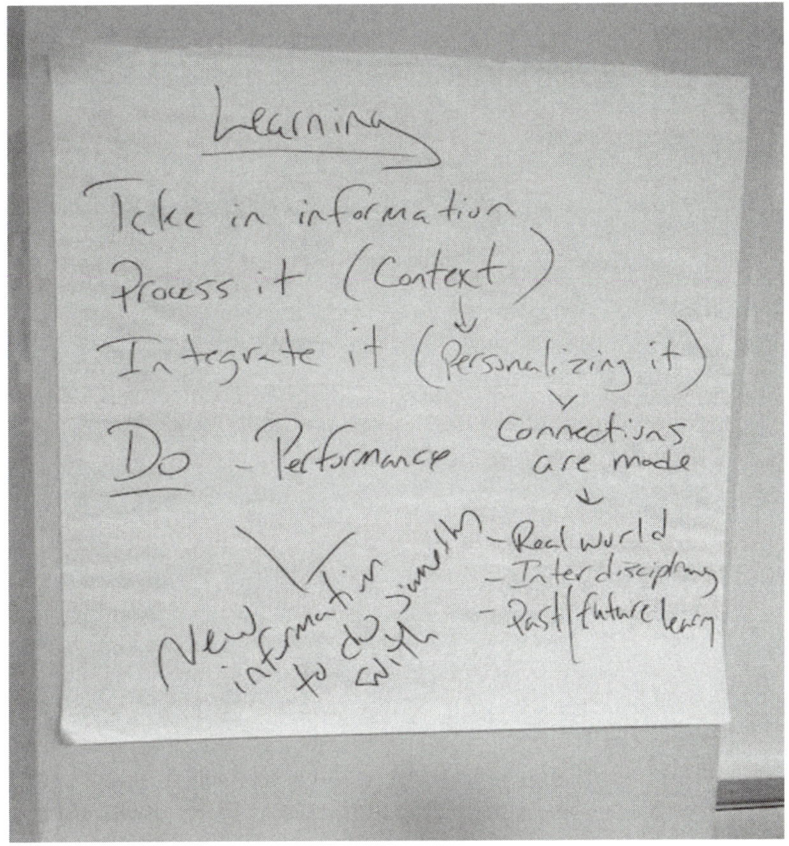

Source: RVL (2018).

Between 2010 and now, we have seen many changes in evaluation and supervision practices. Some require that we "study" students' learning. Other districts and regions have revised teacher performance standards to explicitly include learning outcomes. In our work with educators, we explore their understandings of *learning* while also exploring instructional frameworks. For example, take a look at the indicator examples shown in Figure 2.3 defining proficient/effective expectations. Consider how certain phrases like *advanc[ing] learning* or *constructing new and meaningful learning*, such as in Figure 2.3, might cause confusion or result in differing definitions.

FIGURE 2.3: CHALLENGING PHRASES INDICATOR EXAMPLES

Clearly presents instructional content in a logical and purposeful progression and at an appropriate level of challenge to advance learning of all students

Employs differentiated strategies, tasks, and questions that cognitively engage students in constructing new and meaningful learning through appropriately integrated recall, problem solving, critical and creative thinking, purposeful discourse, and/or inquiry

Source: Connecticut State Department of Education (2017).

Our work in unpacking phrases in district frameworks led to the development of our second strategy.

Strategy 2: Define learning

When *learning* means different things to different people, schools and districts face real challenges in their efforts to achieve coherence and a common vision. After a lesson, Amy asked the observing administrators, "Were the students constructing new learning?" From five participants, she received five different answers! Their different evaluations of the same lesson revealed that they did not share a common definition of learning.

Consider three definitions or understandings of learning presented ahead, from authors and leading educational theorists. How do these understandings mesh with your own understanding of learning?

When learning is occurring, students are doing the following:

1. Grasping a new term or simple concept
2. Demonstrating a discrete/single specific skill
3. Creating complex products/demonstrating complex processes
4. Using critical, creative, and self-regulatory reasoning/thinking skills

Source: Moss and Brookhart (2015, pp. 123–125).

Psychologists Ference Marton and Roger Säljö (1976) looked at how learners *perceive their own learning*. Their perceptions revealed differing ideas of the concept of learning and how learners "set out" to learn:

> In fact, we have found basically two different levels of processing to be clearly distinguishable. These two different levels of processing, which we shall call deep-level and surface-level processing, correspond to the different aspects of the learning material on which the learner focuses. In the case of surface-level processing the student directs his attention towards learning the text itself (the sign), i.e., he has a reproductive conception of learning which means that he is more or less forced to keep to a rote-learning strategy. In the case of deep-level processing, on the other hand, the student is directed towards the intentional content of the learning material (what is signified). (p. 7)

Paul Ramsden (2003) summarizes for us Marton and Säljö's five classifications:

1. **Learning as quantitative increase in knowledge**. Learning is acquiring information or "knowing a lot."
2. **Learning as memorizing.** Learning is storing information that can be reproduced.
3. Learning as acquiring facts, skills, and methods that can be **retained and used** as necessary.
4. **Learning as making sense** or abstracting meaning. Learning involves relating parts of the subject matter to each other and to the real world.
5. Learning as interpreting and **understanding reality in a different way**. Learning involves comprehending the world by re-interpreting knowledge. (pp. 27–28)

Stop and Think: How do you define learning? How does your team define it? What steps can you take/have you taken to create a common definition that aligns with the concepts and goals for learners?

Overarching Goals for All Learners

Once your team has agreed upon a working definition of learning, the next—or, better yet, simultaneous—step is to determine what type of learners we are working to develop or what learning *should* be. Such a definition of learning should be reflected in your team's long-term desired outcomes for students, perhaps in the form of a "portrait of a graduate." This leads to our next strategy: identifying goals for learners.

Hopefully, you are seeking to identify the competencies and skills that will set your students on a path not just for college and career readiness but for a happy, healthy, productive life and what learning needs to look like in our classrooms to ensure they achieve these. To drive a culture of learning and to provide the foundation for high-quality observation and feedback, we must have clear goals established for our learners—our next strategy.

Strategy 3: Create goals for all learners

In 2018, the OECD (Organisation for Economic Co-operation and Development) was seeking to answer "two far-reaching questions" for a vision for year 2030, extending its report from fifteen years earlier:

- What knowledge, skills, attitudes, and values will today's students need to thrive and shape their world?
- How can instructional systems develop these knowledge, skills, attitudes, and values effectively?

The OECD identified three *transformative competencies* to address the growing need for young people to be innovative, responsible, and aware.

- Creating new value:
  - Students need to develop skills including adaptability, creativity, curiosity, and open-mindedness, which will support innovations in business, economics, and new social models.
- Reconciling tensions and dilemmas:
  - Students need to learn to think and act in a more integrated way, taking into account the interconnections and interrelations between contradictory or incompatible ideas.
- Taking responsibility:
  - Students need to develop higher levels of self-regulation, which involves self-control, self-efficacy, responsibility, problem solving, and adaptability as they interact in a world with ever-increasing novelty, change, diversity, and ambiguity.

The OECD (2018) also reinforced the idea that students need to think and process information.

> To learn today, and in preparation for our students' future world, "our students will need a broad range of skills, including cognitive

> and meta-cognitive skills (e.g., critical thinking, creative thinking, learning to learn and self-regulation); social and emotional skills (e.g., empathy, self-efficacy and collaboration); and practical and physical skills (e.g., using new information and communication technology devices)" as tools for self-regulation and management of learning.

In *Deep Learning: Engage the World, Change the World,* Michael Fullan, Joanne Quinn, and Joanne McEachen (2018) provide a comprehensive model for a shift from the concept of traditional learning (content and knowledge driven) to *deep learning,* marked by many of the attributes described by the OECD and organized into six global competencies (an extension of the four Cs you may know from P21/Battelle for Kids): **character, citizenship, collaboration, communication, creativity, and critical thinking**. Ideally, when we observe, we are not attentive to how teachers are building student understanding of content but how they are building student capacity in these six areas, using the content as a vehicle.

Our Three Goals

To create a foundation for observation and feedback, we formed our own three categories or goals for learners. These were created based on current lists of essential skills, what we understand about executive-function skills, and the work of Bandura (1991), along with Zimmerman (1989) and others, in the area of self-regulation. These may help you further refine your own definition of *learning* as well. Though numbered, we are not presenting them as a hierarchy, as they are all equally important.

Goal 1: Students need to learn how to think conceptually (cognition).

Goal 2: Students need to learn how to think about their thinking (metacognition).

Goal 3: Students need to develop the ability to self-regulate and self-monitor.

Zimmerman (1989) summarizes the connections between the three: "The term metacognition in relation to self-regulated learning refers to a learner's ability to think consciously about their cognition and have control over their cognitive processes." He reinforces the idea that these can be taught. For students to become proficient in the essential skills described by the OECD or Fullan et al., they must improve cognitively and metacognitively and develop the habits and skills of self-regulation and self-monitoring. An observer's task is to effectively identify and provide feedback on the way in which a teacher is building capacity and impacting students' progress towards these ends. As this is no small task, we'll review each goal in depth.

Goal 1: Students need to learn how to think conceptually.

Hattie and Donoghue (2016) extend the understanding of surface vs. deep learning from earlier researchers, such as Marton and Säljö (1976), Entwistle and Ramsden (1982), and Biggs (1987). They see the work of learning as the process of students developing foundational surface knowledge that will allow them to move to deeper understanding and to transfer learning to new tasks and situations. Stern, Ferraro, and Mohnkern (2017), authors of *Tools for Teaching Conceptual Understanding*, assert that students need to "use their new knowledge to analyze problems, make decisions, and influence others in ways that matter to them. Once students uncover or discover the relationship between two or more concepts, they can use this knowledge to unlock new situations. This is the goal of conceptual learning: transfer. After students have uncovered a relationship, they need to practice transfer" (p. 57).

Critical thinking is required for deep learning, conceptual understanding, and transfer to occur. Frey, Hattie, and Fisher (2018) further define these levels:

- Surface learning focuses on one idea at a time, whether concept or skill. . . . Surface learning is not superficial learning.
- At the deep level, students see connections, relationships, and schema between ideas and learn to organize skills and concepts.
- When the student begins to apply knowledge in increasingly new and novel situations, the transfer level of learning is reached. (p. 12)

Fullan et al. (2018) view deep learning as the process of acquiring the six global competencies: "It is the process that causes students to use more complex thinking, to tap into creativity, and to solve increasingly enigmatic problems" (pp. 45–46). OECD (2018) includes as an essential skill *transferability*. "Higher priority should be given to knowledge, skills, attitudes and values that can be learned in one context and transferred to others" (p. 11).

In *Feedback to Feed Forward*, we addressed four advancing stages of learning: acquisition, fluency, generalization, and adaptation (Haring, Lovitt, Eaton, & Hansen, 1978). These address levels of competence and learning as a process. Students who are using skills or strategies in new situations are considered to be in the *adaptation phase*, or what we consider to be deeper learning or transfer. You may already be using other classifications such as Bloom's taxonomy or Webb's (1997) depth of knowledge within your school. However, we wanted to go further in understanding what is happening for learners when we are observing by introducing you to one additional taxonomy that you may be less familiar with but that can provide another valuable resource for your thinking.

The SOLO taxonomy (structure of observed learning outcomes; Biggs & Collis, 1982) is a means to "classifying learning outcomes in terms of their complexity" (n.p.). It is helpful and highly recommended for considering how students are moving through the levels of thinking and understanding. Though the names may intimidate some, once simplified, the levels are very logical for planning and implementing lessons and units and, therefore, can aid an observer.

Prestructural (has no idea yet/does not understand)

Unistructural (understands one idea)

Multistructural (understands multiple ideas but not their relationship)

Relational (can relate or join ideas)

Extended abstract (can extend ideas and transfer)

Regardless of the tool you are using, we recommend you take the time to understand how the taxonomy helps to identify what it is we want students to know or know how to do and how these align to surface and deep learning and transfer. For example, notice in Figure 2.4 (an adaptation of Anderson et al.'s [2001] revisions) that we can identify what we want students to know (knowledge dimension) and how they will learn it (cognitive process), going beyond the pyramid (or a going-up-rungs-of-a-ladder concept). Notice that these include our Goal 2 and 3 as essential knowledge. Dianna Fisher, the creator of the graphic, built an interactive version that includes samples of learning objectives, and you can also find an excellent three-dimensional model from Iowa State University.

FIGURE 2.4: THE TAXONOMY TABLE

Bloom's Taxonomy						
The Knowledge Dimension	The Cognitive Process Dimension					
	Remember	Understand	Apply	Analyze	Evaluate	Create
Factual Knowledge	List	Summarize	Classify	Order	Rank	Combine
Conceptual Knowledge	Describe	Interpret	Experiment	Explain	Assess	Plan
Procedural Knowledge	Tabulate	Predict	Calculate	Differentiate	Conclude	Compose
Metacognitive Knowledge	Appropriate use	Execute	Construct	Achieve	Action	Actualize

Source: Fisher (2019).

Whether in your own classroom or as a leader delivering professional learning, the more deeply we understand classifications of levels of learning as observers, the more effective we become in our own instruction and in our support for teachers in recognizing why, when, and how learning is occurring. The objective for an observer is to develop the capacity to see how learning is progressing within the classroom, and to share what is causing those outcomes as well as how those outcomes are progressing.

The value of deep learning and transfer is clear as our students step into a VUCA (volatile, uncertain, complex, and ambiguous) world. Yet, so often, 90 percent of the instruction can be completed by students using only surface-level skills (Hattie, 2012; Antonetti & Garver, 2015). So let's consider why learning is remaining at the surface.

What might prevent learning from progressing beyond surface-level learning?

Potential Reason 1: Fear, Disposition, and/or Compliance

Teachers are told to increase rigor and to share responsibility while also trying to keep pace with curriculum guides (that are potentially brand new) and testing schedules. Because of this, teachers will often skip over or not spend enough time on essential surface-level skills. They do not build in opportunities for students to practice with or revisit concepts, and many think, "I taught it; I have to move on." This results in surface learning or limited learning for many. Recently, we shared with a teacher after an observation that based on our interactions with her learners, at least six to seven of her sixth graders did not understand how to identify evidence that supported their claims. This is a necessary and highly challenging step they must master *before* beginning to write and integrate that evidence, utilize it in future arguments, or form an opinion from a variety of sources. The teacher said, "But I need to get them writing," expressing her frustration that her pacing schedules seem to prevent her from thoroughly covering basic skills.

Potential Reason 2: Skill and Understanding

- Teachers and those supporting them often do not have the understanding of taxonomies or how students think and learn, of how to scaffold to ensure student success, or of how to utilize assessment, feedback, or shifts to support students in deeper learning. They do not know how to build lessons within units that will drive toward conceptual understanding or transfer. In many of the schools we visit, there are teachers and supervisors who are still struggling to understand learning targets and utilize backward design.

- Teachers are following a less-than-stellar curriculum or program. "Curriculum materials are seldom designed to systematically set up this intellectual synergy between the factual and conceptual levels of thinking. Though concepts are mentioned and often defined, they appear to be, 'oh by the way . . .' afterthoughts that one might want to consider. . . . Concept-based teachers know how to adapt lower level curriculum materials to teach for deeper understanding" (Erickson, 2007, p. 10).

Notice that our potential reasons follow the same pattern. If teachers of teachers and leaders of leaders do not support those in need in the essential surface learning, then deep teaching and learning cannot occur.

Potential Reason 3: Student Dispositions

Some students do not want to face challenge or persevere in the type of thinking we are promoting.

Cautions for Observers

To combat these identified challenges and to support teacher and student dispositions, skills, and understandings through observation and feedback, we offer two key cautions for observers.

Caution 1: Learners need foundations

Often "lower-level" or "surface" learning—or what we might consider recall—has been equated with "bad" practice. Look back again at the indicator examples in Figure 2.3. Notice the description that says that students should be constructing new learning through "appropriately integrated recall." Learning generally requires students to use facts (recall) to arrive at conceptual understanding. We also can see forms of memorization at play in both surface *and* deep learning. Keep in mind that why learners are memorizing and how they use the memorized information make the difference.

We have to remember,

> facts and topics do not transfer. Whenever we try to apply our insights from one situation to another we are always abstracting to the conceptual level, generalizing from a specific instance to a broader rule, before our knowledge helps us unlock the new situation. . . . If we remain at the topic and factual level, students stop trying to derive larger principles about what they're learning. (Stern et al., 2017, p. 15)

Educators also assume learners must move up through levels like a ladder to the "better" level.

Charlotte Danielson (2016) reminds us,

> The danger for learning occurs when teaching of facts and procedures is substituted for conceptual understanding. That is, students can simply memorize procedures for getting the right answer, or the facts of history, or the definitions of terms in science. But without conceptual underpinning supporting their memory, it is vulnerable to being forgotten, to not being available to apply to other situations. The concepts just memorized can't in any meaningful sense be said to have been learned. Constructivist teaching, on the other hand, aims for conceptual, flexible, understanding with students in control of powerful understanding. (p. 35)

Teachers need peers, coaches, and administrators who understand how learners build foundations and who can observe for a teacher's impact on learners' abilities to achieve deep learning and transfer.

Caution 2: Do not make assumptions or label learners.

It is easy to say, "Oh, that child isn't a deep thinker because . . .". We must remember *surface* and *deep* are not attributes of individuals, and one learner may use both approaches at different times (Atherton, 2013). As Debbie Silver (2012) reminds us, learners who exhibit ineffective habits such as learned helplessness "do not necessarily lack the requisite skills or ability. Rather, it is their perception of themselves that is flawed" (p. 61), and Eric Jensen (2005) asserts that students will pair negative emotions with each new learning experience if a negative association is made previously.

Interestingly, Stern et al. (2017) also note, "Students often want learning to be black and white. Contradictions and complications are generally unwelcome, and their brains want to sift them out. When faced with a complication, they unconsciously iron out the kinks to make the example fit their preexisting theory" (pp. 63–64). Students who are taught the skills to maintain control of their own understanding, who think metacognitively (Goal 2), and who utilize self-regulation (Goal 3) have the tools and mindsets to overcome challenges, contradictions and complications, and learned helplessness.

Observers can avoid the cautionary scenarios by paying close attention to learners during observations using our foundational evidence collection strategies of listening, viewing, and interacting to ensure that accurate causal attributions are determined for observed outcomes.

Stop and Think: Review our three potential reasons learners may remain at a surface level of learning and our cautions. Are any of these issues present in your school? Has professional learning helped to address or build capacity related to these?

Goal 2: Students need to learn how to think metacognitively.

Metacognition, or thinking about thinking, is not a new concept, with research dating back to the 1970s but actually with origins in Socrates's methods. It is a powerful skill to possess, but "despite the wealth of research on the importance of teaching metacognition, educational practice continues to focus almost exclusively on content knowledge" (Wilson & Conyers, 2016, p. 15). Students can learn how to think about their thinking to where it "can become so practiced, so normal, that as a mental habit, it almost acquires the status of personality trait" (Martinez, 2006, p. 698). In fact, Costa and Kallick's (2009) sixteen habits of mind—what we do when we don't know what to do—includes metacognition along with other essential and related habits such as "Questioning and Posing Problems," "Striving for Accuracy," and "Thinking Flexibly."

Habits, dispositions, and thinking are challenging to observe. As an observer, to understand how students are moving along a continuum toward becoming metacognitive thinkers, it helps to first understand that metacognition, too, has layers:

a. Metacognitive awareness: understanding where you are in the learning process and what needs to be done

b. Metacognitive evaluation: making judgments about your effectiveness with possible anticipation of regulation needed

c. Metacognitive regulation: using your metacognitive skills to direct knowledge and thinking and skills like planning and self-correcting (Wilson & Clarke, 2011)

Our upcoming chapters will make these more visible by providing specific evidence collection strategies and examples.

Goal 3: Students need to develop the ability to self-regulate and self-monitor.

We have separated self-regulation and self-monitoring, although, in terms of mental processing, they are interrelated. If metacognition is thinking about thinking, then self-regulation is acting upon that thinking. To effectively self-regulate, students need to be able to self-monitor (observe and check their own behaviors), self-evaluate (determine if the behaviors are leading to success), and make changes based on the determination. We are seeking to determine how the teacher has enabled (or not enabled) students to engage in self-regulation and self-monitoring. "Students can be described as self-regulated to the degree that they are metacognitively, motivationally, and behaviorally active participants in their own learning process" (Zimmerman, 1989).

"Purposefully monitoring one's own learning is at the heart of metacognition." Self-monitoring is the "ability to track one's thoughts and actions in learning. Students who are adept at this metacognitive skill regularly ask themselves, 'How well do I understand this lesson? How can I evaluate my understanding and what more do I need to learn? How does this knowledge fit into what I already know? Which strategies am I using/can I use?'" (Wilson & Conyers, 2016, p. 89). You can see how critical these questions (and answers!) are for students in order for them to become self-directed learners.

Students can self-monitor countless behaviors, such as attention to task, solving a math problem, or comprehending a reading passage. A 2011 study of metacognition in math instruction provided specific examples articulated by students of their ongoing thinking during tasks. These demonstrate the idea that mental movement through our three goals is not linear and thus difficult to observe and measure. Student notes included the following:

> *"I tried to remember if I had ever done a problem like this before."* (self-awareness)
>
> *"I made a plan to work it out."* (self-regulation)
>
> *"I counted."* (cognitive thinking/activity)
>
> *"I thought about whether what I was doing was working."* (self-evaluation)
>
> (Wilson & Clarke, 2011, p. 39)

Metacognitive experiences may result in two different steps. For example, imagine that you are studying for a test and realize you need to reread sections of a chapter, resource, or text to better understand a concept (cognitive/improve knowledge). Or you might decide to quiz yourself on the content (metacognitive, which will lead to either more metacognitive or cognitive steps). "Cognitive strategies are invoked to make cognitive progress, metacognitive to monitor it" (Flavell, 1979, p. 909). Without the cognitive resources—or until automaticity is built—students will struggle to utilize metacognitive resources. (This is an example of how memorization, fluency work, and surface learning contribute to deeper learning and allow the brain to work more efficiently.) This is what we want to try to capture and analyze as observers to support teachers in this challenging work.

Stop and Think: Does instruction in your building or district/region address all three goals for learners? Have you observed lessons with learner Goals 2 and 3 in mind? Where do you find teachers need the most support in helping students reach the three goals?

Character

While not explicit in our three goals, the competency of character remains important and appears as one of the six Cs. Character is inclusive of a student's capacity to demonstrate grit, tenacity, perseverance, and resilience—all essential elements of social-emotional learning that have been established as fundamental to student success. Goal 3 helps us to focus on the analysis of the self-regulation and self-evaluation necessary for social-emotional success. Debbie Silver (2012; Silver & Stafford, 2017) has written two books with titles that encapsulate everything we are trying to achieve each day in our schools: *Teaching Kids to Thrive* and *Fall Down 7 Times, Get Up 8: Teaching Kids to Succeed*. Our students need the academic, social, and self-skills to thrive, to get up time and again, to be happy, and to be successful in all they set out to do.

These skills are no longer secondary to the curriculum or picked up in an advisory program, lunch bunch, or during supplemental events. "We must attend to language, thinking and emotions simultaneously because children learn best in an environment that acknowledges the interconnectivity of both cognitive and emotional development" (Fullan et al., 2018, p. 23). Students need and deserve a classroom and school environment where they feel successful, where they are learning, and where their learning meets their needs within an ever-evolving, often stressful world. Sadly, in many cases, school may be the only safe and potentially stress-free environment to which some students have access. So while we do not attempt to directly teach classroom practice associated with social-emotional learning in this book, we want to help you establish an understanding of the connections in order to define more clearly what and how to observe in classrooms. What we are coming to see is that "All Learning Is Social and Emotional," the title of Frey, Fisher, and Smith's 2019 publication that so appropriately sums it up.

Student-Owned Learning

The three goals outlined previously describe learners who own their own learning and know how to learn. They are *leaders of their own learning* (Berger, Rugen, & Woodfin, 2014) or *assessment-capable visible learners* (Frey, Hattie, & Fisher, 2018). These students

- know where they are going, understanding current performance and how it relates to learning goals and criteria,
- have the tools for the journey and know they can select from a range of strategies,
- monitor their own progress, seek feedback, and know that making mistakes is expected,
- recognize when they are ready for what's next against the learning intention and criteria, and
- know what to do next, including what to do when they do not know what to do (Frey et al., 2018, p. 15).

Remember our parallel to teachers becoming assessment-capable learners? We realized that learners who know how to learn and who clearly see where they are headed often have high levels of self-efficacy, as they see goals as attainable and experience bite-sized success each day. Just consider the social-emotional impact of this for a moment.

In order to develop this type of learner, specific knowledge, skills, dispositions, and tools need to be in place for both teacher and student. We introduced you to teacher look-fors in Chapter 1 but added student examples (though certainly not an exhaustive list) for you to think about in Figure 2.5. Similar to our work with teachers, you must consider what foundational knowledge students will need; for example, what "criteria" is, or what it means to learn. As an observer, these understandings allow you to utilize your evidence collection, analysis, and feedback to directly support a teacher in this work.

FIGURE 2.5: TEACHER AND STUDENT LOOK-FORS

	Teachers	Students
Skills Need to know how to . . .	• Build student capacity to work independently • Use appropriate scaffolding • Model self-monitoring, using criteria, making adjustments, and utilizing resources and evaluating effectiveness of resources • Plan/facilitate learning vs. delivering content • Give feedback to drive student-owned learning	• Monitor own work, and reflect using a learning target and criteria • Support peers in the day's work and give/receive feedback • Use a resource to move forward • Evaluate effectiveness of resources • Think metacognitively
Dispositions Need to be willing to . . .	• Turn learning over to students • Allow good struggle • Have high expectations/belief that students can achieve and think at high levels	• Take responsibility and rely less on teacher • Seek out or use resources • Take risks, attempt responses, deal with disagreements, or revise reasoning
Tools Need to have available . . .	• Clear and specific daily learning goals • Clear and specific learning criteria • Time throughout each lesson for reflection • Time in each lesson to unpack goals and criteria	• Usable tools for students to monitor their own/peer's work (e.g., exemplars, checklists, models, rubrics) • Usable resources (e.g., word lists students can locate/read)

Stop and Think: Are you facilitating these skills and dispositions and using these tools in your school or classroom to support the vision of learning and achievement of the goals we set for our students?

How the Brain Works

In many schools and districts we visit, as instruction has focused predominantly on content, so too has observation. Little attention has been paid or support provided to teachers in teaching students how to learn. We have also found that most teacher preparation programs have not provided incoming teachers with coursework, nor has ongoing professional learning focused on these outcomes or on how students' brains actually learn and work (nor has any leader preparation that we have seen). So let's begin to chip away at this new idea with Strategy 4.

Strategy 4: Understand how learners learn

We struggled to condense years of research into just a few paragraphs, to share some of the most important takeaways and considerations that influence our observation practices.

For teachers and observers to understand how learners are learning, we have to understand the thing responsible for learning—our brains! Think for a minute of your self-assessment at the beginning of the chapter. What do you know about how our brains actually process information? This was not part of our undergrad or graduate work in education in the 1990s. We know that our brains (especially those of children) are highly impacted by social, physical, cognitive, and emotional influences, and Eric Jensen (2005) got our attention when he said, "Students who attend school from kindergarten through secondary school typically spend more than 13,000 hours of their developing brain's time in the presence of teachers . . . and their brains will be altered by the experiences they have in school" (p. 1). No pressure! So what do we *need* to understand about the brain to maximize our impact on learners? We are finding it is all about connections.

The brain is constantly seeking to make connections and find patterns. Individual neurons carry information and, over time, can become more efficient. Instead of neurons firing one at a time, mindful teaching can allow neurons to form bundles or neural networks that fire together with less effort.

> Deep learning helps the brain build those important patterns of understanding necessary if we expect to encode the new learning into long-term memory and recall it when needed. By manipulating the new learning in various ways through different thought processes and sensory modalities, the learner builds more interconnections within and between neural networks. This mass of interconnections provides multiple pathways for retrieving the new learning from long-term memory. (Sousa & Tomlinson, 2018, p. 59)

Lynn Erickson (2007) recognizes "to stimulate more sophisticated, complex thinking, we need to create a *synergy* between the simpler and more complex processing centers in the brain. This interactive synergy requires the mind to process the information on two cognitive levels—the factual and the conceptual. The conceptual mind uses facts as a tool to discern patterns, connections, and deeper transferable understandings" (p. 10). "The ability to transfer knowledge and skills to new or similar contexts is evidence of deeper understanding and higher order thinking" (p. 13). Yet curriculum and teaching practices often do not build to this level.

The concepts of surface and deep learning and transfer are directly related to what we know about how the brain works. Therefore, it seems logical that anyone who has the power to alter the most complex organ in the human body should understand, to some degree, how instructional choices can impact it in positive or negative ways. Though there is already much research about how the brain works, there is still more to know about applications in teaching and learning. Let's consider some of the agreed-upon basics (we emphasize *basics*) that are pertinent to us as observers, with a few related instructional practices (Figure 2.6).

FIGURE 2.6: BRAIN FUNCTIONS AND TEACHING

What's Involved	Description	Considerations	Related Instructional Practices
Sensory memory or sensory perception	Information comes in from the senses for a moment (less than one second) before an internal decision is made about what to do with it (discarded or enters sensory memory)	"The assignment of meaning to incoming stimuli depends on prior knowledge," and this is where pattern recognition occurs or not. "When we experience something new, our brain looks for an existing network. . . . If the brain can find no previously activated networks into which the new information fits, it is much less likely to attend to this information" (Wolfe, 2010, pp. 108, 113, 118).	Establishing context and relevance, hooking students, capturing attention
Short-term or working memory	Three to seven chunks of information are stored before overload for only five to twenty-five seconds or up to a minute (varies based on age and other factors)	"Prior learning is personal, complex, and highly resistant to change . . . students might not understand a concept as they have a competing, conflicting, or unreliable prior knowledge that dooms their thinking" (Jensen, 2005, pp. 45–46). "Once teachers have a sense of what students already know, they can use that to their advantage to anchor new knowledge to existing knowledge. Anchoring fosters schema as students begin to make connections and see relationships among concepts" (Frey, Hattie, & Fisher, 2018, p. 34).	Establishing context, connecting new learning to prior, chunking, rehearsal Developing use of strategies, building automaticity

What's Involved	Description	Considerations	Related Instructional Practices
	Connection making for explicit learning begins within fifteen minutes of exposure	"Honing working memory helps students think faster, weigh the pros and cons to make better decisions, adapt to new situations, and maintain motivation to achieve long-term learning goals" (Wilson & Conyers, 2016, p. 73). "When things are learned, working memory can be devoted to more complex thinking." We "should value memorization and recall of the content information if it then leads to reducing students' working memory demand so that they go on to understand conceptual relationship, extend their ideas, and think critically" (Frey, Hattie, & Fisher, 2018, pp. 11, 49).	Integrating appropriate recall, surface learning, helping students make connections between the unfamiliar and familiar, opportunities for retrieval
Long-term memory	If the learning is considered to be worth remembering/important, it will be organized, cataloged, stored by the brain	"Critical thinking skills take time to learn because you're asking the brain to make changes . . . learning new skills literally reorganizes brain mass" (Jensen, 2005, p. 116). "Our ability to remember is essentially a process of reconstruction or reactivation. . . . Coverage (going over information superficially) does not build strong neural connections and is seldom remembered, or it is remembered incorrectly" (Wolfe, 2010, pp. 152, 158).	Time for practice and peer teaching, repeated rehearsal/retrieval over time, increasing degrees of challenge/authentic problem solving and experiences

Teachers and observers need to determine how instructional choices can impact *if and how* new information is stored or learned and why. For example, we need to notice if teachers are taking the time to help learners connect to prior learning or just starting lessons by saying, "Remember, yesterday we were working on the legislative branch of government, so today we are going to talk about the judicial branch," and then beginning new content. This is not helping students to activate prior learning, make connections, or identify what they do or do not remember, nor is it helping the teacher to determine what they do or do not know.

Marcia Tate's (2016) ten characteristics of classrooms where students excel and her strategies for a *brain-compatible classroom* from *Worksheets Don't Grow Dendrites* can help teachers to more purposefully plan teaching based on how students learn and also allow observers to more purposefully collect evidence to support teachers in this challenging work. Ideally, instruction includes the following:

1. Positive environment
2. Visuals
3. Music
4. Relevant lessons
5. Rituals taught
6. Students talking about content
7. Students moving to learn content
8. High expectations
9. High challenge/low stress
10. Content taught in chunks with action

Stop and Think: Consider Figure 2.6, and think about the research. What other instructional choices might impact how students attend to and retain new information? What student actions or tasks might increase that impact?

Eager to know more? Beyond the sources cited earlier, additional resources we found useful include the following:

12 Brain/Mind Learning Principles in Action: The Fieldbook for Making Connections, Teaching, and the Human Brain (3rd ed. , 2015), Caine, Caine, McClintic, & Klimek

How the Brain Learns (5th ed., 2017), Sousa

Differentiation and the Brain: How Neuroscience Supports the Learner-Friendly Classroom (2018), Sousa & Tomlinson

Identifying Learning in Action

Though it is important to think deeply about the teaching, observers need to remain highly attentive to what learners look and sound like as their brains are working. It would be great if we could actually see a hamster running on a wheel for each student when we visit classrooms or giant lightbulbs shining or dimming above students' heads throughout a lesson to help us better understand what is happening. While the signposts might not be as obvious as we'd like, rest assured, there are observables that we can hear and see and questions we can ask to ascertain how a learner is progressing. Start by thinking about a skill you have now mastered: What did you look and sound like in each phase of learning? Did someone help you in the process?

"Teachers should carefully consider the phase of students' learning needs and which approaches are more likely to guide thinking" (Frey et al., 2018, p. 19).

As observers, we are trying to observe for

> three inputs and three outcomes; student knowledge of the success criteria for the task; three phases of the learning process (surface, deep, and transfer), with surface and deep learning each comprising an acquisition phase and a consolidation phase; and an environment for the learning. We are proposing that various learning strategies are differentially effective depending on the degree to which the students are aware of the criteria of success, on the phases of learning process in which the strategies are used, and on whether the student is acquiring or consolidating their understanding. (Hattie & Donaghue, 2016, p. 1)

Remember, "Deep learning is not about one particular method of teaching" (Fullan et al., 2018, pp. 45–46). It is about how we lead students through learning to ensure they become lifelong learners, understanding how they think and what they need. Teachers should strive to possess "a wide range of pedagogical capacities and use thinking tools and explicit questions to scaffold learning for that particular student or task so that students are challenged to meet the next level of learning and develop increasingly complex capacities and competencies" (Fullan et al., 2018, p. 67). This leads us to our next strategy and the role of teachers in the learning process. "A key asset in self-monitoring is cognitive flexibility, the capacity to objectively consider two or more concepts simultaneously and to recognize when it may be useful to adjust one's thinking and actions based on new information. . . . Cognitive flexibility allows us to look at things differently—to learn new ways of doing things and solve problems" (Wilson & Conyers, 2016, pp. 90, 95).

As teachers, we have the power to build this *cognitive flexibility* and to actually impact neural activity or effect outcomes.

Strategy 5: Understand how teachers create outcomes

We came across Hattie's (2012) description of teachers as *activators* and liked this concept very much. If your yoga or workout instructors are anything like ours, they are always telling us to "engage your core" or, in other words, tell your stomach muscles it is time to think about getting to work or become an active participant in a position. Highly effective workouts are built from warm-ups that prepare us for what is to come: stretch, engage (turn on targeted areas), and activate (recruit more muscles). They say activation exercises can maximize workouts and prepare your muscles for challenging work ahead—sounds exactly like steps we would take for getting brains ready for learning each day.

Then, we encountered Fullan's concept of teachers as *cultivators*, which we equally loved. This evoked related images in that cultivation ensures that the soil is ready for new seed, maximizing the opportunity for growth, along with visions of tending to the seedling as it grows. Your job as observers, through comprehensive evidence collection and feedback about impact, is to help teachers understand how they are (or can be) serving as cultivators and activators of learners.

Recognizing Impact on Learning

As you think about how the brain works, you are already headed down the path of pondering cause-and-effect relationships and how teaching practices impact a learner's ability to learn. We mentioned social-emotional learning, but we know developing brains are significantly impacted when Maslow's (1943) basic safety and physiological needs are not being met. "Very high levels of stress over time are damaging and can impair cognition" (Jensen, 2005, p. 74), and "stress does impair verbal and working memory" (Jensen, 2005, citing Lupien, Gillin, & Hauger, 1999). We want to acknowledge that we are well aware of the challenges students face in their lives every day that are not within the control of a teacher, coach, or leader.

Over our careers, we have conducted home visits—Amy, as an administrator at an alternative school—looking for students who were chronically absent (finding all of their belongings outside of their homes, evicted). She opened freezers to see if they had food and bought clothes so they had something clean to wear. Patrick once asked students to draw "home" for an eighth-grade group task to create a community within the classroom and learned one student was homeless when he drew a car. He worked with the mother and the school team to ensure they could find housing.

We want to acknowledge the extraordinary emotional, psychological, and physical means educators use to best support students in varying levels of trauma—and how much more frequent this need is becoming. It is important to remember to take care of yourselves (another book, for another day). Remember though, school may be the only place a student can feel safe and successful—things we can control through our classroom environments and instructional choices. Therefore, for our purposes in this book, we want to focus on those things within our control in our classrooms.

Danielson (2016) cites Glasser, Deci, and White, among others, who identify additional psychological needs that need to be met in classrooms (think of the belongingness, esteem, and self-actualization needs from Maslow). Teachers' choices and actions directly impact how students experience the following:

- Belonging and making connections with others
- Competence or mastery: "Part of the satisfaction is the struggle itself: If it's too easy, if there is no challenge, the result is cheapened. Mastery of complex content, then, represents *power*."
- Autonomy or freedom
- Intellectual challenge (pp. 38–39)

The Chicken or the Egg

When it comes to what impacts our learners, figuring out what causes specific outcomes reminds us of the chicken-or-the-egg dilemma—which comes first? For learners to become empowered, we need to challenge them to think deeply, but they need to feel empowered to persevere and work through a challenge. Our challenges need to include collaboration, but for collaboration to occur, students need to know how to make connections with each other and feel safe doing so. No wonder teachers feel overwhelmed!

Our good friend Alisha DiCorpo, assistant superintendent for New Milford Public Schools, was concerned about the level of support for teachers in her district. She worked to shift district thinking and their theory of action by creating the following overarching theme for any professional learning provided (essentially making a theory of action actionable): "*Moving from the 'if' to the 'then.'*" She wanted to focus on providing professional-learning opportunities that would build teachers' understanding of what lies between the *if* and the *then* and how to bridge that gap. We created and coached the district to use a simple visual aid to reinforce how teachers impact engagement and learning every day through choices and strategies and how engagement and learning are related. Use the frame "If . . . then . . ." from Figure 2.7 beginning at the top, and consider how each action and outcome fuels the next, ultimately bringing about high levels of motivation and self-efficacy in the classroom. (Think about Bandura from Chapter 1.)

FIGURE 2.7: IF–THEN RELATIONSHIPS

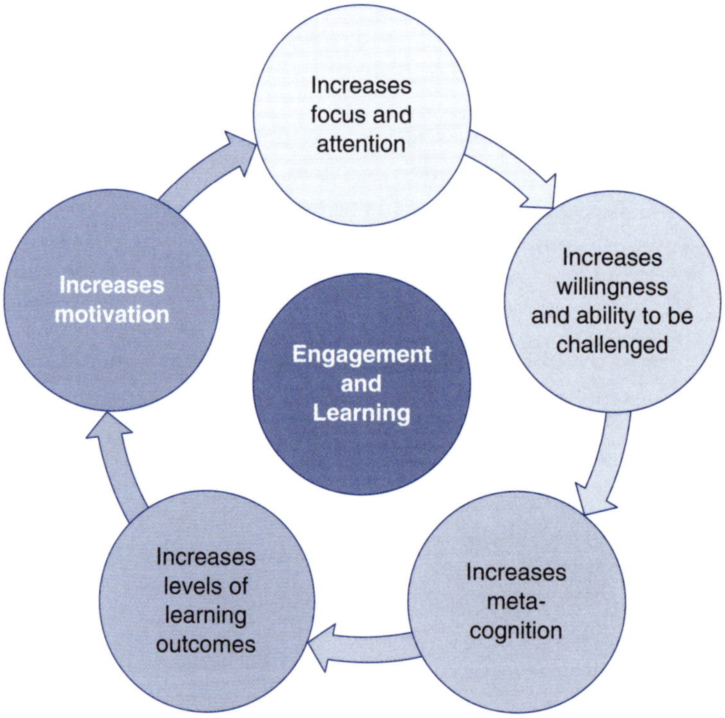

Source: Tepper and Flynn, LLC.

By starting with gaining students' attention, we can help teachers build a cycle for continuous improvement. For example,

> ***If*** *we can start with just gaining student focus and attention (sometimes a heavy lift!),* ***then*** *we will increase student willingness and, ultimately, their ability to be challenged (think: skill and will), thus leading to higher levels of engagement.*

Continue around the circle, thinking about how to move from the if to the then. The process includes strategies and tasks to ensure students are making connections and seeing relevance.

> ***If*** *we increase student willingness to be challenged,* ***then*** *they will be more open to think metacognitively about how they are learning.* ***If*** *they are thinking metacognitively,* ***then*** *we increase outcomes; students don't just master an objective, they are learning to self-monitor and self-adjust.* ***If*** *they achieve even bite-sized success through this process and see goals as attainable,* ***then*** *we increase intrinsic motivation.*

Notice how we can go round and round the circle, increasing outcomes exponentially. (Of course, other factors will influence outcomes, like explicit teaching of the skills needed.)

Engagement

Teachers are constantly hearing that their students need to be *engaged*. But, much like the term *learning*, there are many definitions and interpretations, again requiring that you and your team work to build a common understanding of expectations and look-fors. Consistently, observers share with teachers after an observation, "Everyone was engaged," simply meaning that everyone was completing the task or was paying attention. "There is a difference between being entertained and engaged. An entertaining teacher is the center of attention, whereas a teacher who engages students provides tools and resources for them to be the attentive center of their learning" (Quaglia & Corso, 2014, p. 85).

In *Feedback to Feed Forward*, we devote a significant portion of time to the concept of engagement and provide several frames that you might already use, such as Schlechty's five levels, various taxonomies, or a threefold perspective of behavioral, emotional, and cognitive engagement. However, now that you have added new layers of understanding, you might extend or revisit how you define and measure cognitive or intellectual engagement.

> **Stop and Think:** How is engagement defined in your school? What steps can you take to unify around a single vision and understanding?

Increasing Attention/The Role of Attention

Increases focus and attention

We often hear teachers tell students to pay attention, which is different from asking them to truly engage in learning. A student can look at a teacher and listen but make no meaningful connections, storing (and losing) everything in short-term memory. We know focus or attention is critical, as many of us have designed lessons for years with a "hook" to grab them. And the week before a holiday break, when it is raining, in May . . . there's an even greater need! With the ever-growing competition we face from phones and video games, we feel the pressure to compete to get students' attention. Attention serves as the baseline for higher-order thinking processes, including self-regulating thoughts and behavior, making meaning of new information, and employing new strategies (Miller, 2007, cited by Wilson & Conyers, 2016).

But know this: When you ask students to "pay attention," "the brain is always paying attention to something" (Wolfe, 2010, p. 114). "Paying attention is not easy to do consciously . . . we orient, engage, and maintain . . . and exclude or suppress external and internal distractors. . . . Remember that the human brain is poor at nonstop attention" (Jensen, 2005, pp. 35, 37). Getting students' attention is one thing, but teaching them how to maintain their own attention and focus is another—one that is a learned skill and necessary for them to truly own their own learning.

Wilson and Conyers (2016) define "selective attention as the skill of identifying what is important in any given situation and attention to what is necessary with appropriate focus." They assert,

> The ability to focus on lesson content and to attend to learning tasks is a fundamental aspect of self-regulatory behavior that can be enhanced through deliberate practice. Explicit instruction on selective attention can help students to become better listeners, to take the initiative on learning tasks, and to set a realistic pace for making steady progress on their learning goals. . . . Developing selective attention can also help students enhance the cognitive asset of working memory in action. (pp. 72–73)

We can strengthen selective attention by shifting student focus to their own learning and their thinking about their thinking and helping them to see the importance and relevance in the learning.

The Role of Emotion

"Emotions give us a more activated and chemically stimulated brain, they help us recall things better and form more explicit memories . . . for students to think well, they absolutely must be able to manage their emotional states. This ability is not innate; it must be taught" (Jensen, 2005, pp. 71, 121).

We can evoke feelings or reactions as students experience our choices, tasks, strategies, and classroom environment. Think of the importance of emotion and our physiological state to our self-efficacy from Chapter 1. Though there are some really interesting related psychological studies out there (if this interests you), for all of us who have spent any time with students, we know that feelings are tied to beliefs, which are tied to motivation. Jensen (2005) reminds us, "Mind and emotions are not separate . . . emotions organize and create our reality" (p. 68). So much of what we do as educators creates emotional states, intentionally and unintentionally. Emotions

- constitute the passion for learning;
- help orchestrate our attentional priorities;
- support either persistence or retreat;
- are sources of information about the outside world;
- evoke necessary empathy, support, or fear;
- improve social problem solving;
- allow us to enjoy and even celebrate our learning success; and
- can enhance memory (Jensen, 2005, pp. 58, 68, 69).

If you want to know more about the neuroscience, Jensen's *Teaching With the Brain in Mind* (second edition) is a helpful resource; it wades much farther into the connection between learning and emotion.

Based on what we know about the brain and what we've experienced when teenagers ask, "What do I need this for?" when students see connections, importance, and relevance, we can gain attention and potentially inspire and motivate our students. Marcia Tate suggests teachers integrate any of four "hooks" to gain and maintain students' attention in a lesson, to increase engagement and connection through emotion, meaning, need, or novelty.

"There's no need for the brain to adapt to change if what it must deal with is the same. Novelty creates a stronger opportunity for new learning and pathways in the brain" (Jensen, 2005, p. 120). Whatever the brain perceives as unusual, it remembers and wakes up to pay attention (Sprenger, 2018). As observers and teachers, be careful—we've seen very excited middle school students get so lost in launching rockets that they completely forgot to use data and collaborative decision making to improve models, ripping fins off and scrambling to add tape just to get a chance to relaunch.

Increasing Willingness and Motivation

Increases willingness and ability to be challenged

So teachers have students' attention; what's next? Notice in Figure 2.7 that the second circle represents the work toward getting a student to say, "Okay, I am willing to try." Think about the dance you did in November (or March!) when one of your students finally said this. We know this is a big step for some and takes time, especially for those students who have developed learned helplessness. For example, we step into countless high school classrooms where students sit and wait for the teacher or just accept that they "aren't good at math."

Once we have their attention, we have to provide them with tools, habits, and support to turn that into perseverance driven by intrinsic motivation. "Real engagement comes from within a student who is intentionally aiming for a shared learning target and is required to reason—engage with the content—in ways that empower the student to self-assess and self-regulate" (Moss & Brookhart, 2015, p. 20). The motivation comes from experiencing small successes, especially those achieved by reaching beyond what they did before, or in other words, "Nothing is more motivating than a hard earned success" (Silver, 2012, p. 20).

Increases meta-cognition

But sometimes students won't succeed. The magic happens in those moments. We know from Bandura that students' belief in their own abilities—self-efficacy—is driven by the understanding of *causal attributes*, or what caused the outcomes. We want students to seek answers as to why they did not succeed, not simply give up or sit with their hand up waiting for the nearest adult. This is where all of those metacognitive skills can kick in! We know all learners can become self-motivated, autonomous, and more successful when they have choice and control over aspects of their learning environments and experience (Quaglia & Corso, 2014; Silver, 2012). It is also equally as powerful for students to determine what is causing success so those actions and choices can be replicated.

You may notice a parallel here between Chapters 1 and 2. All learners—teachers and students—can own their learning. When evidence collection is grounded in the fundamental understanding of how learners learn, observers and those who support observers have the power to drive toward this goal.

Stop and Think: Look through each of the circles in Figure 2.7. Consider, as an observer, what each stage might look and sound like (teacher and student actions and behaviors). Utilize the skills, tools, and dispositions from Figure 2.5 to help you.

Determining Causal Attribution

As we make the shift to observing and providing feedback with attention to teaching *and* learning, the analysis and focus need to remain on how the teacher is impacting or causing the outcomes. The goal is to help teachers see the causal attributes as strengths and areas of growth through our feedback. We know from Bandura that this is the source of self-efficacy and can lead to increased levels of collective teacher efficacy.

So far in this chapter, you have encountered several factors that impact learners, and we know there are plenty of things we encounter every day that are not in our control. But to help teachers more clearly see what is within their control, we organized instructional practices into categories, or five focus areas, that impact engagement and learning (Figure 2.8), introduced in *Feedback to Feed Forward*. As you move through each one, think about what the related teaching and learning look and sound like in a classroom and how teacher choices within each area could potentially impact students. Heading into observations, thinking about factors that influence learners and their interconnectedness better prepares you for evidence collection, which, in turn, will help you determine how the teacher impacted engagement and learning while you visited.

FIGURE 2.8: FIVE FOCUS AREAS

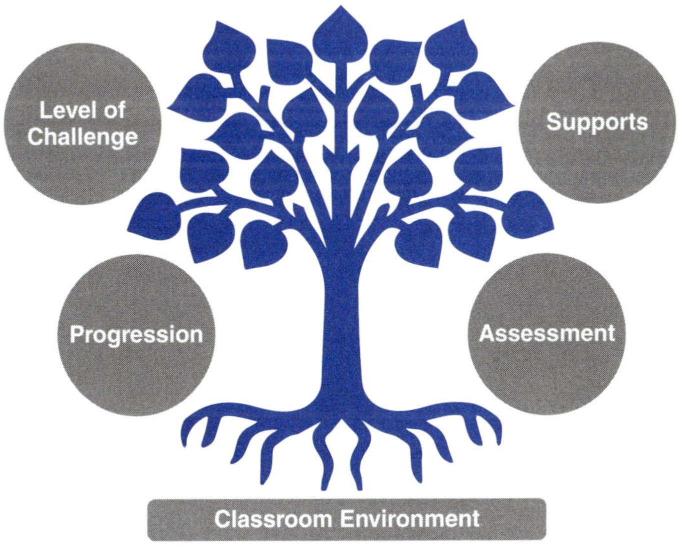

Level of Challenge
Supports
Progression
Assessment
Classroom Environment

Source: Tepper and Flynn, LLC.

Let's briefly consider each one.

Level of Challenge: Think about what you read earlier from experts about the role of learning facts and the need for appropriate surface understanding, memorization, or recall. Certainly, students need to be challenged to read complex texts, make connections, apply thinking in new ways, and think conceptually. "Motivation is sparked by the desire to achieve mastery of a challenging skill or concept. Learning cannot occur in the absence of challenge—its stagnation, not progression" (Frey, Hattie, & Fisher, 2018, p. 52). However, if learners are facing tasks or texts that are too hard (outside their *zone of proximal development*, or ZPD), they will struggle to move forward, and it will decrease their level of efficacy and motivation. This is directly related to the next focus area.

Progression: When you read the word *progression*, perhaps you jump to the idea of the gradual-release model shown in Figure 2.9. Even in classrooms promoting high levels of inquiry and levels of student ownership, we know the benefits of scaffolded instruction that progress in a similar fashion. We also know a successful lesson does not have to unfold in this way. However, if a teacher skips essential components of a progression, for example, moving from "I do" to "You do it alone" omitting a "We do" or "You do together," students may not be set up for success, as depicted in Figure 2.10 as a nonexample of effective gradual release.

FIGURE 2.9: GRADUAL-RELEASE MODEL

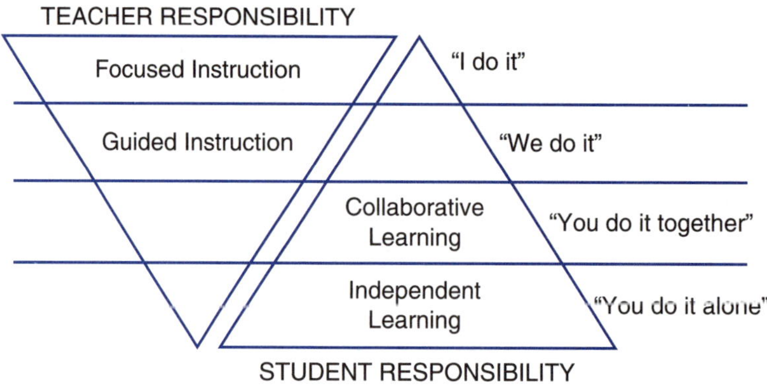

Source: Fisher & Frey (2013).

FIGURE 2.10: GRADUAL RELEASE NONEXAMPLE

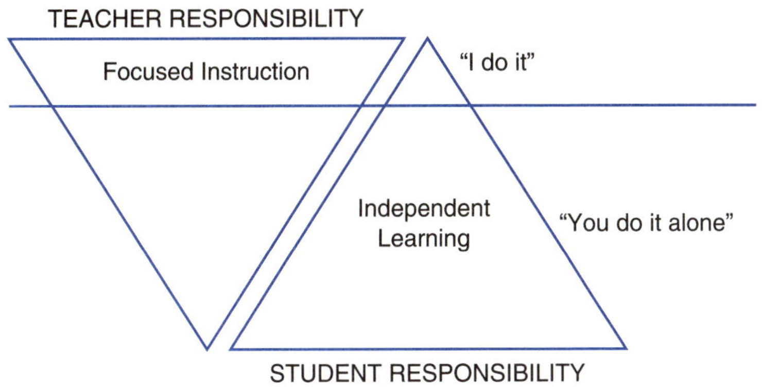

TEACHER RESPONSIBILITY
Focused Instruction
"I do it"
Independent Learning
"You do it alone"
STUDENT RESPONSIBILITY

Source: Fisher & Frey (2013).

It is also important to note that a logical progression within a unit or year is not necessarily occurring in a straight line, and it is absolutely essential for you to remember that "conceptual learning is not linear; it's iterative . . . learning happens through repetitions of the inquiry process, giving students multiple chances to develop ideas and deepen their understanding relative to a single learning goal" (Stern et al., 2017, p. 40). We can't expect to always see students moving neatly along rows in the figure as teachers or observers. A learning progression is unique to each individual and can be messy, and that is what makes teachers' and observers' jobs challenging.

When we think of progression, we also think of how time is used and use of routines such as dedicated time to communicate or determine a day's learning goals and criteria for success and opportunities for reflection throughout. "Students need to be drawn into the analysis and unpacking of learning targets, building a clear vision of where they need to go" (Berger et al., 2014, p. 41). If the teacher—not the students—owns the learning targets and success criteria, it doesn't matter how well they are crafted and worded (Pearson & Gallagher, 1983); they won't allow students to determine and act upon "Where am I going?" and "How am I going?" It is important to know that "clear and shared understandings of what success looks like helps to develop dispositions and attitudes for accepting greater levels of challenge" (Frey et al., 2018, p. 66).

Supports: As students progress through a learning cycle and as we strive to ensure that they are working within their zone of proximal development, they may require anywhere from small to significant support to reach goals. They may require more teacher- or student-driven scaffolding, such as review, revisiting of modeling, or more practice, or they may seek support that might include resources, tools, or peers. Clearly, a lack of appropriate and useful supports can quickly leave students unable to move forward. Teacher-to-student feedback is a form of ongoing support that "fuels perseverance by providing students additional avenues of support and alternatives to the futile 'wheel spinning' that effort alone cannot overcome" (Frey et al., 2018, p. 89).

Assessment: Ongoing formative assessment conducted by teachers followed by action (such as giving feedback, adjusting instruction, differentiating, or pointing to or providing resources) ensures students continue to work within their zone of proximal development (Vygotsky, 1978), maintaining engagement and motivation. Students who self- and peer-assess strengthen metacognitive skills and reach deeper levels of understanding by providing feedback to peers and teaching each other.

Classroom Environment: If learners aren't building the habits or mindsets to persevere and they lack self-efficacy, then they will not be able to meet increased levels of challenge or be willing to use the supports and resources you have made available to them. We have to ensure time is taken throughout the year to explicitly teach and reinforce the skills and dispositions required for students to take ownership of learning. Without this step, teachers will not be able to meet the goal of generating self-regulated learning. We want students to maintain an "outlook of practical optimism" or "an approach to learning and life that focuses on taking practical positive action to increase the probability of successful outcomes" (Wilson & Conyers, 2011, p. 148). Ultimately, all of these impact student motivation, which we know is tied to a willingness to persevere and engage in challenging tasks. We also know that when students are successful and meeting attainable goals, motivation is increased.

Stop and Think: Does feedback you receive or provide address causal attribution? If so, what evidence is provided to support the cause-and-effect relationships?

(See Resource 2.1: Learner-Focused Feedback in the Resource Center, **resources.corwin.com/learnerfocusedfeedback**)

Give It a Try

Beyond taking stock of your own personal understanding of the content in this weighty chapter, we offer a few other role-specific suggestions:

Teachers

- Review Figure 2.7 (If–Then), and think about which is the greatest area of need in your classroom right now. Talk to your peers, and see if they have similar challenges.

- Determine times when you can observe in each others' rooms to practice utilizing the *Feedback to Feed Forward* Strategies 6–14 reviewed in Chapter 1, choosing one to two at a time, or observe for each of the five focus areas (Figure 2.8).
- Self-assess your own use and further research strategies related to how the brain works. Choose one new strategy to implement, and review the impact it had on your learners.
- Identify opportunities to co-plan for strategies that increase engagement and learning based on what you have learned in this chapter.
- Video application: Watch video of your own classroom and analyze your learners carefully for signs they are learning.

Coaches

- Utilize Figure 2.7 (If–Then) as a foundation for determining coaching focus areas and a preliminary observation tool.
- Mindfully practice utilizing the *Feedback to Feed Forward* Strategies 6–14 with a partner or team.
- Practice using the five focus areas (Figure 2.8) as a frame to determine causal attribution to refine coaching focus areas/goal setting.
- Co-teach, model, or observe new strategies related to how the brain works for your teachers.

Supervisors

- Work together at a school, district, or regional level to arrive at a coherent vision for teaching and learning, and establish a plan to build a common understanding of this vision with teachers.
- Ensure that professional-learning experiences provide the adaptive messaging (or *the why*) behind expected effective practices based on what we know about how students learn and what they need.
- Use Figure 2.7 (If–Then) and Figure 2.8 (the five focus areas) or the lists of instructional strategies in this chapter as a foundation for schoolwide data collection and conduct walk-throughs to look for trends and to build professional learning.
- Work to refine your evidence collection utilizing the foundational *Feedback to Feed Forward* Strategies 7–14.

In this chapter, we explored several critical concepts about how students learn in order to provide the foundation for your purposeful evidence collection and impactful feedback. Remember to ground your observation practices in the overarching goal we have established for our students: to become leaders of their own learning as self-directed assessment-capable visible learners. We want to help teachers understand "how they are going" in leading students toward this goal and clearly determine what is next as they become assessment-capable learners themselves.

Stop and Think: Complete this thinking frame borrowed from Ritchhart and Church's (2011) *Making Thinking Visible*, and feel free to create one of these for each chapter ahead.

I used to think learning was _____, but because ___, now I think ______.

Revisit your self-assessment from the beginning of the chapter and the concepts introduced throughout and consider, "Where are you now?"

- What does it mean to learn?
- What do we want students to learn?
- How do learners learn?
- How do teachers impact students' ability to reach outcomes and goals as learners?

What's Ahead

As you move forward, we will help you further understand

- what effective instruction looks and sounds like in terms of teacher actions and student outcomes, and
- how effective teaching and learning are defined in your instructional framework.

Then consider the following: What do you still need to understand on a deeper level? What does your team need to understand? What is your next step toward acquiring that understanding?

In the chapters ahead, you will build on new learning from this chapter and from our *Feedback to Feed Forward* strategies to help you consider what you can plan before you ever arrive at a classroom (Chapter 3) and how you can adapt your evidence-collection practices and strategies based on what is happening in a classroom when you arrive and as the lesson unfolds (Chapters 4 and 5).

How Can You Prepare for Evidence Collection? 3

From the field . . .

As someone who recently shifted into a coordinator role as a complementary observer and prior to our district's work in aligning our evidence collection processes, I had difficulty in determining how to effectively gather data, where to find it, and how to choose what types of data to collect. The process became more manageable when I realized it needed ***to start prior to stepping foot in a classroom****. The steps that allow for a more focused and organized method of data collection are my discussions ahead of time with my teachers about items (practices, outcomes) for which they want feedback and my planning of the use of my inking tablet (with templates I create for myself). The tablet allows me to place myself where the learning is occurring and more readily collect both quantitative and qualitative evidence to support the teacher's growth toward his or her goals.*

—Jesse Darcy, Math Coordinator, Grades 5–12

"You hit home runs not by chance but by preparation."

—Roger Maris

You've seen it: baseball players take one crack at a pitch and make hitting home runs that soar into the stands look so easy. What you don't see is the players spending hours in batting practice to achieve those glorious home run hits. Teachers work equally as hard behind the scenes to meet individual student needs, ensure high levels of challenge, and increase the level of rigor in lessons—complex work that is rooted in effective planning. Winging it (or simply replaying the previous year's lesson) would likely result in a pop-up to the second baseman.

The same can be said for effective feedback. Now that you have built a foundation from Chapters 1 and 2, you have begun the steps toward proactive thinking and planning for highly effective and comprehensive evidence collection that will result in feedback that feeds forward. We know this type of feedback does not happen by chance, so to help you knock it out of the park, we have dedicated a whole chapter to *planning* for observation and feedback.

Assessment-capable and highly efficacious teachers recognize and reflect on how their actions are impacting their students. To help a teacher understand his or her impact through feedback, we know as observers that we must collect rich evidence of engagement and learning. As things evolve in a lesson, you will adjust your strategies and evidence collection (addressed in Chapter 4 and 5). Chapter 3 offers proactive steps you can take before you arrive at any classroom or begin to watch a video lesson and strategies that will help you to maximize your observations with evidence collection that is efficient and effective. We will explore two new aspects: (1) the evidence collection tools you are using and (2) how you can plan to look, listen, and interact with learners based on expectations. Expectations for teaching and learning might be outlined in an instructional framework of teacher performance standards and should be aligned to disciplines and content standards.

After reading Chapters 1 and 2, we hope you have taken the opportunity to set a plan in motion, to

- develop an understanding of how students think and learn,
- deconstruct your rubric to develop a deep understanding of expected teaching and learning and general look-fors,
- investigate strategies related to neuroscience, and
- practice basic evidence collection strategies.

You will find through your work in the chapters ahead that you will continue to strengthen your capacity and skills related to the items in the list. Don't forget that our suggested steps, standards, and skills take time to master, so be patient with yourself. Practice, reflect, and revise!

Strategy 1: Mindfully plan from Chapter 1 serves as a foundation for this chapter. Let's continue that thinking and uncover more elements you can plan in advance of an observation. As you read, you can also consider possible applications for steps you can take before viewing lessons on video.

Preobservation Planning

Often, observers will engage with a teacher in a preobservation meeting before a visit. From this conversation, you can gather a great deal of information about the teacher's expectations for learning for the lesson, thought process in planning to meet learners' needs, how students will be applying the learning or demonstrating understanding, and so forth. Together, you can discuss the unit context and previous and upcoming lessons and brainstorm about what might unfold (e.g., potential areas for misconceptions or needs for extensions). A teacher can also request that you watch for a particular practice or student behaviors. Ideally, in a culture of learning, teachers arrive at meetings ready to discuss these points.

These do not have to be formal meetings, but it is valuable to make time for a quick chat so that you can align your evidence collection to teacher goals, new learning, or needs. Know that if you are consistently meeting with a teacher *after* observations, you will find you can often immediately utilize the additional planning strategies in this chapter. This will allow you to conduct more frequent unannounced visits, which often provide more accurate snapshots of instruction.

Regardless of whether you are planning an announced or unannounced visit, we highly recommend that observers engage in some preparation to do the following:

- Quickly chat with a teacher about what is happening in the upcoming week, ask if she or he is trying out new strategies, and determine if there are good times to visit or not visit (e.g., avoid test days and field trips).
- Review your notes from goal-setting meetings, previous visits and conversations, coaching sessions, and next steps.

- Plan with your assistant or other team members to determine how you can block your schedule in order to spend uninterrupted time observing lessons live or on video

Planning Your Tools

From Chapter 1, you have determined who you will visit and when, and with some quick preparation and conversation, you have goals or look-fors planned for the week's visits. Beyond this, you will need to plan your steps and processes for *how* you will engage in evidence collection during the observation. You may be thinking, "I know I am going to talk to students when I come to visit, but what will I be talking to them about?" or "What else will I be doing?" You can use our set of strategies from *Feedback to Feed Forward* as a foundation:

- FF Strategy 14: Listen to teaching and learning. What will you look for, watch, or see?
- FF Strategy 15: View learning in action. What will you listen for or hear?
- FF Strategy 16: Interact with learners. What will you ask students to determine if they are engaged, and at what levels, or if they are moving forward in understanding? How will you interact with them?

As you take steps to organize yourself beforehand, think about how you will plan for the use of your evidence collection tools. You do not want to arrive without the essentials you need or struggle in the middle of a lesson. To successfully use any of our strategies, you will need to plan how to record the evidence that you will collect (FF Strategy 13: Maximize the use of your notepad or tablet).

Many observers, especially those new to evidence collection during observations, feel overwhelmed and ask us for examples of notecatchers, templates, or guides in support of our recommended strategies. Some observers set up their notes ahead of time with reminders ("Time" in the left column, "Learning Target" at the top), while others have set up columns with "T" for teacher on one side and "S" for student on the other, and some teams have created elaborate templates. Often, goals for observations can guide the design of an evidence organizer if you require one (discussed in just a bit). Regardless of what you use, it is important to think ahead about how to maximize your tools to ensure that you are able to capture the evidence in the moment and actually leave the room with it.

You might find that a template you planned or designed is too cumbersome and you are missing too much of the lesson trying to complete it. For example, we have watched a principal try to carry a full instructional framework around and add notes, with difficulty, to the bottom, under "aligned indicators." Or sometimes, you become so engaged with listening to or speaking with students, you forget to record what happened or what was said at all. (This is where pause and replay on video is beneficial!) Because these things occur, you'll want to set yourself up for success by planning ahead, thinking about where that evidence might be recorded (e.g., always have your devices fully charged.) Some observers are challenged just by juggling the tools they must carry, which takes practice. It seems simple, but we always make sure we have pockets, a watch, and extra paper and pens to plan for any possible situation or tech malfunction. As you practice with the skills, strategies, and tools, try something, reflect on its usefulness, and then modify.

Templates

There are many protocols and templates available to observers. Some excellent options that help you organize *what* to collect include these:

- Donahoo's (2017) Template for Documenting Students' Learning
- Marzano's Walkthrough Protocol (LSI, 2017), based on forty-one key teaching strategies
- Hattie's (2012) Walkthrough Tools
- Big Picture Figure 1.4 (Tepper & Flynn, 2019)

We never want to dictate what will work best for you. However, it is important to remember why we are visiting classrooms—to provide feedback that will help teachers understand how they are going, where they are going, and what is next based on the impact on learners. So if you are using a template or predesigned tool, make sure not only teaching moves and practices are included but *student outcomes* look-fors as well. The following criteria can help guide you in the use of any evidence collection template or tool. Ideally, the tool within the observation process

- should not result in simply checking off items on a list or limit your evidence collection because a box is too small,
- should not be required to do too much processing or analysis to answer template questions or think about where evidence should go as you are observing and collecting,
- should not cause you frustration or impair your ability to interact authentically with students or distract students (kindergartners are mystified by rapid typing), and

- should result in the collection of a comprehensive and usable set of specific evidence, examples, and quotes that will allow you to analyze how a teacher is impacting learners.

Remember from Chapter 1, we are working to help teachers understand through *relevant* evidence

- how/why claims are being made about the overall effectiveness of instructional practices (which could include clear and objective support of a performance-level rating),
- how they are impacting student engagement and learning (causal attribution), and
- how they are progressing toward district/region, school, or professional goals.

These are rooted in our determination as to how students are progressing toward the three goals outlined in Chapter 2:

> Goal 1: Conceptual thinking: this will involve your monitoring of cognitive understanding (acquiring and using new concepts, skills, knowledge, etc.)
>
> Goal 2: Metacognitive thinking
>
> Goal 3: Self-regulation and self-monitoring

Stop and Think: What tools do you use when observing lessons (or does an observer in your room use)? Are these choices allowing you or the observer to meet the overarching goals mentioned previously and collect needed evidence?

Planning by Using Expectations

Though templates are very helpful for efficiency and to organize your thinking, always work to ensure they are aligned with the expectations for teaching and learning outlined in your instructional framework. A framework, especially one that includes not just expectations for teachers but also student outcomes, is a tool that can be used for coaching, growth, supervision, and support, not just evaluation. We have worked directly with nonsupervising support staff, like coaches and peer teachers, who successfully leverage the framework in nonevaluative ways, building a common understanding of effective teaching and learning across a team.

It is important *not* to add new lists of expectations with differing language or to complicate the process. Based on what we know from Bandura (1994), self- and collective efficacy increases as learners develop clearer self-perceptions and understandings of their role in outcomes (causal attributions)—all rooted in a clearer understanding of expectations. If you and your team have engaged in our suggested tasks to unpack your instructional framework or understandings about your learners (see Chapter 1), you are ready to begin working on Strategy 6.

Strategy 6: Plan evidence collection based on your framework

Let's look at an example of how to determine what evidence can and should be collected by using expectations articulated in your instructional framework. This work can be done in conjunction with our suggested initial deep-dive deconstruction of the teacher performance rubric or as a separate step, isolating and unpacking targeted attributes or indicators. Regardless of the method, we recommend that you and your team engage in the work together to calibrate how you define and collect evidence of effective teaching and learning for each indicator and attribute. Let's look at a sample indicator from an environment domain in Figure 3.1 and consider whether your framework contains similar language.

FIGURE 3.1: ENVIRONMENT INDICATOR EXAMPLE

	BELOW STANDARD	**DEVELOPING**	**PROFICIENT**	**EXEMPLARY** ***All characteristics of* Proficient, *plus one or more of the following:***
Environment supportive of intellectual risk taking	Creates a learning environment that discourages students from attempting tasks, responding to questions and challenges, or feeling safe to make and learn from mistakes	Creates a learning environment in which some students are willing to attempt tasks, respond to questions and challenges, and feel safe to make and learn from mistakes.	Creates a learning environment in which most students are willing to take risks and respond to questions and challenges, and feel safe to make and learn from mistakes.	Creates an environment in which students are encouraged to respectfully question or challenge ideas presented by the teacher or other students.

Source: Connecticut State Department of Education (2017).

The language does not directly reference engagement and learning, but we know a learning environment can impact levels of thinking, discourse, and understanding. For this indicator, we want to plan ahead and think about what it is we need to understand about the teacher and the impact he or she is having on the students and the classroom environment.

- To make an accurate claim or rating, what are the key levers or the difference in ratings? These will dictate what we must collect. Read the "Proficient" and "Exemplary" descriptions. Notice how both teaching practices and student outcomes are reflected in those. We have to determine how the teacher is creating an environment that supports students and how many are willing to take risks.
- How do we, our team, and our teachers define *intellectual risks* and what that looks like in the classroom?
- What and how are the students thinking? You will want to get into their heads through your evidence collection, as much of risk taking is related to mental processing and an unwillingness to give up. For example, think of trying to determine a student's use of Costa and Kallick's (2009) habit of mind called *persisting*, or the self-talk or strategic mental processing that we use when we don't know what to do. We want to determine not only if a student is trying and trying—a first grader's definition of persistence—but rather *how* they are trying and *why*. What do students really think about the work and the effort it will take to complete it? What is motivating them? (Think back to "If . . . then . . ." from Chapter 2. Is it just for the grade or a fun task at the end? Do they have a growth mindset, seeing that the journey is the reward, and recognize how this will help them in the long or short term?) Which mental habits are they using to tackle the task? What do they tell themselves when it gets hard?
- What are the root causes to student behaviors, mindsets, or actions? Why are they taking risks or not? Is it related to the environment or possibly a lack of knowledge, clear learning expectations, relevance, and/or authentic applications (which may reside in a different indicator/expectation)?
- What do students perceive or know about *how the teacher creates* a particular environment or expectation? For example, they may share with you that they are aware that the teacher will call on anyone—not just those with hands up—but will wait to allow them to think and let them have a lifeline (like "phoning a friend") after they have tried to look in their notes but are still stuck.

The challenge lies in determining all of this through evidence collection—but know it is possible. Figure 3.2 provides an example of a graphic organizer you and your team can use to prepare for collecting evidence related to a selected indicator or attribute. Notice how it will allow you to plan ahead for the use of the three basic observation strategies:

FF 14: Listen to teaching and learning

FF 15: View learning in action

FF 16: Interact with learners

FIGURE 3.2: EVIDENCE COLLECTION PREPARATION: EXPECTATIONS

Expectations	Teaching/Cause		Learning/Effect or Impact		
Framework Language	Listening: Teacher action you hear causing/ impacting student action or behavior	Viewing: Teacher action you see causing/ impacting student action or behavior	Listening: What could you hear?	Viewing: What could you see? What would student work tell/show you?	Interacting: What can you ask students?
CCT 1a (CSDE, 2017) "Creates a learning environment in which most are willing to take risks"	Providing wait time Providing positive growth mindset feedback ("... yet") Modeling of responses Offering reminders of supports/ resources available	Attending to Ss who raise hands or not Providing stems for Ss to use in sharing Providing/ helping Ss use resources/ supports Designing appropriate tasks/ scaffolding	Attempting verbal answers, not skipping them ("I am thinking ...") Growth mindset statements ("I don't have it yet ...")	Raising hands/ participating in discussions Attempting to work or answer even if incorrect or unsure Contributing to group work Getting up/ seeking to use resources	What do you do when you don't know how to answer or how to solve the problem? What does it mean to persevere?

Planning to Interact With Learners

Interacting and engaging with learners in the moment through questions is powerful—a benefit of live observations (shown in the last column of Figure 3.2).

However, you won't always have a chance to talk to students. In Chapter 4, we will talk about when this might be the case, but some examples include the following: They are engaged in a Socratic circle, the teacher is giving directions, or you are watching a video of the lesson. It is important to be ready if and when opportunities arise. If you are watching a video lesson, you can always consider what the teacher asked students and what you might have asked had you been in the room.

The opportunity to question learners serves to make their thinking immediately visible to you and helps you to better understand how a teacher is impacting student engagement and understanding. We know this is one of the most challenging but important parts of observation; therefore, we wanted to get you started with a bank of some common questions that are always requested and which we have developed from our many years observing lessons. Our session participants often follow us around in classrooms just to hear what we ask students. You can use or adapt our suggestions or go through the exercise of creating them as a team based on your district's instructional framework and expectations outlined in your "Effective" or "Proficient" descriptions or school goals.

> To get at the heart of learning processes such as student engagement, a formative walkthrough employs critical points of inquiry, like this one: Are students regulating their own learning to help get themselves to the lessons target? The question compels the observer to gather evidence about whether students 1) understand what they are supposed to learn in the lesson; 2) are required to do, say, make, or write something that will help them learn it; and 3) have specific success criteria against which to regulate the quality of their own work. (Moss & Brookhart, 2015, p. 20)

Remember, there is no magic list of questions, as you will come to see in upcoming chapters regarding evidence collection in real time. However, you will find our lists in Figure 3.3 to be highly useful tools regardless of your experience as an observer. We organized our suggested questions by our five focus areas and by related and specific instructional categories. This should allow you to align the questions to your own framework indicators. You can also organize questions aligned to "critical points of inquiry," as Moss and Brookhart suggest. We are not providing an exhaustive list, but, if you are not sure what to ask students, the ones included will provide a huge boost to your toolbox immediately. We know that as you practice using them, you will have many new ones to add.

Head to the Resource Center for a printable version of Resource 3.1: Focus Area Questions at **resources.corwin.com/learnerfocusedfeedback**.

FIGURE 3.3: FOCUS AREA QUESTIONS

Focus Area 1: Environment

Instructional Area	Potential Questions
Routines/behavior expectations	*How did the "class rules" or "class expectations" get created?* *What happens when someone is not following classroom expectations?* *What things are not permitted in this classroom?* *Where are _____ kept?* *How do you know how to rotate/select books/use materials?* *What should happen when you hear the chime/bell/clap?*
Risk taking	*What does it mean to persevere?* *What do you do when you are stuck/don't know an answer or what to do?* *Do you have a voice in the classroom, such as sharing your opinion or disagreeing with others? What happens when you do?*

Focus Area 2: Level of Challenge

Instructional Area	Potential Questions
Construction of new learning	*What is new about today's learning or lesson?* *How are you using what you know?* *What problem are you trying to solve? What big question are you trying to answer?* *What is challenging you? What is challenging about the task?* *What is the easiest part of this?* *What is your plan? How long will this take you?* *What do you know now that you didn't know when you started or when the lesson or unit started?* *What questions do you still have?* *What does a good reader/writer/historian do? Why?*

Focus Area 3: Progression

Instructional Area	Potential Questions
Learning expectations	*What is your job today as a reader/writer?* *What strategy are you working on today?* *What are you learning? What is today's learning goal/target?* *What do you want to accomplish today? What is your goal today?*

(Continued)

FIGURE 3.3: (Continued)

Instructional Area	Potential Questions
Context/connections	*On which standard are you working? In what unit are you working? How does this day's learning fit in the unit?* *What were you learning/doing before I arrived? How did that help you with what you are doing now?* *What did you learn yesterday that is helping you with today's learning? How does this connect?* *Where are you headed next?* *How will you use the new learning?* *Why is this important?* *How will today's learning/task/strategy help you as a reader, writer, scientist, and so forth?* *Why are you completing this?*
Directions/process	*What are you supposed to be doing to complete this?* *What steps are you taking to complete it?* *What do you do when you are done?*
Group work	*What steps will you take or have you taken as a group?* *How will you get started?* *What roles/responsibilities are there?* *What expectations are there for participation? Does everyone need to share/present/contribute?*

Focus Area 4: Assessment

Instructional Area	Potential Questions
Teacher checks	*How are you showing the teacher what you know?* *Did you have a choice in how you would complete the task or what you would create?*
Criteria/self- or peer checks	*How do you know you have it?* *How do you know when you are finished?* *How do you know you have the right answer? How can you check your answers?* *What does mastery look like?* *How was the rubric/checklist/example created?* *How are you using this rubric/checklist/exemplar to help you?* *What steps are you taking to improve or work toward your goal? Why?* *How can you use the rubric/checklist/exemplar to help your friend?* *How do you give feedback to a classmate?*

Focus Area 5: Supports

Instructional Area	Potential Questions
Choice	*How are you grouped?* *How often are you given choices about your work, what you read, who you work with, and where you sit?* *How or why did you choose your partner/seat/resource/product (e.g., to create a video vs. a brochure)?*
Resources	*What do you do/Where can you look when you don't know the answer or are stuck?* *What will help you learn this? Is there a strategy or a resource?* *What can you use when you aren't sure how to complete the task?* *How are you using your notes, the website, or the stems to help you?*
Feedback	*How did the teacher just help you?* *[After hearing an audible aha or seeing erasing] What did you just learn/discover?* *What was your error?* *How did your partner just help you?* *What were you told about your work today?* (*We love this one we found from Hattie's *Visible Learning for Teachers* (2012, p. 193).)

Stop and Think: What have you asked students during an observation, and why? Teachers, how have observers interacted with your students during observations?

Notice that the questions also can serve as an excellent resource for teachers to check for understanding. But, be selective! We do not ask every one of these during a lesson. These examples are provided to assist you in opening the door to authentic conversations with students. It is important to not just rattle questions off as a checklist to be completed. Also, the questions offered should not necessarily be asked in any particular order. Always keep in mind what you are trying to learn from the learner, and remember, you will also need to be mindful of language, social, and developmental levels or needs of the students with whom you interact and adjust how you engage with them.

It is also important to recognize that nothing exists in a lesson in isolation, so sometimes, questions and answers from the lists will overlap and provide related evidence. For example, when inquiring about directions, expectations, or process with "*What do you do when you are done with this task?,*" you tip into criteria and assessment and a related question, such as "*How do you know when you are done?*" This also gives you insight into extension work or support for all levels and if there is an appropriate level of challenge.

Did you notice how some of the questions are related to what you read in Chapter 2 about teaching, the brain, and how students learn? For example, *What did you learn yesterday that is helping you with today's learning? How does this connect? How will you use the new learning? Why is this important? What will help you learn this?* Chapters 4 and 5 will provide you with additional strategies for evidence collection within the context of the lesson that will help you observe for surface and deep learning.

> **Stop and Think:** Which questions in Figure 3.3 are aligned to **Goal 1**: Critical Thinking/Cognition? **Goal 2**: Metacognitive Thinking? **Goal 3**: Self-Monitoring? Did you notice overlaps? Teachers, how often do you ask your students these questions during your own lessons?

As an observer, if you ask a student after seeing him erasing "What was your error?," his answer will reveal a cognitive understanding or misunderstanding of the content. If you follow up and ask, "How did you figure that out?," you move into uncovering his metacognitive and self-monitoring skills. If you then inquire, "What are you going to do differently?," you begin to see how he might be self-regulating. Consider how powerful it would be for teachers to have these conversations with their learners.

Imagine how your students might answer the questions from Figure 3.3. Those answers, regardless of what they are and regardless of whether we are teaching or observing, provide rich information as to how students are thinking and understanding. This, in turn, allows you to analyze and determine the impact instruction is having based on the evidence and their responses.

We know the power of planning questions before teaching a lesson. Similarly, by planning questions ahead of an observation, you will save valuable mental-processing time that you can devote to listening and asking follow-up questions during an observation (steps we will tackle in Chapter 5). You might even go one step further with your teams and determine what student responses might sound like against framework performance levels. For example, look for an indicator on your framework related to communicating the learning expectation. Expected practice (potentially found in "Proficient" or "Effective") may include student understanding or even articulation of the expectation.

Figure 3.4 shows an example of how you could create a tool to understand look-fors, measure the outcomes, and align evidence (such as student responses) to the framework. It is important to remember that this process is meant to support *growth*, not evaluation (though this step could help in calibrating ratings). Observers should also set goals to interact with a high number of learners to determine how many responses fall in each of the categories.

FIGURE 3.4: PROGRESSION OF STUDENT RESPONSES

	More teacher and task driven ⟶ More learning and student driven			
Possible Questions	**Below Standard (not clear)**	**Developing (general understanding)**	**Proficient (specific understanding)**	**Exemplary (specific and broader context understanding)**
What strategy are you working on today? What are you learning? What is today's learning goal/target? What do you want to accomplish today? What is your goal today?	I don't know. I think she put it up on the board. The teacher said we are supposed to finish these notes right now.	It is up on the board: [reading] "Today . . ." We are working on bacteria notes and doing a lab today to learn more.	We watched a video earlier on bacteria to learn . . . and yesterday we . . . Today, we are reviewing our research.	We are just at the beginning of the phenomena. Today's work is helping us to better understand. . . . We need to know this because . . . I'm still unsure about . . . so I am . . .

Planning Using Learning Goals

You can further prepare for observations and refine your evidence collection and interactions with learners by thinking more about expectations. Many regions, districts, and schools have adopted new standards, curriculum, and/or programs. With these expectations come required new levels of rigor, organization and desired outcomes, and a shift in teaching practices. Teachers need support in implementing the changes and require feedback that is rooted in the very teacher's guide or curriculum from which they teach every day. Therefore, observers must develop an understanding of what the teacher is following and the specific related expectations and outcomes to determine what "Proficient" or "Effective" teaching and learning look like and sound like in the context of a particular program, related standards, or curriculum. Through classroom observations, observers are generally required

> to look for an alignment between lesson plans and curriculum goals and to encourage teachers to adopt best-practice instructional

> strategies to deliver that aligned content. Walkthrough information then becomes a search for evidence to improve instruction. This effort is not trivial by any means and is an important part of ensuring students receive a rigorous and relevant education . . . it is when we add what the students actually learned . . . we see the whole picture. (Moss & Brookhart, 2015, p. 100)

Many schools, districts, or regions have also purchased or adopted other approaches, models, programs, or curricula aligned to specific disciplines, such as these:

Math: Bridges®, Math in Focus®, Everyday Math©, Eureka Math (aka EngageNY), and Investigations®

Literacy: Workshop, Fundations®/Wilson®, Read 180®, Superkids, and ReadyGen®

Science: Full Science Option System (FOSS™)

If this is true at your school or in your region or district, it is critical that everyone receive support for implementation based on the expectations for student outcomes and related instructional strategies within the disciplines, models, or programs, especially in the first few years. For many, Year 1 is often time just to orient to the new expectations. (You may have seen teachers or been the one reading from the teacher's guide during a lesson.) However, once acclimated to a new process in Year 2 and Year 3, teachers can begin to focus on personalization or differentiation—adding extensions or small-group support as needed and proactively planning lessons.

Your understanding of the new instructional approaches, program, or model ensures you become a valuable resource as an observer. If you are a teacher supporting your peers in this work, you already have a leg up as an observer because you teach the same model or program every day. With your teams, it is important to work to determine how you can prepare to collect evidence that is aligned to the program- or model-specific teaching and learning. An excellent resource for observers of Workshop, for example, is *Leading Well: Building Schoolwide Excellence in Reading and Writing* (Calkins, Ehrenworth, & Pessah, 2018).

Planning Based on Disciplines

Now it is time to extend this thinking and your planning one step further. Programs, models, and curricula are rooted in standards and discipline-specific learning goals for students. Consider how unpacking *discipline-specific literacies* will increase your effectiveness as an observer. Let's get started with determining look-fors for evidence collection *based on disciplines*.

Discipline-Specific Literacy

Timothy Shanahan and Cynthia Shanahan (2008) identify three levels of how literacy progresses, and though students need basic and intermediate literacy to be successful, it is the third to which we are paying close attention in this chapter. The levels are as follows:

1. Basic Literacy: Literacy skills such as decoding and knowledge of high-frequency words
2. Intermediate Literacy: Literacy skills common to many tasks, including generic comprehension strategies, common word meanings, and basic fluency
3. Disciplinary Literacy: Literacy skills specialized to history, science, mathematics, literature, or other subject matter (p. 44)

It is important to note that discipline literacy cannot replace basic and intermediate for those readers who are arriving to our classrooms without foundational skills.

In early grades, we devote much of our time to teaching students how to read, but beyond fourth grade and as they move into middle and high school, they must be able to read to learn. For years, we were focused on *content area reading* (a textbook still on Amy's shelf), and many students were arriving to the later grades without basic vocabulary or comprehension skills. Science and history teachers were suddenly required to teach reading strategies and were not always willing or able to do so. "Literacy avoidance in content area classes is at odds with student learning needs and the reality of the subject matters" (C. Shanahan, Shanahan, & Misichia, 2011, p. 395). Today, more students than ever in Grades 4–12 are still arriving in our classrooms with lagging reading skills, in addition to gaps in basic discipline-specific *content knowledge*.

Content area reading was often a strategy to ensure students learned content, but the day has passed when we are just teaching content to our students. It is critical for teachers and leaders to understand that how and what we read from discipline to discipline varies; middle and high school teachers who are often specialists recognize this but haven't necessarily integrated this understanding into their teaching. As is true with experts in each field, how we think, speak, write, and create products across disciplines differs greatly. For example, Timothy Shanahan and Cynthia Shanahan (2008) determined in their research that

> math reading requires a precision of meaning, and each word must be understood specifically in service to that particular meaning . . . chemists were most interested in the transformation of information from one form to another. That is, when reading prose, they were visualizing,

> writing down formulas, or, if a diagram or a chart were on the page, going back and forth between the graph and the chart. (p. 49)

Possibly, somewhere in your instructional framework, you may find an attribute or language that references specific literacy strategies or practices that should be integrated into lessons. This is not just about teaching reading or vocabulary. It is important to understand that this includes the specific skills students need for each discipline, leading us to our next strategy.

Strategy 7: Plan evidence collection based on discipline-specific expectations

To begin this process, think about the type of texts read, the thinking required, and the processes experienced by experts in the discipline or field. Think about these questions: *What do the experts do every day? What makes the text they read and write challenging and complex?* Remember, **"A high school student who can do a reasonably good job of reading a story in English class might not be able to make much sense of biology or algebra books, or vice versa"** (T. Shanahan & Shanahan, 2008, p. 45).

Notice how disciplinary literacy is defined in the footnotes of the two indicator examples in Figure 3.5.

Stop and Think: Is there an expectation in your school, district, or region for *literacy strategies* to be implemented outside of ELA instruction? How are these defined?

Similarities

First, it is important to recognize what all disciplines have in common. Consider the example in Figure 3.2 is from a framework that is utilized for observation of a lesson in any discipline. Notice the provided definition in the footnote gets you thinking regardless of what is being taught—students need to build their capacity to use academic vocabulary, read and write, and listen and speak. Think about what you read in Chapter 2 about the skills students need. These become the unifying factors across disciplines, regardless of grade levels. Remember Fullan et al. tell us deep learning occurs when students are engaged in the six Cs.

FIGURE 3.5: DISCIPLINARY LITERACY INDICATOR EXAMPLE

	BELOW STANDARD	DEVELOPING	PROFICIENT	EXEMPLARY *All characteristics of* **Proficient**, *plus one or more of the following:*
Literacy strategies[11]	Plans instruction that includes few opportunities for students to develop literacy skills or academic vocabulary.	Plans instruction that includes some opportunities for students *to develop literacy skills or academic vocabulary in isolation.*	Plans instruction that integrates literacy strategies and academic vocabulary.	Designs opportunities to allow students to independently select *literacy strategies that support their learning.*
Literacy strategies[19]	Presents instruction with limited opportunities for students to *develop literacy and/or academic vocabulary.*	Presents instruction with opportunities for students to develop literacy skills and/or academic vocabulary in isolation.	Presents instruction that integrates literacy strategies and academic vocabulary within lesson content.	Provides opportunities for students to independently select and apply *literacy strategies.*

11. **Literacy through the content areas:** Literacy is the ability to convey meaning and understand meaning in a variety of text forms (e.g., print, media, music, art, movement). Literacy strategies include communicating through language (reading, writing, listening/speaking), using the academic vocabulary of the discipline, interpreting meaning within the discipline, and communicating through the discipline. Research shows that teacher integration of effective discipline-specific literacy strategies results in improved student learning.

19. **Literacy strategies:** To convey meaning and understand meaning in a variety of text forms (e.g., print, media, music, art, movement). Literacy strategies include communicating through language (reading/writing, listening/speaking), using the academic vocabulary of the discipline, interpreting meaning within the discipline, and communicating through the discipline. Research shows that teacher integration of effective discipline-specific literacy strategies results in student learning.

Source: Connecticut State Department of Education (2017).

We can build student capacity in character, citizenship, collaboration, creativity, critical thinking, and communication—but in unique ways exclusive to each discipline—and teach students how to use their knowledge across disciplines. Think about it: We are teaching students how to use evidence and reasoning all day long. In classrooms truly attentive to the differences between disciplines, we are asking them to do so and to use these skills in very different ways—we are asking them to transfer! This is not about everyone using a Venn diagram in every discipline; it is larger than that.

"One of the reasons that disciplinary literacy is so important is that it has everything to do with deeper learning. Disciplinary literacy is not the application of strategies to the disciplines; it is a way of learning that drills deeply into the very essence of what it means to come to know content" (Cossett Lent, 2016, p. 5). We came across a great chart created by Cossett Lent that shows how deep learning and disciplinary literacy are related in *This Is Disciplinary Literacy*. Figure 3.6 shows an excerpt to help you make the connections.

FIGURE 3.6: DEEP LEARNING AND DISCIPLINARY LITERACY

Deeper Learning	Disciplinary Literacy
Relies on collaboration	Within the classroom community that mirrors the work being done in the field by experts
Application: Students learn to become self-directed within a team as they plan, share, and assess learning within a discipline	

Stop and Think: What do you know about the skills, thinking, vocabulary, processing, and goals of your discipline?

Differences

Let's consider the *differences* between disciplines. This understanding will ensure you are highly prepared to observe lessons effectively discipline to discipline, adjusting your thinking before you arrive based on what you know the learning should look and sound like. We need to ensure teachers (especially our non-ELA middle and high school teachers) are receiving the support they need to achieve desired outcomes to effectively support students. "Obviously, there are many barriers to successfully addressing the nation's literacy needs among adolescents, perhaps none more important than the preparation of a teaching force capable of delivering the needed instruction" (T. Shanahan & Shanahan, 2008, p. 46).

Once you have reflected on your own knowledge and understanding, work with your team to develop a shared understanding of the general differences across the disciplines; some disciplines you may want to unpack include foreign language, career technical education, physical education, and the arts. Look to excellent resources for this work from Vicky Zygouris-Coe (2015) and Tim and Cynthia Shanahan (2008) for comprehensive comparisons across disciplines, along with Rachael E. Gabriel and Sarah L. Woulfin (2017) for English/language arts look-fors.

Let's go further with a selected discipline and think about the specialized skills and mindsets needed for history/social studies with examples of what you might see or hear in a classroom related to these discipline-specific elements. Figure 3.7 provides some possible examples.

FIGURE 3.7: SOCIAL STUDIES DISCIPLINE-SPECIFIC CONSIDERATIONS

Elements of Instruction	Considerations
Text	Primary/secondary sources; multiple sources; graphics, such as images, tables, charts, and maps
Vocabulary	Words with connotation or that reflect bias/political beliefs, differing points of view, descriptions of eras or periods (e.g., the Enlightenment)
Skills/thinking and speaking	Argument- or research-based writing, comparing texts or corroboration (e.g., interpretation, validity, accuracy), evaluating bias, understanding historical context and perspective, evaluating cause and effect or consequences (and discerning between chronological versus cause/effect), looking for patterns, making connections, supporting claims with evidence
Assessments	Ways to measure the skills and historical thinking (e.g., students engaging in Socratic circles or debates), writing letters or journals from alternate perspectives, reflections or observations, and argumentative essays

The goal of ensuring students master logical argument, development of claims, and use of supporting evidence is consistent across disciplines, an example we cited earlier. However, expert historians may not arrive at the truth or the same conclusions as one another (versus the idea of a law in science or theorem in math). They "work backwards—they start with answers, search for the questions, and present several arguments from primary sources before they make an overall argument for a particular interpretation of events." Teachers should provide opportunities for students "to analyze primary and secondary sources to support a claim." Whereas "mathematicians use proofs to argue something is true . . . scientists always follow the scientific method when inquiring or arguing" (Zygouris-Coe, 2015, p. 344).

Timothy Shanahan and Cynthia Shanahan (2008) further support that historians

> consider who the authors of the texts were and what their biases might be. Their purpose during the reading seemed to be to figure out what story a particular author wanted to tell; in other words, they were keenly aware that they were reading an interpretation of historical events . . . [they do] not read the text as truth, but rather as an interpretation that has to be judged based on its credibility . . . historians infer cause-and-effect relationships when they study events and what precedes and follows them. These relationships are not necessarily visible in the events themselves . . . so they must be surmised (pp. 50, 55).

Though scientists also examine cause/effect, there is greater human element involved in the examination by historians (C. Shanahan, Shanahan, & Misichia, 2011).

Collecting the Evidence

Let's look at an example in Figure 3.8 of how to take your thinking from Figure 3.7 to prepare for what you could see and hear in classrooms based on what we understand historians do in the field.

Our observer is headed into a high school U.S. history lesson. The department utilizes units from the Stanford History Education Group (2018), an excellent resource that builds lessons from an open-ended question and provides primary documents for investigation. The students are working to answer this question: "Is Andrew Carnegie a hero?" By design, the lesson is promoting the integration of the unique literacies required of historians. Consider what evidence you plan to collect before you arrive based on what you know about the discipline goals and expectations for students.

You see that by having an understanding of the basic similarities—along with the differences in how experts or professionals in a particular field read, write, think, and speak—you might arrive in a classroom with a picture in your head of expected students' behaviors and dispositions and related teacher actions.

FIGURE 3.8: EVIDENCE COLLECTION PREPARATION: DISCIPLINES

Expectations	Potential Teaching/Causes		Potential Learning/Effects or Impacts		
Discipline-specific literacy	Listening: Specific teacher action you hear causing/ impacting student action or behavior	Viewing: Specific teacher action you see causing/ impacting student action or behavior	Listening: What could you hear?	Viewing: What could you see? What would student work tell/show you?	Interacting: What can you ask students?
Thinking like historians	Direct instruction on or promoting investigation of historical context Feedback/ reminders to use metacognitive skills for bias, author's perspective Promoting/ supporting varied historical-event interpretations but use of evidence	Modeling how to read primary sources, corroborate sources Providing multiple sources from varying perspectives Providing graphic organizers to promote cause/effect, compare/ contrast, thinking to support analysis of events or people's intentions	Debating with each other citing evidence and/or cause–effect relationships (e.g., "Because . . ." statements or talk moves to build/argue/ support interpretations)	Writing claims and integrating supportive textual evidence Completing graphic organizers to understand why/cause and effect/ consequences	How are you developing your claim? How has your perspective changed? How are you supporting your decision? What are you learning from the primary documents to help you better understand the historical figure? Who wrote the docs? What was their perspective, and why?

This allows you to more effectively observe how teachers are building these capacities. Consider how students in fourth-grade social studies could be taught to read and think in similar ways as this high school class. Younger students can learn "how to reconstruct meaning from historical documents, identify the main questions, and also analyze the intentions of the people involved, and the complex ways in which they interacted" (Zygouris-Coe, 2015, p. 262).

Stop and Think: To practice, look back in Figure 3.8. Try to align evidence or look-fors listed to expectations in the indicators or attributes on your instructional framework. (For example, compare/contrast how thinking or supporting critical thinking might fall under an indicator related to intellectual engagement.)

Planning Based on Standards

We have spent some time with social studies, so let's dive into another content area to see the intersection of discipline-specific learning/literacy and standards by examining science and the Next Generation Science Standards (NGSS). In her comparisons between disciplines, Zygouris-Coe (2015) reminds us that scientists "should make claims based on data/evidence and their knowledge of scientific concepts" (p. 345). Students will develop initial claims that they will continue to examine, challenge, confirm, or revise based on ongoing investigations. To crosswalk the standards and discipline goals with your team, complete a similar list to Figure 3.7 to determine text, vocabulary, skills/thinking, and assessments that are science specific.

Lessons and units aligned with the NGSS help students to make sense of the world and should engage them with the core ideas in crosscutting concepts using science and engineering practices (similar to the idea of CCSS Math Standards of Practice). The core ideas are broken down into four domains and are

> the fundamental ideas that are necessary for understanding a given science discipline. The core ideas all have broad importance within or across science or engineering disciplines, provide a key tool for understanding or investigating complex ideas and solving problems, relate to societal or personal concerns, and can be taught over multiple grade levels at progressive levels of depth and complexity (NGSS, 2019).

Instruction should allow students to use content understanding to answer questions or solve problems versus learn content from a book with a goal of regurgitating it on a test or memorizing facts. We want to see transfer, application of thinking and processes, and connection making. As they move through lessons and units, they ideally acquire new understandings, engage in discourse, ask scientifically rooted questions, and are able to make more connections to previous lessons, scientific laws, and data. When you see this occurring, you know you are in a brain-based classroom and building the six Cs every day! We took a group of teachers from different disciplines and grade levels into an NGSS-aligned lesson for an observation, and afterwards, they said, "Why can't every classroom be like this?"

To serve as a support for teachers implementing new standards and instructional practices like NGSS, an observer must prepare for observations by not only developing an understanding of discipline-specific skills and dispositions and the new standards but also of the inquiry process itself. Ideally, an observer should also determine beforehand or upon entering a classroom (strategies further explored in the next chapter) where within the phenomena or unit the lesson resides. Is it the very beginning, so students are working to activate what they know to build a foundation of connections? Is it further along so that they have started to revise their hypotheses together about why something is occurring or not because they now have observed, researched, and collected data? This is critical as engagement and learning will look different at each stage, especially if teachers are using a 5E Instructional Model (engage, explore, explain, elaborate, evaluate).

Let's use the same chart you encountered for social studies to look at an example of planning evidence collection for a middle school science lesson in Figure 3.9 (on the next page). The observer knows the students are partway through a unit about energy and are considering ways to transport penguins and are potentially at an "explore" step in the 5E model for this visit. One related standard is PS3-3: "Students who demonstrate understanding can apply scientific principles to design, construct, and test a device that either minimizes or maximizes thermal energy transfer."

Stop and Think: How has your feedback (given or received) after an observation connected to the expectations of teaching and learning within a discipline, program, model, curriculum, or standards? To goals?

After reading this section, consider which disciplines, literacies, and/or standards you need to understand to a deeper level than you do now. Which should you spend more time investigating to improve your evidence collection and feedback? How can you do that with your team?

Highly efficacious teachers and teams who are assessment-capable learners clearly understand how their performance (as related to their impact on students) aligns to expected outcomes, recognize strengths and areas of need, and can determine goals based on any gaps. The more observers understand about the expected outcomes, the greater the resource they become for teachers working to set instructional and professional goals.

FIGURE 3.9: EVIDENCE COLLECTION PREPARATION: STANDARDS

Expectations	Teaching/Cause		Learning/Effect or Impact		
Content area goals or standards	Listening: Teacher action you hear causing/ impacting student action or behavior	Viewing: Teacher action you see causing/ impacting student action or behavior	Listening: What could you hear?	Viewing: What could you see? What would student work tell/show you?	Interacting: What can you ask students?
NGSS	Using push questions or further *why* or *how* questions or connecting to cross-cutting/ core ideas Providing criteria for supporting hypotheses Conducting a think aloud teaching needed foundational skills	Listening to and facilitating group work/ discussions Allowing Ss to explore their own hypotheses or predictions Providing resources for research or support Modeling needed foundational skills/strategies	Providing explanations using evidence, scientific concepts, laws Predicting, creating hypotheses, or revising Asking each other probing questions Using talk moves to uncover further need for data/agree or disagree with conclusions	Developing models Using quantitative data/ evidence in conclusions Engaging in data collection/ recording, analysis Engaging in hands-on experiments	How have you changed your predictions? What have you learned through your experiments/ data collection and discussions so far that have changed your understanding of how thermal energy is transferred? What are you predicting?

Give It a Try

Teachers

- Work and plan together in your teams to develop a common understanding of your standards and discipline-specific literacies. Calibrate what mastery of these look and sound like. Determine strategies and tasks that will promote outcomes aligned to the expectations and plan how/when you can observe in each other's classrooms for these outcomes.
- Review the list of questions in Figure 3.3, and add additional ones. Create a list of those you can plan to use in your own instruction.

- Video application: Before viewing, plan how you will collect and organize your evidence and your goals for viewing the lesson. Pay close attention to the questions you are asking your students and questions you could have asked.

Coaches

- Lead teachers in the work to develop a common understanding of the expectations of standards and discipline-specific goals. Think about how you are helping teachers to narrow the focus of their team and individual goals or to select the "right goals."
- Practice utilizing the questions in Figure 3.3 in observations.
- Observe for instruction that demonstrates understanding of discipline-specific literacy.

Supervisors

- With your team, revisit the questions in Figure 3.3 and practice utilizing them in your observations. Practice utilizing direct student quotes in your feedback to support your claims about teacher impact.
- Identify resources that will allow you to build your understanding of how to observe specific programs, curricula, disciplines, and standards in action.
- Teams can take Figure 3.8 one step further for each discipline and break down look-fors or complete a chart like this for each of your framework indicators.
- Plan and coordinate professional-learning opportunities for teachers to deepen their understanding of expectations aligned with the framework, standards, programs, disciplines, and goals.
- Evaluate the quality of your feedback for alignment with standards, curriculum, disciplines, and goals.

What's Ahead

All of the work that you do in observations to collect evidence should culminate and result in high-quality feedback developed within the context of the expected teaching and learning. It should promote reflection and growth to ensure teachers can create environments for student ownership of learning. This can only occur if you

- plan evidence collection to the levels outlined in this chapter, using your three foundational strategies (look, listen, and interact) and new strategies (Strategy 1–Strategy 7),

- engage with (or set up video to allow you to hear and see) a significant portion of the learners during your visit, and
- leave the observation with the evidence you need to determine teacher impact on their engagement and understanding.

This is only the beginning. After an observation, it is important to objectively analyze the evidence to determine teacher impact, isolate root causes, and develop actionable feedback for the teacher you observed to promote reflection and growth. Though Chapter 6 provides a feedback sample, if these steps challenge you, we highly recommend that you utilize the foundational skills and strategies from *Feedback to Feed Forward* for the development of feedback based on your increasingly more comprehensive evidence collection.

You are now well on your way toward becoming a more effective observer of teaching and learning by thinking through how you can prepare for more efficient and comprehensive evidence collection. You have explored strategies by organizing your tools and how you will look, listen, and interact with learners based on expectations of teacher performance standards, the discipline, and the related standards. Work through our suggestions in bite-sized steps, and adapt the strategies for viewing video lessons.

Try something out, reflect, refine, and try again. We know that we have given you a great deal to think about, research, and try. Do not feel as though you need to master all of our suggestions and strategies in your first attempts!

As an observer, remember that just as with teaching in a classroom, planning can only take us so far. Though preparation allows a teacher to become proactive and purposeful, consistently they have to monitor and make decisions as the lesson unfolds. The same is true in our practice as observers. In the next chapter, you will explore strategies for adjusting your evidence collection upon arrival in a classroom.

4 How Can You Adapt Evidence Collection Upon Arrival?

From the field . . .

I know that when I walk into a classroom, being able to quickly assess if learning is happening is important to ensure I can best support teachers. At the forefront of all observations, I want to make sure I can leave understanding "What are the students learning?," "Why are they learning this?," and "How will it be assessed?" Through my use of the evidence collection strategies, I have been able to better observe and provide specific feedback. I can quickly gather if learning is happening in the classroom because I am able to shift the types of questions I ask while working with students.

As an instructional coach, my work begins and ends with supporting teachers in their practice. Asking specific questions of the students right at the outset of a lesson has changed my focus in the classroom and helps me identify how the teacher is impacting student learning. It also has strengthened my skills for when I am teaching and modeling as I am thinking about what is happening for learners and can more quickly adapt. Overall, the strategies have given me the tools to be a better coach in my district.

—Elizabeth Stewart, Instructional Coach, Grades 6–8

"Intelligence is the ability to adapt to change."

—Stephen Hawking

Think back to a day with your students when you were teaching and things weren't going as you'd hoped. You were trying out a new tech tool that no one could access; you were attempting to create a rubric with your students, but they only wanted to talk about Halloween costumes, weekend plans, or prom; or you were working to finish those flower pot gifts for Mother's Day with eighteen five-year-olds, and chaos was ensuing. Add in, perhaps, that you had visitors to your classroom while this was happening. You may have planned for hours and had all of your supplies, sites, or resources ready to go, yet still, the lesson did not go as expected. You needed to read the situation, make decisions, improvise, and respond to what was happening. In classrooms, teaching and learning are dynamic and unpredictable, to say the least, and ever-changing, not just day by day but minute by minute.

To master the ability to respond and make adjustments during a lesson, teachers must be adaptable, flexible, and responsive—skills we are also seeking to develop in our students. Those who support teachers need to possess these skills as well. When we went searching for the definition of *adaptability*, we arrived at an *ability or willingness to change*.

For you to be an effective observer, you first must be *willing to adapt* to what is happening in the moment and not just continue to do the same thing throughout the observation. You have to *have the capacity* to effectively react and shift your evidence collection strategies. For teachers to respond as adaptable facilitators of learning, they must develop an accurate and clear understanding of how they are impacting students. This means that anyone who supports them through observation and feedback, whether as a peer, coach, or supervisor, must work diligently to do the same and collect specific and comprehensive evidence from students *as* they learn.

Your Goals as an Observer

Let's take a step back and review what it is you are working toward as an observer to understand how and why you should respond and adapt during a lesson. The key to becoming an effective support for teachers is to collect evidence that is *relevant*. Remember to always consider this: How can I serve as a valuable second set of eyes? What does this teacher need to know about what is happening with students right now?

Relevant evidence helps teachers understand

- how and why claims are being made about the overall effectiveness of instructional practices (which could include clear and objective support of a performance-level rating),
- how they are impacting student engagement and learning (causal attribution), and
- how they are progressing toward district/region, school, or professional goals.

Through these understandings, we build reflective practice, help teachers determine actionable next steps for growth, and continually improve outcomes for students.

To accurately measure how students are progressing toward our three goals (conceptual thinking, metacognitive thinking, and self-regulation), you must be able to adapt during an observation, as the related student actions, behaviors, and habits are always evolving. Chapter 3 set you up with a bank of surefire questions you can have at the ready. These provide a great place to start, especially for observers who are unsure of what to collect. They also provide a jumping-off point for you so that you are able to adapt questions to the immediate context of the learning. If you can become proactive in your approach to evidence collection and feedback, you will save mental energy for when you need to make an adjustment.

This chapter represents a more challenging level of observation and contains seven strategies (Strategies 8–14), but you are up to the task with practice and ongoing reflection! Keep Chapters 2 and 3 handy, as the basic strategies and concepts about learning, along with your preplanned questions, form the backbone of upcoming suggestions and strategies. Regardless of whether you

- held a preobservation conference or had a chance for a quick chat before you arrived that provided insight into what might be unfolding in the upcoming lesson, or
- you just popped in without notice and you know the teacher's goals, you will need to respond to what you see once you arrive.

Ultimately, as an observer, you should strive to increase your own metacognitive skills related to classroom observation so that you are purposefully collecting evidence. This is not to say you should confirm existing beliefs, make judgments, or selectively follow or disregard critical findings. We are saying that as an observer, think like a teacher; don't just become a witness to instruction. Check for understanding of the students' progress toward their learning target, and determine how they are thinking and learning. Remember, we are trying to determine how teachers are creating these outcomes and helping them to grow.

You will find the value in adapting your observation practices upon arrival will increase the quality and impact of your evidence collection.

Adapting During an Observation Ensures That . . .

- Your questions to students and attention to look-fors can immediately become contextualized based on the intended learning for the day (versus asking generic, though high-quality, questions)
- You can quickly develop questions of varying levels (from Bloom's or depth of knowledge, for example) based on intended learning
- You will have an easier time engaging in authentic conversations with students rather than running through a litany of questions
- You maximize your time in a classroom

The strategies introduced in this chapter will help you to make necessary adjustments while you are observing a lesson, understanding when, how, and why they are needed. We will walk you through

- Additional foundational strategies you will need
- How to adapt based on *when* you arrive during a lesson
- How to adapt based on *what is happening* when you arrive

We want to start with steps you can take within the first few minutes as you respond and adapt to the *immediate* learning and lesson unfolding. In Chapter 5, we will address how you might shift as the lesson continues to unfold.

We recommend, as always, that you try out our strategies, reflect on your effectiveness, refine, and try again, remembering that no two days—or teachers, lessons, or learners—are the same. We know it would be impossible to provide examples to prepare you for any and all scenarios, and with today's creative and innovative lessons, we would certainly miss something. Therefore, we worked to provide strategies and scenarios that we believe are transferable regardless of what you encounter when you arrive. These should allow you to adapt and personalize them to your own practices, schools, and classrooms. If you are viewing video lessons, you can use the new learning from this chapter to determine if and how the teacher adjusted during the lesson in response to the learners.

Stop and Think: To move forward in this chapter, it is important to have a clear picture of your tendencies. How willing are you to shift when something you have planned is not working as expected? Do you have the skills to make adjustments to improve your evidence collection in the moment?

Adapting 101: The Basics

Have you ever come down the hall, walked into a noisy classroom, and found students literally everywhere—working in groups, standing on chairs, and building objects? You look around and struggle to locate the teacher, who is fully embedded with one team. It generally takes a few seconds (or minutes, for some) to acclimate and figure out how to use your time. If you have been in this situation, you've already been making decisions as to how to refine your planned evidence collection strategies based on what is happening. Perhaps you walked in, and not only are students working in groups but the teacher has also pulled a small group for differentiated instruction. You want to see how she is meeting needs, but you also want to see what the student-led groups are doing. You have to make a decision about where to go first.

To facilitate your ability to adapt, before you head into classrooms you should have predetermined the following three things:

- A potential focus area based on
  - previous coaching,
  - your goals as an instructional leader, or
  - the teacher's, school's, or district's/region's goals. These could be based on any of our five focus areas (see Figure 2.7). Perhaps your goal may be to keep an open mind and a broad perspective, as the teacher has not yet set goals or is new to you. This is where you can remember to maintain your big-picture thinking (purpose, process, and understanding) from Chapter 1.
- A bank of general questions you can ask students or methods for interacting with the learners
- An understanding of teaching practices and outcomes related to the discipline

In Chapter 1, we reminded you of three foundational strategies for gathering evidence from learners:

- View learning in action
- Listen to teaching and learning
- Interact with learners

When we bring new observers into lessons, upon arrival, they like to follow these in order, as if they are sequenced steps (which is totally acceptable), although you can use them interchangeably. New observers look around first, listen to what is happening, and then make a decision about how to engage with learners. Depending on what is happening, it may neither be immediately appropriate to interrupt students nor possible to lean over and see their work (more on this in a bit). But to get you started, some steps we always take as soon as we arrive (though not necessarily in this order) regardless of what is happening, include the following:

Steps to Take Upon Entering a Classroom

1. **Determine how many students you will interact with.**

   Count the students in the room, and set a goal for the number with whom you want to interact if the instructional structure is going to allow for it. Even if you remain a short time, you will not accurately determine teacher impact if you only engage with one or two learners.

   Students were on the carpet listening to a think aloud in the third-grade reading lesson, so we quickly counted nineteen learners and looked around to see various reading anchor charts from the unit of study. During the turn-and-talk, we worked to listen to four partnerships and then set a goal to interact with half in the remaining ten minutes during their independent reading time.

2. **Draw a map noting the location and grouping of students.**

   If you like to utilize a mapping evidence collection strategy, draw the seating or locations of students and teacher. However, be ready; they may get up and move within minutes, requiring you to draw a new one.

   When we arrived at a second-grade math Pearson Investigations lesson, students were seated around the carpet watching the teacher play the new math station game she called "Compare" with a partner. Students then went back to their seats and worked with a partner to practice the game. We wondered and got ready to ask, Do you always work with the same partner? Does your seat change?

3. **Scan the room, quickly noting students' affects.**

   Scan the room quickly. Where is the teacher? Where are students? Immediately, watch body language and behaviors; they are starting points. We like to check on those who "appear" quiet, frustrated, and/or finished to learn more.

   We walked in as students were finishing a formative assessment in a high school chemistry lesson, and one student's body language was clearly showing frustration. He was slouched and not continuing his quiz. The teacher was monitoring and noticed students were struggling, and she was giving hints and feedback around the room. We took the opportunity to check in with the student. "What is challenging you right now?" He shared that he had no idea how to solve the problems and had left #3 blank. We then swept the room to see that nearly every student had skipped #3 and noticed how many students were also showing overall signs of frustration or had hands raised seeking teacher assistance. This led to a great conversation with the teacher about scaffolding, the unit design, and what she learned from the check/what essential understandings students were missing.

4. **Locate the learning target.**

   Locate the standards and objective/learning target(s), remembering that these are not always posted. Look at walls or boards, at an anchor chart up front from an introduction, for a PowerPoint slide, or in student notebooks. If you don't see it, ask students, if possible.

   During a quick transition between direct instruction and the first independent task in a high school financial literacy class, we jumped up and were able to ask five different students about the expectations for the day's learning: What are you learning today? They were able to communicate the goal easily, without reading it: "We are learning how our credit gets built and how our choices affect our credit scores in positive and negative ways. We are going to read scenarios to give advice to the person about their credit and what they should do and why." They pointed out a board behind them with the goal and agenda posted that we had not seen.

5. **Find out what the task expectations are.**

   Quickly get a handle on directions and task expectations/criteria. Be sure to ask more than one student to confirm/match answers.

   - *In one sixth-grade social studies lesson, it was clear everyone was not doing the same thing, so it was important to spend*

(Continued)

(Continued)

time understanding the various product options. Some were practicing a skit, and others were developing a public service announcement, while others were creating a brochure to demonstrate understanding. Remember also, students may have flexible pacing—"When do you need to have this finished?"—so they also could be working on different phases of the same task. Ask, "How did you choose what you are creating?" and "What will you be doing with the finished product?"

- *In a tenth-grade health class, everyone was finishing independent projects on their computers about healthy lifestyles related to healthy relationships. (We often walk into lessons where there are various tasks at hand.) We asked students, "Is everyone doing the same thing?" (Answer: "Yes.") "What were your steps up to this point to complete this?" We looked through the rubrics and directions they had on their desks to orient ourselves to the expectations.*

Stop and Think: What are the habits or strategies you utilize as soon as you enter a classroom or begin an observation? What has an observer done upon arrival when visiting your classroom?

(Visit **resources.corwin.com/learnerfocusedfeedback** to review Resource 4.1: Adapting 101 strategies from *Feedback to Feed Forward*.)

The more often you visit classrooms, the easier it becomes to quickly acclimate and adapt to what you are seeing and hearing. In those rooms you visit frequently, you will also get to know where things are located and the typical routines. As you look, listen, and plan how you will collect evidence, one of the first elements you'll need to consider upon arriving to a classroom will be "At what point am I arriving in the lesson, period, and unit?" Based on this and thinking about Chapter 2, engagement and learning will look and sound different. In addition, the instructional design or teacher's level of responsibility may look and sound different. Therefore, as expected, your methods of evidence collection will look and sound different. This is what we consider **Evidence Collection 2.0**, the backbone of learner-focused feedback.

Metacognition in Motion

In the strategies ahead, we practice making our own metacognitive processing visible to you to demonstrate how we respond and adapt our evidence collection practices, beginning with how we make choices in evidence collection.

Strategy 8: Purposefully choose your evidence collection methods

As part of Evidence Collection 2.0, Strategy 8 serves as an extension of FF Strategies 14–16 (listen, view, and interact). We continue to see observers (especially when new to observation) struggle to determine what to do and when to use each strategy during a lesson and how to maximize the use of each. Remember, the fact that you are *willing* to adapt or utilize different evidence collection strategies is a huge step! Now, let's focus on your ability to adapt. When you are in a room, you become a valuable second set of eyes for a teacher—try not to see yourself as an impediment. You should be thinking, "What is it the teacher needs to know about what is happening right now about the learning?"

At first, you may choose to look over the shoulder of a student you know well, listen at random to a group in the corner, or talk to the student sitting closest to you. These methods are totally acceptable as you build your capacity as an evidence collector of engagement and learning. You will become more comfortable, fast-moving, and interactive and will grow to more purposefully collect evidence during each lesson if you think about your thinking. This is challenging because, simultaneously, a lesson is playing out and students are thinking about their thinking. Let's consider what is happening in the classroom when listening and viewing are especially important with a few examples in Figure 4.1.

FIGURE 4.1: LISTENING AND VIEWING BASICS

Listen when . . .	View when . . .
T is providing direct instruction T is questioning the group T is providing learning objective and criteria T is providing feedback T is conferring Ss are responding Ss are talking in groups or partnerships Ss are asking questions Ss are making comments (e.g., of frustration or ahas) Ss are restating	T is modeling T is moving or teaching individuals or small groups Ss are participating or raising hands (or not) Ss are working on a task or reading, building, creating, or producing something Ss are working on pace or not (e.g., are finishing quickly, not starting, or skipping answers/ sections) Ss are transitioning between tasks or moving in the room

Classroom Example 4.1

Subject: Middle School Science

Recall our mention of middle school students launching rockets in Chapter 2 in our discussion of the role of emotion in learning. The observer entered the classroom just as the teacher was introducing the lesson, and within minutes, students moved into their groups to work. From the moment he arrived, the observer needed to make decisions. He decided to first look around, and he observed the notes on the board. He noted direct quotes as he listened to the teacher. He made a conscious choice to interact with learners *after* the teacher finished and the students had gotten started, as he didn't want to interrupt either the teacher in the first few minutes or the students as they transitioned to gather what they needed. He pondered asking preplanned questions based on what he was seeing and hearing or possibly adjusting his evidence collection. Within the first few minutes back at their tables, he'd decided to wait and just view and listen as they were building on yesterday's lesson to purposefully observe how they were proceeding.

He noticed students were rushing, not using their notes or drawing new models as the teacher recommended, and were not consulting with group members or talking about the science behind their decisions. Figure 4.2 shows the evidence the observer collected just by listening and viewing.

FIGURE 4.2: LISTENING AND VIEWING EXAMPLE

Listening to the Teaching and Learning	Viewing the Teaching and Learning
• T gave directions and expectations for first 2 minutes: to use data to make adjustments for relaunches of rockets, to set goals for distance targets • 5 of 7 groups Ss talked in groups, but only 1 of 7 were talking using scientific concepts to support changes • T gave feedback to Ss as they relaunched • T noticed Ss weren't using data and redirected, "Remember to use your notes and draw a model of your new proposed rocket first"	• Ss moved to groups and got out supplies—all Ss working within 1 minute • Within 3 minutes of group work, the first group was ready to relaunch • Ss were not using resources—only 4 Ss had their notes out on the desks • All groups were making physical adjustments to the rockets (pulling of fins, adding more tape) • Only 1 group was creating a model

Note: You will encounter charts like these throughout the next two chapters. They are quick snapshots of interactions from a few students and may not represent full conversations the observer had with students or show the variety of answers or evidence collected from many students.

Our observer started to use Strategy 8 when he adjusted his evidence collection based on what he was noticing and learning from the students. Once he saw the groups failing to use data or prior knowledge, he decided to interact with them, asking what they had learned previously and how they were or could be using that to make decisions, along with what they noticed about their previous launch—thus getting to an overview of their overall scientific thinking. (We will tackle this technique in more detail in Chapter 5.)

Our observer learned a great deal just watching and listening, but several students were unhappy about answering his questions because they wanted to get to the next launch opportunity. Even this, in itself, became evidence they were missing the forest for the trees. Though they were excited, most were not concerned about the scientific basis or data-driven steps. They were not using effective reasoning or collaboration, previous learning, or detailed review of their previous launch. Clearly this teacher was working to shift his instruction to align to NGSS (deep learning), but students were fixated on the "fun activity." Students saw our interruptions as standing in the way of getting to the launch quickly—launches that were again not meeting their goals for flight or height reached from the ground. (The observer decided to spend time watching the launches after a few minutes at the group tables.)

There are times when we should avoid or limit interrupting, such as situations where students are

- in a race or timed situation (these students perceived they were in a race),
- listening to a teacher give direct instruction or directions,
- engaged in a Socratic-type structure, or
- watching a video.

In these moments (as with watching a filmed observation), rely on your viewing and listening skills and your strategies to provide you with rich data.

Cautions

A few words of caution regarding overcoming bias (FF Strategies 7, 8, and 9): Though we are working on our thinking about thinking, it is important to remember that sometimes our thinking can be flawed or misleading.

> **Caution 1:** As observers, you too can get caught up in a fun activity, the buzz of students talking, or newly aligned NGSS lessons. Though we like to see students enjoying a task and we know the value of humor and positive emotions on engagement, this can cloud our ability to collect

real data as to how the teacher is impacting learning and how deeply students are thinking.

Caution 2: Beyond not getting caught up in the moment, don't make assumptions—they will not always be correct, and your evidence collection and feedback need to remain objective. Be careful with first instincts or judgments with things like, say, body language. Notice them; you are human and an educator, but be sure to look at the slouched student's work or ask him or her questions. Sometimes, they are thinking deeply and are ahead of the group!

(View Resource 4.2: Potential First Assumptions for some examples of first assumptions **resources.corwin.com/learnerfocusedfeedback**)

Caution 3: We have also seen our observers begin teaching when they see students struggling. (This is our nature!) When observing for growth versus evaluation (when you should not interfere in the teaching and learning), observers can take steps to support and better understand learners. We have been known in the midst of observing to do the following:

- Helped students with decoding and reading strategies when we see them skipping difficult words in their texts
- Pulled math manipulatives to reteach a concept
- Noticed that third-grade students were lined up at the teacher's desk with completed poems saying, "I'm done," and the teacher replied, "Okay, start another one." Amy modeled for her how to give feedback to redirect them to learning criteria (e.g., asking students, "What should your haiku include? What are we trying to do with our words in a haiku?"), and the teacher immediately tried this out.

Sometimes, we as observers, when asking questions that push student thinking, will see learning change immediately. For example, if you notice students aren't using notes, ask about them. They take the notes out and begin using them—it is a win–win! We are in the business of making a difference for our learners. You just need to let the teacher know how you altered outcomes and talk more about how she or he might conduct note checks for quality and usefulness, possibly model the use of them during the task, and utilize feedback to remind them to use the notes. An observer can inadvertently alter evidence collection if fellow observers are unaware that you changed the outcomes for those students.

If the observation is for the purpose of evaluation, it is critical to observe and interact, but resist the temptation to teach. We want to develop a clear understanding of what the teacher most needs in his or her instructional practices. We want to see if a teacher notices students struggling and then what she or he does about it.

Regardless of the purpose of your observation or what is occurring during your visit—direct instruction, students watching a video—it is important for you to make decisions and consider how to best use your evidence collection tools of viewing, listening, and interacting interchangeably.

Stop and Think: As an observer, what might prevent or has prevented you from interacting with the learners directly during a lesson?

Making It Count

You have valuable minutes, sometimes only ten to fifteen, and you want to make them count when observing a lesson. Think about these strategies from *Feedback to Feed Forward*:

FF Strategy 10: Place yourself where the learning is occurring (moving)

FF Strategy 11: Do what it takes to collect evidence (using all means available)

Be sure to maximize your available time while you are in a classroom. Things are constantly evolving and occurring. If you are 100 percent present during a lesson, you will recognize many opportunities to collect valuable evidence of the engagement and learning occurring moment to moment. We want to extend the idea behind these strategies to the use of time. Early in our sessions, we often see observers hanging near the door or just looking at learners. Sometimes, this is related to

- earlier training models when we did not speak to students,
- stamina (sometimes observers get worn out or they are taking longer to acclimate to a room/tasks),
- fear of "bothering," and
- not knowing what to collect.

We will often approach observers and prompt them, giving permission to get involved, and will often model or provide examples of possible entry questions to learners based on what we see happening.

Know that this is about being alert and nimble. If you hear "Turn and talk to your neighbor," "Write your answers on your whiteboards," or "Gather what you need, find a spot, and get started," these are prime opportunities for you to learn something about the learner, so get moving. The moment there is an opportunity to collect evidence of the learning occurring, you want to take it with the least amount of disruption possible. Think about Adapting 101 from earlier in this chapter, and consider these prime possibilities:

- When you first arrive and the lesson has not begun: Students present? Chat with them about what they might be learning in this next lesson. Students not present? Look around. How is the room organized? Are classroom expectations, messages, or anchor charts posted?
- Transitions large and small: Are students gathering material or waiting for materials to be distributed? Get over there, and ask about the learning target and expectations for the day. Are they putting on coats, headed to PE, or transitioning to a new location, such as the playground, the computer lab, or the media center? We have had some of our best conversations walking with students.
- Once a student finishes a math calculation or writing a sentence, flips a page, or finishes speaking

We can work toward having meaningful quick bursts of conversation with learners throughout a lesson, using Strategy 9, especially if we are mindful of when and how we are interrupting. Our next strategy builds on FF Strategy 16: Interact with learners.

Strategy 9: Engage in conversations through questions

We realized the need for Strategy 9 after noticing observers mechanically asking students questions as if marking items off of a checklist, polling, and then moving on to the next question and the next student. We realized that observers who did this were not understanding that the goal of the questions is to interact with learners in a conversation. They were missing out on the data, and understanding that can come from really engaging with students, hearing and seeing how they are thinking—what they have to teach us.

Questioning is one of the most important instructional tools available to us as teachers; it can push thinking and serve as a valuable check for understanding. You are seeking to understand the following through conversation (versus survey):

- Level of rigor or depth of knowledge of learning, thinking, discussion, or artifact creation
- Level of connection making
- Level of struggle and success (e.g., appropriateness of scaffolding, supports, differentiation)
- Level of use of metacognitive skills and self-monitoring/self-regulation

Remember, this process is not a "Gotcha!" for teachers. We are working to make student thinking visible and looking for causes of outcomes.

You can have a powerful one- to two-minute conversation if you ask powerful questions. Sometimes you need to start small: "How are you today?" or "What are you working on?" But there are twenty-plus others awaiting a chat with you, so you want to cut to the chase pretty quickly and ask meaningful questions. Remember, too, the more frequently you visit classrooms, the more students will be ready and willing to talk. But know for some, your presence and questions may scare the living daylights out of them, and they will answer you with one-word responses, though they may understand a great deal more than they are conveying. You may ask a great question, but the student just stares at you, puts in headphones, or even starts to growl (this happened to Amy). This leads to our next strategy.

Strategy 10: Set high expectations for responses

We added this strategy based on what we continue to see in our trainings. Observers get wowed by surface thinking or if all students can articulate the directions. We should absolutely celebrate the small successes and the baby steps (or giant leaps) based on what we know about our individual learners (especially those who struggle every day) and what our teachers are accomplishing. And sometimes, if you remember from Chapter 2, surface learning should be celebrated as a necessary step for deeper learning. (Mastering your 9 times tables or a sight word list should merit a party. Automaticity has great value. As we know once it is applied in the context of new learning, students can become more efficient and effective.)

Remember also, a few months can make a difference in students' ability to articulate responses or thinking, especially in lower elementary, and understanding only increases across a unit of study. But the strategy here is to expect that your students can and will think conceptually and answer your "Why?"

and "How?" questions because of teaching that is building their ability to do so. This is rooted in the fundamental belief within a culture of learning that all students can learn. If they cannot yet, we search for causal attribution and how a teacher is moving toward that goal.

Our expectations were forever changed one February after visiting several kindergarten classrooms in different districts to watch writing lessons.

School 1:

O: What are you creating?

S: A how-to book.

O: Why? What is that for?

S: We are all experts in something, so this is to teach someone how to do something new.

O: What are you teaching? How did you decide you were an expert?

S: How to make a snowman. First, we made a list of all things we know how to do. Then, we chose one we have done a lot of times and are very good at. We drew pictures after to be a better expert and not miss anything.

O: Who will be reading your book?

S: We will post them in the hallway for all of the other grades, and they will be able to choose what they want to learn about.

O: What are you and your partner working on now?

S: We are reading each other's to see if it is missing something.

The observer then spent time listening to students reading each other's work and then asked specific questions about the sequenced steps in each how-to. Based on observers' questions, students realized that some steps had been left out of the how-to book.

School 2:

O: What is your goal as a writer today?

SI: We are writing about the artist we studied last week to share with the other class.

O: What do you remember about the artist that was important?

S1: Georgia O'Keeffe painted flowers and used lots of colors . . . wait let me get the book to show you. Look, see how . . .

S2: She was different and had her own way. So we can be different when we draw.

S3: She wanted to be an artist when she was twelve, and that's what I want to be.

Amy taught full-day preK back in the early 1990s, and the expectation was for her students to work on number, letter, and sight word recognition, fine motor skills, and crafts. Now, we enter classrooms and find five- and six-year-olds formally writing and making cross-discipline connections and using the text in their writing, understanding learning purpose and criteria, and peer reviewing! Notice how the students were aware of where they were headed and were making connections.

If five- and six-year-olds can share at this level, why can't fifteen- and sixteen-year-olds accomplish this and beyond? The key is in helping teachers see how they can create these outcomes and build these capacities.

In both previous scenarios, we walked in during independent work time and had not seen the introduction, yet students in those classrooms had a clear path in mind. Let's now consider how you would adapt your strategies based on the point in which you enter a lesson or learning progression.

Timing Is Everything

When you enter a classroom, notice what is happening in the learning progression at that moment so that you can adapt your evidence collection strategies accordingly.

Strategy 11: Use what you know about the timing of your arrival

For common understanding of *learning progression*, let's use the gradual-release model (Figure 2.9) to think about how teachers release responsibility to students, ensuring they are working in the zone of proximal development (Fisher & Frey, 2013; Pearson & Gallagher, 1983; Vygotsky 1978).

Be aware . . .

1. In contrast to observations in elementary classrooms where morning meeting and then reading occurs at the same time in the same way each day, when observing classrooms in block periods, the time of your arrival will not necessarily indicate any given activity or point within the progression of the lesson. Although you arrive shortly after the bell rings, students may already be deeply engaged in continuing a project from the day (or week) before.

2. Teachers do not need to follow this model or see this as linear, nor does every lesson need to begin at "I do." Remember what we understand about learning as iterative: "The gradual release of responsibility instructional framework is recursive, and a teacher might reassume responsibility several times during a lesson to reestablish its purpose and provide additional examples of expert thinking" (Fisher & Frey, 2013).

3. The use of the strategies presented ahead also needs to be weighed against a few other possible situations, such as if you are arriving in a "you do" or "you do together" segment of the lesson. For example, you may arrive

   a. On a culminating type of day when students are demonstrating, utilizing, or transferring understanding (e.g., You walk in, and they are all getting seated to begin a debate, or they are on day two of viewing each other's presentations.)

   b. During an inquiry-based or discovery lesson

   c. During a portion of a flipped gradual-release model

The National Council of Teachers of Mathematics (NCTM; McCaffrey, 2016) suggests that teachers *can* effectively reverse the order of the known model (picture an independent Do Now ["You do"], share with a partner ["You do together"], and then teacher instruction ["I do"] based on check-ins with students). However, this will only result in a successful progression if teachers are capable of

- designing high-quality tasks that will serve as effective checks for prior understanding of essentials or preassessments of upcoming skills/concepts before beginning instruction,
- providing opportunities and building the capacity for an effective "We do together" that they then monitor for students' levels of understanding (partner discussions and compare), and
- using data on the spot (using student evidence to determine a starting point and potential differentiation).

Stop and Think: Why or how might you need to adapt your evidence collection strategies based on the teacher's level of ownership versus the student's? For example, if you step into an "I do" with more ownership on the teacher's part, you will not necessarily have the opportunity to interact with students or interrupt the direct instruction.

For our purposes in this chapter, we utilize a standard gradual-release model, but generally, you will find you can apply our strategies regardless of the teacher's progression.

Arriving During the Introduction or Minilesson

You may have arrived early as students are filing in or transitioning to the next subject, in time to catch the introduction to the day's learning. This is a luxury in that, sometimes, stepping in mid-lesson can cause you to feel overwhelmed, or your bias kicks in: "It's too noisy. The teacher has no control," or "Hurray, they are in groups!" By stepping in at the outset, you are able to get your bearings and potentially see the establishment of learning expectations and criteria. (*Note:* Just because you arrived at the outset does not mean you will hear the learning purpose in the first few minutes, but remember that effective instruction includes continuous reiteration of the purpose along with reflection.)

You may see and hear explicit instruction, such as a teacher modeling or thinking aloud to demonstrate the new skill or strategy, an "I do," and a "we do together" portion. Though teacher led,

> there is no time in teaching when "telling" is enough. The key to quality instruction is explaining. Students need an explanation of their teacher's cognitive processes and metacognitive thinking. . . . It is teacher behavior that serves as the transition to guided instruction. [Teachers], you are observing, listening, and using your knowledge of the content, of novice learners, and of their likely misconceptions or partial understandings to help you formulate the questions, prompts, and cues you'll need to scaffold student learning. (Fisher & Frey, 2013, pp. 20, 34)

Keep in mind that this is the time when we will hear activation of prior learning and hopefully hear and see students' connection making beginning (Figure 2.6).

Figure 4.3 provides some ideas for what you can be thinking during the introduction of a lesson. (Remember, you are strengthening your own observation metacognitive skills in this process.) Notice that Figure 4.3 and strategies

FIGURE 4.3: OBSERVER THINKING: INTRODUCTION

Viewing Teaching and Learning	Listening to Teaching and Learning	Interacting With Learners in the Moment
Think:	**Think:**	**Think:**
• Where are students seated? • What do they have with them? (supplies, notebooks, journals, whiteboards, articles, resources) • Are they partnered? • What does the teacher have out? Is she showing or creating an example/nonexample? • Is the teacher looking at responses on whiteboards or work in front of students? • What do I see the teacher do in response to student understanding? (e.g., keep a few students behind for reteaching)	• What is the strategy, skill, or understanding the teacher is introducing? What are the steps? • Is the teacher checking for understanding or giving students opportunities to articulate? (e.g., prior learning, connection making, misconceptions, understanding of learning targets) • Is the teacher listening to sharing in turn-and-talks, cold calling responses? • What do I hear students saying in response to questions, or what questions are they asking? • What is it telling me (and the teacher)? • What do I hear the teacher do in response?	• How is the teacher setting them up for success? • Do they know what the goals are for the day's learning and how they will get there? • Can you become a partner with a student or jump into any partnership's conversation without delaying the task? • Can students explain learning expectations and/or connections they are making to previous lessons or concepts?

integrate the big-picture thinking from Chapter 1, considering purpose, process, and understanding.

Arriving During Independent Work

We love walking into classrooms when learning is in full force, to see students grappling, problem solving, talking, and growing, but it requires you to hone your evidence collection skills to be able to jump right in with them. Keep in mind a few things:

- The more you and your team visit classrooms, the more comfortable students will be talking to you and the faster you can acclimate.
- You should use your strategies to view and listen first before interacting directly with students. Pay attention, and choose opportune times to do so.

- *Caution:* Compliant students who are focused on rewards and grades or completion of a task will often find your questions troublesome. Be considerate of their receptiveness.

Many observers are intimidated by the busyness and feel they are interrupting or bothering students, so we have compiled a set of strategies and scenarios to help you best adapt to any instructional structure or situation you might encounter as you walk through the classroom door.

Upon arrival, you might find students doing the following:

- Involved in hands-on learning individually, as partners, in small groups, or as a whole group (e.g., engaged in science experiments/labs, using math manipulatives, practicing dribbling a basketball, acting out a scene in a play or skit, practicing a piece of music, building something)
- Using technology, such as working on a phone, Chromebook, laptop, or iPad (e.g., blogging, creating a website, creating a graphic design, giving feedback to a peer, working in Google Classroom, reading an e-text or PDF, writing)
- Engaged in group or partner discussion (e.g., planning a project, practicing foreign-language vocabulary, researching, partner reading/feedback)
- Engaged in whole-group discussions (e.g., Socratic circle, debates, Philosophical Chairs)
- Leaving to go somewhere (e.g., outside, alternate location for class, media center, next class)
- Presenting to classmates
- Working with the teacher in a small group or conferring one on one

You might find these are difficult or inappropriate situations in which to engage with students; collecting evidence of learning may not be possible. But you might also find windows of opportunity. Agriculture science, or really any performance-based courses, provide these unique situations. Amy stood in a barn holding a baby goat while students tended to their work cleaning up the stalls and chatted about their learning. We have walked to fields discussing the day's plan as students prepared to build a new fence to keep deer out of a garden and transitioned with students outside as they walked out back to the tractor they were learning to drive. Strategy 11: *Use what you know about the timing of your arrival* was built on FF Strategy 10: Place yourself where the learning is occurring.

Though you will probably be moving around a good bit if you arrive after an introduction, you may still utilize the thinking in Figure 4.3. However, you can also look to Figure 4.4 for additional thinking prompts. If you walk in after the introduction, you need to quickly get a handle on what happened before you arrived (for example, you see a model or think-aloud poster by the carpet, or you see notes on the board) and find ways to adapt your evidence collection immediately to allow yourself to get your bearings and determine learners' progressions and understandings.

FIGURE 4.4: OBSERVER THINKING: INDEPENDENT WORK

Viewing Teaching and Learning	Listening to Teaching and Learning	Interacting With Learners in the Moment
Think:	**Think:**	**Think:**
• Where are students seated? • What do they have with them? (supplies, notebooks, journals, whiteboards, articles, resources, worksheets, computer) • Are they partnered or in groups? • Where is the teacher? • What is the teacher doing while students are working? • Do you see any student body language or behaviors revealing motivation or thinking?	• Do you hear learners making their learning audible? (ahas, frustration, discussion, questions) • If in partners or groups, what are students saying to each other? • Are they asking questions of each other or to the teacher? • What feedback is the teacher providing to students? Are there mid-lesson teaching adjustments?	• Where are they in the learning progression? Are they on pace for the task/day? • Do they know what the goals are for the day's learning and how they will get there? • Can they explain learning expectations and/or connections they are making to previous lessons or concepts? • Can they make connections to today's tasks or introduction from before you arrived? • How has the teacher set them up for success?

Do you remember our chemistry example from earlier in the chapter? Even if you walk in when students are taking a quiz or test, there are opportunities to collect evidence. Not only can you see how learners are experiencing the assessment and their correct or incorrect answers, you can also see how they are being asked to apply or transfer the learning in the quiz questions.

Classroom Example 4.2

Subject: High School Child Development

We stepped into a class quiz and saw everyone with the same words—matching them with definitions—that we later saw they had copied, word for word, in their notebooks.

Though recall has a role in learning, we know from research and what we understand about the brain that this is not the most effective way for students to learn vocabulary, and it is not personalized. It does not provide opportunities for them to generate their own lists, create their own meaning, and develop conceptual understanding, nor does it prepare them to utilize the terms and concepts in new ways. The quiz format was not the best way to measure understanding, as we saw students guessing and then using process of elimination. Beyond this, if a student matched them all correctly, it does not mean that they "know" the word.

This quick visit helped us see next potential steps for the teacher and was an opportunity to talk about surface and deep learning.

Using the Learning Goals

The learning goals established for a day's lesson and unit form the foundation of our evidence collection, whether we are an observer or a teacher. At the outset of a lesson or within moments of entering a classroom, regardless of where you step into the progression, your work can begin if you know where students are headed. Once you understand learning expectations, you have plenty of information to adjust your evidence collection strategies. Remember, student understanding of learning expectations starts them on their journey of determining where they are going and how they are going. You can view or hear student success or progress (or lack thereof) in direct alignment to the target through their work, your questions to them and their responses, or if you hear them restate learning goals. Utilizing objectives or learning targets forms the foundation of our upcoming Strategies 12, 13, and 14.

You strengthen your snapshot conversations when they are directly related to student understanding of the expectations (and their progression). The rest of the chapter is built on the premise that you can engage with students while you are in the room without being disruptive. You may have planned a number of questions (Chapter 3) and are ready to ask students, "What are you learning today, and why?"—a powerful question. However, we want to introduce you to the next layer in your evidence collection practice—to think about how you can ask direct and specific questions aligned to the day's learning. Think back to our second graders learning to play a station game from earlier in the chapter. Observers started with "What are you learning?," but students responded "To play a game." We simply shifted our questions to "What will you learn by playing this game?" and "What is this game helping you to do better?"

Classroom Example 4.3

Subject: Fourth-Grade Reading

Let's look at another example. We arrived with several observers at the tail end of a minilesson. Let's look at the evidence one observer collected. Figure 4.5 shows the evidence collected within the first six to seven minutes of arrival.

FIGURE 4.5: EVIDENCE COLLECTION BASED ON EXPECTATIONS

Viewing Teaching and Learning	Listening to Teaching and Learning	Interacting With Learners
There was a posted objective: "I can make an inference about a story using prompts." There was a chart on the board with examples under each. It says | I know | It tells us 4 or 5 Ss' hands were raised for each question	T: How do you know if it's time to make an inference? S1: If you're in the middle of the book. S2: If you are stuck. T: What are we looking for? S: What does the book want us to learn?	O to S1: What strategy are you trying out today? S1: Where the inference is. O: What is an inference? S1: What the character wants us to know. O: How do you figure that out? S1: By reading it to see if he is greedy or not.

Viewing Teaching and Learning	Listening to Teaching and Learning	Interacting With Learners
T called on 3 Ss Ss moved to their seats within 3 minutes of our arrival/were reading within 1 min. T began conferring immediately w/ 1 S 3 of 23 Ss were writing on notes in a notebook/ on a sticky	T: You are always looking for this, for a spot where I don't know what was said.	O to S2: When would you try to infer something in your book? S2: When you get stuck or when a reader wants to know about a book. O: How will you use the prompt to help you infer? S2: I'm not sure.

Stop and Think: What did you notice so far from the ongoing evidence collected?

After talking to a handful of students and listening to the transition from the minilesson to independent reading, our observer was thinking about her thinking immediately. Her self-talk was leading to decision making within just a few minutes of arrival. Based on the students' answers (on the carpet and in response to her questions) as to when readers would make inferences, along with the teacher's restatement, and the fact that only three responded on the carpet, the observer wants to be sure everyone understands when readers need to infer and how to do that—or to find who may need more support in this. They may not successfully infer at this point, and that's okay, but she wanted to determine what they understand about the concept. The observer quickly plans in her head:

View: Look at student notes on stickies; pay attention to where the teacher goes and for how long.

Listen: Listen to students read; try to capture some of the teacher's conversation with individuals.

Interact: Ask students about their process and use of the strategies.

Let's look at a few things our observer is considering. She knows

- the chart/prompt is an effective tool to help students make connections to schema (neuroscience/research),
- inference requires critical thinking as text complexity increases (discipline-specific literacy and deep learning),
- inferring is figuring out meaning when it is not explicitly stated, so students are on the right path when they say they might do this in the middle of the book, that they may be learning something, or when we may be stuck, but
- they don't understand exactly when to infer, what an inference is, or how to use the prompt to make an inference.

We will revisit this lesson in Chapter 5 to see more evidence the observer collected as the lesson unfolded.

Foundational Understandings

Think back to what we discussed about how our brains work and the critical need for students to be able to anchor or construct new learning based on previous learning to allow them to make connections and build neural pathways. As an observer, once you are acclimated to a classroom structure, point in the lesson, and learning and task expectations, you can begin to ascertain how students are recalling and using prior learning, Strategy 12.

Strategy 12: Interact to determine prior learning

> *"You cannot reconstruct or reactivate a neural circuit or network if it was never activated in the first place."* —Wolfe, 2010, p. 117

Through your questioning aligned to the day's learning expectations, you want to determine student understanding of essential skills and foundations, depth of activation or prior learning, and their connection making. Are they set up for success and to master the posted or stated target? Are they aware of what they knew and didn't know when starting the lesson or task? The moment we arrive in a room and determine the learning target, our wheels should start spinning as to what knowledge, understandings, or skills the students need in order to master the day's expectations. We want to quickly determine where they are in the learning progression, lesson, and unit. (You could see how frequent visits and/or quick chats before help with this.) We want to determine what was taught before this lesson and what students need within this lesson. Often, teachers are rushing to turn learning over (remember, they are told time and again in feedback that they must share responsibility and talk less), or they assume students remember previous concepts.

Classroom Example 4.4

Subject: High School Algebra II

Let's consider an example to illustrate this. The observer walked in and saw the posted learning target: *"I can solve an algorithm problem using a quadratic function or by extracting the square root."* Students confirm this is today's learning and are working in pairs to solve equations and also explain why they chose their solution method. The observer has only fifteen minutes or so, so she chooses to

> **View**: visually sweeping the room and seeing hands raised for help, erasing, and some sitting, but not working
>
> **Listen**: hearing the teacher and paraprofessional reteaching content to individuals

Then, she consciously chooses to **interact, determining questions based on what she was seeing and what they were expected to learn.**

> **Interact**: head to check first on the students who are looking for help or just sitting first

We chose this lesson as an example to show that effective observation does not always rely on content expertise. You may or may not be well versed in quadratic functions yet must support teachers in various disciplines. We also encourage teachers to visit peers across disciplines and grades because when you understand teaching and learning, your support can be of great value. Based on your expertise or background, you may or may not know all of the essentials or foundations students require to achieve this target. Immediately, two things potentially could be deduced:

1. These students have been exposed to two methods, as they now need to select the best or most appropriate one. We see this type of target

and thinking for all grade levels of math, especially for those grounded in the Standards for Mathematical Practice 1: *Make sense of problems and persevere in solving them. "They can understand the approaches of others to solving complex problems and identify correspondences between different approaches."* (CCSSI, 2018) (discipline-specific understanding)

For example, in one classroom visit, our bar setters—kindergartners—told us they were working toward finding the most "efficient and effective ways" to find a sum and could explain what that meant. In other disciplines, ideally, you will see similar thinking promoted because it requires conceptual understanding (cognitive thinking), along with metacognition and self-regulation. For example, the workshop approach for reading and writing provides students the freedom to utilize varied strategies based on need and appropriateness, and students K–8 have explained to us why they were or were not using a particular strategy on a given day (e.g., based on genre, where they are in the book or writing, and reading needs).

So let's return to our algebra II lesson for further thinking from the observer's conclusions so far.

2. To determine the best or most efficient method, the students need to be proficient in solving each of the various methods. Some starter questions (beginning with those students who appear to struggle or are just sitting) will help the observer get to their foundations and background knowledge. This will help her to understand if supports or effective scaffolding are in place or needed and the root causes of their challenges. Some observer questions include the following:

O: What does it mean to extract the square root?

S1: I'm not sure.

O: When did you learn about extracting the square root? What do you remember about it?

S1: A while ago, but I forget how to do it.

S2: I was absent, so I don't remember.

S3: We learned this before break. I think this is for review.

O: How do you know which method to use?

S4: I think she wants us to use the one we think is easiest.

O: [Points to a skipped problem and asks specifically about it] How can you decide which method to use for this one? [Helps to make their processing visible]

S4: I don't know how to solve that one. [The student isn't looking for clues that will help him make the determination.]

Based on the answers given, the observer is starting to collect evidence that the students do not remember and are not successful at solving for one of the methods.

If students are unsure, depending on the time you have and if this is nonevaluative, you can take a few next steps:

a. You can dig deeper and break down the essential understandings further with questions such as, "*What is a square root?*" or "*What is an algorithm?*"
b. You can ask the students where the information might be in their notes or books and have them locate the resources (or learn there aren't any), asking, "*What can you do if you don't know?*"
c. If you have a strong relationship with this teacher, you can provide her with immediate feedback that may change the outcomes for these students on the spot. Also, in middle and high school, teachers may teach this exact lesson again forty-five minutes later, and this can build reflection about the incoming learners' needs and potentially allow them to revise the plan for next period.

When we begin a lesson, we expect (hope) our learners are holding on to previous concepts taught, yet many times, we start with something they encountered only twenty-four hours earlier but have absolutely no recollection of. We know this could be linked to several causes related to how the teacher helped students make connections and move the new learning from working memory. An observer becomes a valuable second set of eyes to determine what is causing the outcomes in the moment, and often, it is a lack of prior knowledge or connection making.

We always like to ask how and when students know something to accurately assess progression and scaffolding, student connection making, or transfer. For example, the observer asked the algebra II students, "*When/how did you learn this?*"

But other times, you might see students who are excelling, and their answers demonstrate highly effective scaffolding:

> S: Ms. R has been teaching us how to do this for a few weeks, and now we are using everything we learned to . . .

Though students require scaffolding to be successful, they also need to persevere in the face of challenge as they are constructing new knowledge or using previous knowledge in new ways. A means to drive that motivation—to try when things are difficult—lies in how a teacher helps students to see the context of the day's learning and personal relevance.

Strategy 13: Interact to determine relevance and context

> *"The brain will not adapt to senseless tasks."* —Jensen, 2005, p. 117

Russ Quaglia is dedicated to learners connecting to their schools and classroom and is a well-known advocate for student voice and choice.

When students connect what they are learning to their futures, they are 15 times more likely to be academically motivated (QISA, 2013).

> Those with aspirations are determined. With genuine aspiration comes the vision of a destination clearly seen and the passion for exerting oneself on behalf of that future. They commit the energy, time, and resources required to meet their objective. In schools that foster students' aspirations,
>
> - students know learning is about more than test scores,
> - teachers know students' hopes and dreams, and
> - teachers make learning relevant for student.
>
> Aspiration is the ability to dream and set goals for the future while being inspired in the present to reach those dreams. (Quaglia & Corso, 2014, pp. 20, 116)

Helping students see and internalize a day's lesson in the context of immediate, short-term, and long-term applications or connections is directly related to their understanding of the concepts, strategies, and skills that came before. "In other words, an understanding of the relevancy of one's learning moves students forward from declarative (factual knowledge), through procedural and conditional knowledge—from *what* to *how* to *when*" (Frey, Hattie, & Fisher, 2018, p. 44).

Beyond this, you are also seeking to determine who is making the connections (often, it is just the teacher) and if the current work is transferable and relevant, involves an authentic task or audience, connects to them in some way, or is linked to previous concepts. When we think about our second-grade math students from early in the chapter, we wondered if they were making connections or simply playing a game. We asked, "Why are you playing this new game, Compare?" By also using our earlier question, "What are you learning by playing this game?" along with student answers, we learn they are not, in fact, making any connections and see it only as a fun game that will become a new station. As they lined up to leave, we asked them what it means to "compare something," and they were unsure.

Let's build on earlier suggestions and strategies and look at how you can engage in a conversation (Strategy 9) with students to determine their understanding of essential concepts and the *why* behind the learning and how students will use the day's learning in future applications. Notice in Figure 4.6 how the observers adapted their preplanned questions to align to the learning expectations and how these can lead to more authentic conversations within the context of the learning.

FIGURE 4.6: ADAPTED QUESTIONS FOR CONTEXT

Grade and Learning Target	Preplanned Question	Adapted Questions
MS science: "I can determine how heat is transferred by researching and explaining".	O: What did you learn yesterday or this week?	O: What do you already know about how heat is transferred? S: I know that heat makes molecules move . . .
	O: Why are you learning about this? O: What is coming next? What will you be doing next?	O: Why do you need to understand the transfer of heat and how that works? S: Because we have to solve a problem of transporting a penguin, and we have to figure out how to keep him cold. O: What have you figured out so far toward your goal of how you will keep him cold?

(Continued)

FIGURE 4.6: (Continued)

Grade and Learning Target	Preplanned Question	Adapted Questions
Sixth-grade writing: "I can continue my research to answer my question"; "I know what I still need to find out about my topic."	O: What's coming next?	O: What will you be doing after you research your topic? S: We have to develop our claim with supporting evidence. O: Then what? Will you share your viewpoint on your topic with anyone? I see you are in favor of driverless cars, but your tablemate is not. S: I don't know. The teacher will read them. [when asked, the T had plans for them to debate but hadn't shared with the Ss yet]

Though both sets of questions are effective, notice that the slight shift can allow observers to

- engage in authentic conversations with students in the context of the day's learning, and
- more efficiently make student thinking visible related to the day's learning.

Adapting questions and strategies can also

- create an immediate teaching moment for a teacher.

You can see how much more relevant the evidence is that you can collect from learners because you are creating a conversation within an aligned context. Figure 4.7 provides an example of a nonevaluative interaction with a student and an action the observer took based on it. In essence, the observer is teaching and helping the students see relevance and connections.

FIGURE 4.7: NONEVALUATIVE ADAPTED QUESTIONS

Grade and Learning Target	Preplanned Questions	Adapted Questions
Fifth-grade math: "I can multiply a fraction by a fraction."	O: Why are you learning about fractions?	O: When would you ever need to add or multiply fractions outside of school? S: Like if you are an architect. O: Why would an architect need to do that? S: You know, to build things. O: Do you want to be an architect? S: No. O: What interests you? S: I want to run a hotel. O: Hmm, when would situations come up in a hotel when understanding how to multiply or add fractions will make a big difference? S: I can't think of one. [The observer then gave an example of forty sets of sheets being ruined by housekeeping because they mismeasured the bleach when doing the laundry. The manager would have to show the team how to use fractions so the bleach/water solutions were correct.]

The teacher in the example in Figure 4.7 was following a math program that provided a real-world example for the lesson. However, after this lesson, the observer helped him see how he could further personalize learning and the given examples to help students make connections that are meaningful. (Remember that in Chapter 3, we talked about how critical it is for observers to understand program, curricular, or model expectations.)

Consider an example of when and how you could customize your questions within a workshop lesson. In reader's and writer's workshop, the day's new strategy may not be appropriate for use during a learner's independent or partner work. For example, the new strategy introduced while you are observing writing is elaboration or adding details, but several students are just starting a new story upon return to their seats. It may not be appropriate for them to focus on elaboration. Ideally, a student can answer why they have selected a particular strategy and will not be working on the introduced one. (S: "I am organizing my ideas and then working on my introduction and hook.") You also might want to consider the language the teacher uses so you might adjust your question to students, asking something like *"What is your job for today as a writer/in your writing?"*

Stop and Think: In the lessons you've taught, how often have you ensured that students you were teaching were making personal connections to the day's learning? How do/can you engage them in this kind of connection making?

Language plays a huge role in both our teaching and observing, so let's take that one step further. Do you or your teachers take the time to unpack the learning target, context, and essential academic vocabulary each day? (Think about skills, dispositions, and tools from Chapters 1 and 2.) Let's consider the next strategy related to students' foundational understanding, Strategy 14.

Strategy 14: Interact to determine understanding of essential vocabulary

As an observer, you can also develop a clearer picture of student understanding and prior learning, along with teacher scaffolding and differentiation, if you think about core literacy and language skills. In Chapter 3, you explored discipline-specific literacy strategies and use of academic vocabulary. But here, we are also reminding you to pay attention to some of the basics.

Often, we have found that students appear to be working successfully, but once we interact with them with questions aligned to verbs or vocabulary words that appear in the learning targets, we find they do or do not understand basic vocabulary that represents essentials or foundations (which could be directly connected to a gap in prior learning discussed earlier). When you read or hear the learning expectations, immediately identify vocabulary or phrases that might challenge students, even if you heard the teacher unpack the learning target with the students. You will find that using common sense or asking the obvious is the best way to start.

We want to truly understand what students know and don't know, and sometimes, their first answers aren't always accurately demonstrating what they know. Remember from Strategy 9, work to ask follow-up questions or lower-level questions in case students are nervous talking to you. Consider some examples of questions observers have asked to determine student understanding of vocabulary in the context of the day's learning in Figure 4.8.

FIGURE 4.8: QUESTIONS FOR VOCABULARY UNDERSTANDING

Grade and Learning Target	Adapted Questions	
Third-grade math: "I can tell elapsed time on an analog clock."	O:	What does *elapsed* mean?
	S1:	It goes by.
	S2:	I don't remember.
	O:	What is the difference between an analog and digital clock?
	S1:	That one is round [pointing to wall clock].
	S2:	This one has numbers around it, and a digital just has numbers for time.
	O:	Why do we need to learn how to read analog clocks?
	S1:	I don't know.
	[Observer backs up.]	
	O:	What's an analog clock?
	S2:	A clock that tells time.
Sixth-grade art: "I can create an illusion of depth."	O:	What's an illusion of depth?
	S1:	To make a person think it looks like something.
	O:	What does it mean to show depth?
	S1:	We need to make it look like rock.
	S2:	It has shadows and dark parts.
	O:	How can you use color to create an illusion or make something appear to be like a stone?
	S2:	I can use the gold for the brighter points and the black and gray for the deeper parts.
HS science: "I can create a website to demonstrate homeostasis."	O:	Could you read me that learning target on the board?
	S1:	. . . homstats . . . homeasis
	O:	Oh, that's *homeostasis*. What is that?
	S1:	I don't know, but I think I should.
	S1 to S2:	What's homeostasis?
	S2:	It's, it's, um, it's hard to explain. We've learned about it.

In the last example (Figure 4.9), though we are excited that students are using technology to build an authentic product, we want to help the teacher understand that the posted objective is a task, not a learning goal. However, we have an issue if students cannot read or define vocabulary appearing within the learning expectations, especially a term they are working to demonstrate. Clearly, something is missing in the learning progression. Immediately, you can gain additional information about the students and the learning environment by asking follow-up questions.

FIGURE 4.9: FOLLOW-UP QUESTIONS

Strategy	Evidence and Thinking
Interact	O: Where can you look if you don't know?/ What can you do if you don't know? S: I guess I could look at my notes [in desk, in bag, can't find . . .]
View	Do the notes serve as a valuable resource or learning tool, and why, or why not? Watch students look through their notes, and ask your question again.
Interact	O: What did you figure out about homeostasis? S1: I can't find it in my notes. Don't hesitate to ask a student if you can look at earlier notes, resources, journal entries.

(In the Resource Center for Chapter 5, you will find an expanded version of the evidence collection from this lesson in Resource 5.1: Observation Example: PullingStrategies Together at **resources.corwin.com/learnerfocused feedback**.)

Regardless of when you arrive during a lesson for an observation, you will want to determine what students understand about the day's learning expectations and essential foundations related to those expectations.

Student Ability to Meet Expectations

Throughout this chapter, though each teacher is working toward deeper learning and student ownership, you have encountered some examples from lessons where students were not successful or thinking at deeper levels.

Though we want students to engage in good struggle, which potentially can occur after we leave a room, as an observer, you can sometimes spot immediate observable outcomes or dispositions that, with a slight instructional shift, could be improved. Remember, we are always looking for how the teacher is impacting or causing those outcomes and how to build on strengths. For example, within minutes, you can begin to think about and collect evidence aligned to the five focus areas (Figure 2.8) that impact engagement and learning. (View Resource 4.3: Focus Area Evidence Collection at **resources.corwin.com/learnerfocusedfeedback**.)

After looking at the varied answers provided by students throughout the examples in this chapter and considering also that their ongoing work and conversations were as varied, notice how you can develop the ability to very quickly determine how/if student needs are being met or how they are progressing in the moment. This is what we want teachers to learn how to do well. Think about it; teachers also have the benefit of really knowing their learners. The observer's questions support feedback that can help the teacher learn how to plan for and respond to needs. You become an invaluable second set of eyes to support teachers in the work of using data, planning for needs, monitoring student learning, and making decisions. Chapter 5 will serve to further support you in this work.

Give It a Try

Teachers

- Practice visiting your colleagues' classrooms for just six to seven minutes to practice some of the evidence collection strategies recommended at the beginning of the chapter under "Adapting 101." Select one new strategy at a time from Strategies 7–13 to practice.
- Video-record your lesson or review a peer's video to listen, and view how the learning is being set up for students through the learning targets. Observe for opportunities to make adjustments earlier in the lesson. Did the teacher or you make an adjustment or need to make one? What happened?

Coaches

- Observe teachers you are coaching currently, and practice "Adapting 101" strategies.
- Self-assess against Strategies 7–13, and practice utilizing each in the first six to seven minutes. Share your thinking and your evidence with your teachers.

Leaders

- Visit classrooms with a partner or in a group and mindfully use the new strategies to collect evidence in the first six to seven minutes. Debrief with each other what strategies you used, what you collected, and what questions you would want answered based on your initial evidence collection.
- Notice what strategies you can continue to use once you have settled into the classroom and lesson and how you need to adjust further (as a prep for Chapter 5).

What's Ahead

You have been equipped with the strategies and know-how not only to plan your actions before an observation but also to begin making decisions and adjustments upon your arrival in a classroom.

Remember, it is challenging to adapt your evidence collection practices on the fly in response to classroom environment, lesson structure, the point at which you arrive, learning expectations, and learner behaviors. Try to practice isolated strategies suggested here with a metacognitive lens. Try to become very conscious of your own decision making and reasoning while you are observing. Think: Why are you choosing to record that evidence at that moment? Why is it relevant? Why are you choosing a certain location or talking to an individual student? What are you learning about the learner? Think about how rich your conversation will be with the observed teacher when you can share your self-talk as well! Find time to reflect on your own willingness to be flexible and your own capacity to act upon what you are hearing and seeing to adapt your evidence collection.

As you head into Chapter 5, we are taking it up another notch! You will build on the idea of adapting and responding to what you see and hear in the classroom, not just in the first few minutes but as the lesson and student learning unfold before your eyes.

5 How Can You Adapt Evidence Collection as a Lesson Unfolds?

From the field . . .

Reflecting back to my early years as an evaluator, I remember intently focusing on teacher talk and action to provide useful feedback to improve instruction. Consequently, what students were doing, thinking, and understanding lived in the background of my feedback. Shifting toward an observing-for-impact philosophy has improved my practice as an evaluator and sends a positive message to students that my presence in the room is directly connected to their learning. I have learned to interact with students within the context of the lesson as learning progresses to collect evidence to help the teacher understand what is happening for learners.

At one time, my feedback to a teacher may have read, "Directions seemed unclear." Now, my feedback is more detailed. For example, "Five students left number two blank. When speaking with the students, four shared they did not understand the directions, and one student shared she was absent yesterday and had no idea how to approach the problem." Now, ***I focus on***

(Continued)

(Continued)

the why *behind outcomes I see and might ask the teacher if he or she knew why students were not as successful before sharing what I learned. Who better to help teachers understand the impact of their instruction other than the students who are in their classrooms every day?*

—Chris Tranberg, Assistant Superintendent

"The art of life is a constant readjustment to our surroundings."

—Kakuzo Okakura

At this point in the book, you've started to build both your will and skill in terms of adapting to your surroundings, and you realize observation is both an art and a science, just like teaching. The strategies introduced in this chapter are considered to be the most advanced observation practices as they require

- deep understanding of effective teaching practices that build student capacity in the skills addressed,
- deep understanding of how students learn,
- mastery (ultimately) of basic observation practices using our suggested strategies,
- comprehensive knowledge of the expectations of teaching and learning found in your instructional framework,
- close attention to the details, expectations, and progression of the executed lesson as it unfolds, and
- a high level of both mental and physical flexibility while observing a lesson and a willingness to adapt.

However, we have only scratched the surface in the process of adapting your evidence collection in the last chapter, addressing how you might adjust your practices in the first six to seven minutes in a classroom. The strategies we provide in this chapter can be utilized whether you are observing for fifteen minutes or forty-five minutes, though research supports shorter, more frequent visits (Marshall & Marshall, 2017). Though those first minutes are powerful, what should you do for the rest of your observation? We will be tackling specifically how to use what is available to you to make evidence collection decisions and adaptations as the learning and lesson unfolds. This will include the use of student work, task materials, resources, student discussions, and teacher actions and conversations.

What makes this high level of observation challenging is that it requires that you conduct an error analysis in the moment. This allows you to craft questions and vary how you are collecting evidence to ultimately better determine the causes of the outcomes you are observing—all in real time. Every lesson, every day, and every student is different. But remember, we are asking the observed teacher to do this every day—to make decisions and adjustments based on what is learned about the learners. (Think Hattie & Zierer's [2018] mindframe: I am an evaluator of my impact.) In Chapter 2, we identified one critical attribute of learners as *cognitive flexibility*.

Teachers must possess and apply the same skill set in the facilitation and cultivation of learning; they "must adapt continually in managing the learning of behaviors of a room full of diverse students by recognizing teachable moments and responding to the needs of students to slow down, speed up, or approach learning from a different direction" (Wilson & Conyers, 2016, p. 106). "The teachers of assessment-capable visible learners are adaptive learning experts" (Frey, Hattie, & Fisher, 2018, p. 140). The *teachers of teachers* of assessment-capable visible learning are adaptive learning experts as well.

Let's review again what it is we are trying to accomplish through our observation and feedback. Remember, we are working to collect relevant evidence that helps teachers understand

- how/why claims are being made about the overall effectiveness of instructional practices (which could include clear and objective support of a performance-level rating),
- how they are impacting student engagement and learning (causal attribution), and
- how they are progressing toward district/region, school, or professional goals.

Let's look at an excerpt of feedback provided after a new observer visited a high school English classroom. In this thirty-minute observation, students were working in groups to create posters that were to be displayed showing essential questions and visuals to demonstrate themes of the books they were reading. The observer was attentive not just to the teacher but also the learners and included quantitative and qualitative data. Consider how the observer collected the evidence and whether this feedback supports the bulleted goals just listed.

When the lesson started, twenty-five students out of twenty-seven were looking at the teacher while two were looking at their Chromebooks. Mr. A told students that they needed to find three quotes in their books related to their theme and create a visual to represent their theme. Students started working in groups at 10:30. All but three students were engaged within their groups and were on task. Of the three who were not engaged, two were off topic, and one wasn't participating in the discussion.

Five out of the six groups had all students at their tables engaged while one table had two students engaged in an outside conversation. Mr. A went to each group to check in. "What type of visual can you use to show your information? What do you want your classmates to understand about your theme? What makes for a good essential question?" Mr. A left students to discuss.

By 10:35, all groups had decided on a theme, and students were searching their books for quotes. Students at four of the six tables were reading different quotes for approval while the other two tables just announced a quote without discussion and wrote it down. Mr. A asked a group, "Why did you choose that quote?" One student answered, and the rest of the group agreed with her answer. At 10:50, four of six groups had two quotes written down while the other two groups only had one. Mr. A worked with two students who appeared to be unengaged with their group and was able to get them back on task by asking them if they had a role and if so what it was. At 10:55, Mr. A gave a seven-minute warning for students to finish and be ready to present to the class.

Stop and Think: Is this helping the teacher learn how he impacted the student outcomes?

You may have determined that some things are missing from the feedback. However, can you spot when our observer used our suggested evidence collection strategies? She is on the right track. But what else could the observer have collected as the lesson evolved, and why? Let's break the feedback down based on what you have learned so far.

Analysis of Observer's Feedback

The Essentials (Chapter 2)

The observer put herself where the learning was occurring. She

- ✓ listened to the teacher and students, and
- ✓ viewed the teacher at tables, student behaviors, and group work.

However, notice she did not interact directly with learners.

Planning (Chapter 3)

You might not have been able to discern the observer's planning in this feedback. However, evidence that she planned her tools ahead of time might be as follows:

- ✓ She is working on collecting more comprehensive evidence.
- ✓ She is trying to make it easier to move around the room when students are in groups.
- ✓ She decided to use a laptop but also to carry a pad.
- ✓ She set up a template ahead of time to remind herself to collect time stamps (something she has been forgetful of in the past); this led to more success in time stamps.

Adapting 101 (Chapter 4)

The observer made decisions immediately upon entering by

- ✓ counting students,
- ✓ paying close attention to the teacher movement, and
- ✓ quickly getting a handle on the task expectations.

However, we are left wondering what impact the teacher had on the learning, as the focus of the feedback was on the teacher's actions and student on-task behaviors.

In our support of this observer's growth, we asked the following:

- What did the introduction to the task entail? How did it set students up for success in the group task? How do you know?

(Continued)

(Continued)

- What was the quality and depth of the conversations in the groups?
- What did the conversations sound like after the teacher feedback?
- Was each group's chosen theme accurate and well supported with quotes?
- What did they see as the purpose of the task? What will they do with the posters?
- What did they see as the new learning that the posters would promote?
- Were students thinking deeply or critically? How do you know?

Notice how these questions align to our big-picture goal from Chapter 1 of observing for purpose, process, and understanding. The answers are essential to best support this teacher. These can only be answered if an observer is willing to interact directly with learners and make adjustments to evidence collection based on what is being revealed about thinking and understanding minute by minute.

Regardless of when you arrive, you can see that as you remain and settle into a lesson and classroom, you will continue to utilize the strategies we presented in Chapter 4. If it's been some time since you read Chapter 4, go back and review Adapting 101, as those strategies will help you as you progress through this chapter.

Observing for Learning

Ultimately, we need to be able to help teachers think through the question, "Did the students reach the desired level of learning?" (Antonetti & Garver, 2015, p. 135). We also must be attentive as to whether students are learning how to learn (and why or why not) and how students are progressing toward our three overarching goals. Let's further explore reasons as to why we need to adapt observation practices to help you better understand what it is you are working to collect and determine.

"Students don't become assessment-capable learners by copying what their teachers have already written. That's hands on but minds off. Getting students to think, and to notice their thinking, is vital if students are going to gain a sense of where they're going" (Frey et al., 2018, p. 35). This understanding should drive our evidence collection as lessons unfold.

Observing for Deep Learning

One of the most important and difficult jobs we have as observers is to determine at what level and *how* students are thinking and learning. Goal 1 (conceptual thinking) focuses on critical thinking and transfer, or deep learning. Remember, this will include your monitoring of cognitive understanding (acquiring and using new concepts, skills, knowledge, etc.).

When we observe a lesson or review lesson plans, we are thinking about alignment to standards, which will often serve to increase the level of rigor, and we consider how a teacher is building student capacity in the essential skills such as the six Cs. Figure 5.1 from Battelle for Kids, now a blended entity with the Partnership for 21st Century Learning, shows the integration of these two elements.

FIGURE 5.1: DEEP-LEARNING INTEGRATION

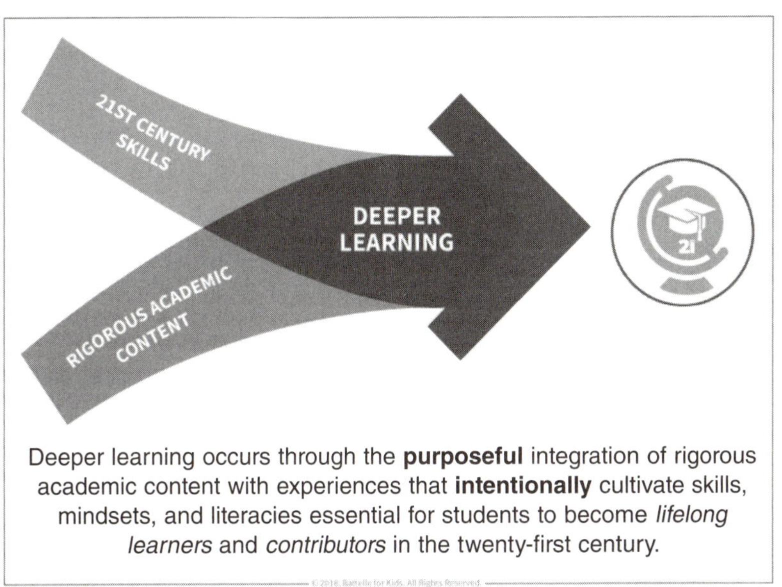

Deeper learning occurs through the **purposeful** integration of rigorous academic content with experiences that **intentionally** cultivate skills, mindsets, and literacies essential for students to become *lifelong learners* and *contributors* in the twenty-first century.

Source: Battelle for Kids (2018).

There are countless examples we could provide for how we observe for deeper learning and this integration, but some of our previous and upcoming examples help to illustrate how we incorporate this understanding into our observations. A common problem with instruction is a lack of backward design—when the teacher neglects to prioritize the intended learning. Often, many teachers identify an interesting or fun project, task, or tool for students. But if students, despite being engaged in collaboration, creativity, and communication, are not experiencing deep learning, then there is a problem. Teachers may not know how to begin with a learning intention (or standard, for that matter) or may have limited understanding of taxonomies to measure cognitive demand. They often perceive that students will be or are utilizing critical thinking, which may not, in fact, be accurate.

We recently sat in and observed a feedback meeting, and the middle school social studies teacher lamented that he did not get to everything he wanted to during the observed lesson. He showed us the construction paper banners that students would create to be hung in the room with the roles of the president on each. He said this was a good task "because 'create' is at the top of Bloom's." However, the text to be included on the paper was at a recall or knowledge level; ultimately, they were only creating triangles out of construction paper. They need this knowledge as a foundation, not as a culminating project. Though he is working to use a taxonomy to develop learning tasks and objectives for higher learning, this teacher needs ongoing support and professional learning in planning for conceptual understanding.

General Look-Fors

Remember, Fullan, Quinn, and McEachen (2018) define deep learning as "valuable learning that sticks" (p. xvii) and "is the process of acquiring the six global competencies" (p. 16). To guide us in our thinking about what we might see beyond our first few minutes, we can use a list they provide us containing characteristics of classrooms in which students are moving toward deep learning. Look for the following:

1. Students asking questions
2. Questions valued above answers
3. Varied models for learning
4. Explicit connections to real-world application
5. Collaboration
6. Assessment of learning that is embedded, transparent, and authentic (p. 79)

Frey et al. (2018) describe the characteristics of visible learners as those students who can do the following:

- Be their own teacher
- Articulate what they are learning and why

- Talk about how they are learning—the strategies they are using to learn
- Articulate next steps
- Use self-regulation strategies
- Seek, are resilient, and aspire to challenge
- Set mastery goals
- See errors as opportunities and are comfortable saying that they don't know and/or need help
- Positively support peers' learning
- Know what to do when they don't know what to do
- Actively seek feedback (p. 8)

Consider which characteristics from the lists could be collected through viewing and listening to learning, but notice that, to clearly determine items from the "They can" list, an observer (and teacher) needs to interact with learners.

Stop and Think: Think back to the list we provided in Chapter 2 from Marcia Tate's brain-compatible classrooms. Take a few minutes to look through your instructional framework. Do the expectations in this list and the ones listed here appear anywhere in your indicators?

Observing for Metacognitive Thinking (Goal 2)

In our algebra II lesson (Classroom Example 4.4), you have already encountered an example of when the observer was working to determine if the students were thinking about their thinking and if students had resources or tools they could utilize to move forward (Goal 3: Self-Regulation). These actions should be a staple in your practice as an observer. Let's switch gears and think about how this looks in ELA and jump back to our fourth-grade reading lesson on inference (Classroom Example 4.3). As students encounter complex text in all grades, it is important for them to use metacognitive strategies before, during, and after reading. Inappropriate text, a lack of close reading, or a lack of the use of strategies can quickly result in a task that is too easy or too hard. In the reading lesson, the observer was collecting evidence of the students' critical thinking and cognitive understanding when inquiring about the students' understanding of how to infer to best help the teacher see how they were applying strategies.

Classroom Example 5.1

(Continuation of Classroom Example 4.3)

Subject: Fourth-Grade Reading

Strategy	Evidence and Thinking
View	As students continued reading, the observer noticed a student write a word down in her notebook, *beastly*.
Interact	O: Why did you write that down? S: Because I don't know what it means. O: What can you do when you are unsure about words . . . what do you do after you write it down? S: I can ask the teacher.
View	The observer noticed a student by herself with picture books on her desk, while most other students were reading varying levels of chapter books. The observer noticed several challenging words on the page the student was reading.
Interact	O to S: Can you read this page to me? The student missed the compound words *lighthouse* and *searchlight* because of a struggle with *light* (a lower-level sight word). O: When you don't know a word, what do you do? S: I skip it.

Both students are aware and mindful of when words are too difficult. Our *beastly* example is one step closer, as the student had thought it was important to write that down and learn what the word meant. The observer questioned her about potential strategies she could use other than the teacher and reminded her of using the context and parts of words, and together, they were able to determine the meaning. You can see how rich it would be to provide teachers with not only information about the progress toward the learning target but also if and how students are using previously taught reading strategies.

Observing for Self-Regulation and Self-Monitoring (Goal 3)

Sometimes, students appear stuck but are almost there. This is also what we want to uncover for a teacher! An observer learned this while watching small groups work in a sixth-grade science class as group members raised their hands with questions waiting for the teacher.

Classroom Example 5.2

Subject: Sixth-Grade Science

Strategy	Evidence
Interact	The observer approached each of the groups: O: What do you need? S: We want Ms. T to help us because we can't figure out . . . O: But she is working with that other group right now. What can you do if she is busy? S Group 1: Well, we could Google the periodic table and . . . S Group 2: We could look back in the chapter. S Group 3: It's probably in our notes.
View	The observer stepped back and watched all groups. In each group, students used the tools they suggested and were able to continue working.
Listen	By the time the teacher arrived at each of these groups, they said, "We figured it out."

This teacher was working hard, moving from group to group to address needs and questions, so afterwards, we let her know of our interactions and suggested to her that she remind students of (or has them articulate) the tools available to them before beginning the task. This will help her focus her energy on those who need additional support.

One of our favorite questions to students is "What do you do when you don't know what to do?" And many times, the answer is "Wait for the teacher." Though we want to see that students are open to help and seek feedback, we also want to ensure they are also working on their own to determine "How am I going?" and "What's next?" The students in the previous example knew what they didn't know and what a next step could be (essentials of becoming assessment capable). Through the questioning by the observer, they were able to solve their own problems by the time the teacher arrived to check on them.

Observing for All Three Goals

Remember from Chapter 2, Stern et al. remind us that "conceptual learning is not linear; it's iterative." Even in a ten- to fifteen-minute observation, you may watch or hear a learner move through various phases of cognitive or metacognitive processing while you are in a room. Take a minute to look back at the math research study in Chapter 2 (Wilson & Clarke, 2011), which captured students' thinking and demonstrated in real time they were moving between cognition, metacognition, and self-regulation continually.

Let's look at a high school example, similar to our fourth-grade reading lesson of how an observer mindful of all three learning goals collected evidence in an English lesson. Remember, in Chapter 4, we introduced you to Strategy 13: Interact to Determine Essential Vocabulary. As you remain in a classroom during a lesson, you can often gain insight into how students build their vocabulary knowledge or understanding of words, just as the observer did in the fourth-grade classroom.

The CCSS shifts brought new attention about the ineffectiveness of our previous "drill and kill" instructional methods for vocabulary, but formal lessons still occur where every student is working on the same twenty-five words, copying the same definition (as in that Child Development Quiz in Classroom Example 4.2). In this English lesson, students were getting ready to create or locate visual aids for new vocabulary words, a recommended strategy, and the teacher was allowing for choice—important instructional starting points. But students were all working out of the same level vocabulary workbook, working on the same twenty-five words. Because they had the workbooks open on their desks, we were able to adapt our evidence collection to what they were using (a strategy we will further explore in a bit). After asking a student about the directions and requirements of the task, the observer went on to collect evidence based on what the learners were revealing.

Classroom Example 5.3

Subject: Ninth-Grade English

O:	Which word are you working on right now?
S:	[pointing]
O:	What is that word?
S:	Cad . . . cad . . . not sure.
O:	Ah, that's cadaverous. Thinking about what it means, do you hear a familiar word in there? [helps O determine previous teaching of roots/prefixes]
S:	[attempting]
O:	I see you have the definition on your screen. What part of speech is this?
S:	Adjective.

O: What's an adjective?

S: [attempting] A thing?

The observer was also interested in how the teacher was differentiating and asked students about their familiarity with the twenty-five words:

O: How many of these words do you know already and can define?

S1: None.

S2: Maybe half.

S3: All of them.

O to S3: These are challenging. How do you think you learned them already?

S3: My grandmother buys me tons of books, and I read a lot.

O: That definitely makes a difference! What are you reading right now?

Notice how the observer was able to create a conversation with a learner that revealed a great deal about students' levels and needs. This was a nonevaluative visit, so the observer took a few steps to support Student 1 and collect more evidence for the teacher. Notice, the observer is using what she understands about cognitive knowledge (inquiring to see if the students have learned about roots and prefixes or know parts of speech) to see if the student is using (or equipped to use) that knowledge to think metacognitively. Ideally, like our expectation in fourth grade, students say to themselves, "I don't know this word; what strategies can I use to figure it out?"

Regardless of grade level, students often can't pronounce words on the paper in front of them, and vocabulary instruction such as this will not result in students building a deep understanding of words. Certainly, the observer will want to work with the teacher on the quality and rigor of the learning target in the ELA lesson but also on longer-range goals, such as utilizing research-based strategies for more effective differentiated vocabulary instruction.

Observing for Causal Attribution and Impact

Remember, regardless of whether you are a teacher or an observer, you are always seeking causal attributions (or what is causing outcomes). Consider how the observer's actions and questions helped to determine causes for behaviors and responses she was encountering. The way that we do this as a lesson unfolds is to spend time with learners—listening, viewing, and interacting—as they learn. We seek causal attributions in this way to determine how instructional practices and choices are impacting learners to avoid making assumptions that can lead to faulty conclusions and/or less-than-effective next steps. Don't forget from Chapter 1, it is equally as important to identify what is causing positive or effective outcomes as it is to identify what is causing less-than-effective outcomes.

Note: Throughout this chapter, you will find a few examples of lessons that resulted in highly effective and impactful teaching and learning. Notice how the observers determine why the teaching was impactful. However, you will also find lessons that are not as effective. Notice how observers are identifying and weighing teacher strengths and jumping-off points for next steps in their think alouds in either case. You will want to engage in the same kind of thinking but should resist the urge to convert this into what is called a "praise sandwich" in your feedback—either all praise and no meat or the layering of a less-than-effective practice or needed change (one to two pieces of thin meat) between various statements of praise.

There are rich opportunities everywhere you turn that will allow you to learn more about the learners, which will help you better determine teacher impact and next steps. Let's revisit the algebra II observation (Classroom Example 4.4) to see how our evidence collection adjustments can point us toward causal attributions. Using our five focus areas (Figure 2.8), we show the observer's thinking as the lesson evolves in Figure 5.2.

FIGURE 5.2: ONGOING THINKING ALIGNED TO FOCUS AREAS

Focus Area	Observer's Thinking (first six to seven minutes)	Evidence Collected	Observer Thinking (next ten minutes)
Environment	Is the physical environment conducive to the learning? Are students working cooperatively or respectfully together? Are they willing to persevere?	Ss are seated in groups of 4, working in pairs, and some are helping each other. Ss are waiting for the T to help.	What could help them persevere?

Focus Area	Observer's Thinking (first six to seven minutes)	Evidence Collected	Observer Thinking (next ten minutes)
Level of challenge	Are students engaged in good struggle? Is the work too hard or too easy?	Some Ss don't know how to solve the problems [hands raised, stopped working], some are working independently and quickly, and some are trying.	Are they willing to try? What do they not understand? Are they working in their zone of proximal development? At what level are students thinking?
Progression	Are students missing foundations or essentials required to master the stated objective or task?	Some were absent. Ss said there was a short introduction before O arrived.	Why are some successful and others not? What happened before I walked in?
Assessment	Does the teacher know what learners know and don't know? Do students know what they don't know or how they are doing?	T monitoring partnerships Ss aware they don't know how to do it, they're not sure what they need or how to move forward.	What is the teacher noticing about student understanding? What will she do about it?
Supports	What's available to students if they are struggling?	The para, T, and other peers are working with Ss.	What are the para–S, T–S, and S–S conversations? What is the quality of the feedback? Are they moving students forward? Do Ss have notes or work from previous lessons they can use? How are they partnered?

Remember, as you consider the observer's thinking using the five focus areas, you can see how the evidence collected and the considerations of the observer are helping her to establish understanding of the three goals for learners.

Goal 1: What concepts do students not understand?

Goal 2: Do students know what they don't know?

Goal 3: What steps are students taking when they are stuck?

In the first six to seven minutes, notice that the observer only has collected preliminary evidence ("some") and will work to quantify this and collect more specific evidence. In the next ten minutes, the observer noted the following.

Classroom Example 5.4

(Continuation of Classroom Example 4.4)

Subject: Algebra II

Strategy	Evidence and Thinking
View	At 10:35, T stopped the class and asked everyone to pull out their notebooks to the notes from when they covered quadratic function and extracting square root. 5 Ss could not locate their notes; 4 were absent on one of those days and do not have notes for those lessons. 10:35–10:43 On the board, in 3 minutes, T showed them how to solve using each and then had them return to their partner work. Ss who did not have notes are erasing and copying from the board.
The teacher noticed a possible cause of student confusion was that students weren't using notes and thought reviewing one problem together would solve the problem—a strength to build upon. If you remain even for just a few more minutes, you can continue to adapt to collect relevant evidence for the teacher as to whether her adjustment was effective for those who did not understand (more on this strategy in a bit). The observer can adapt evidence collection to see if outcomes changed.	
Listen	S1 to Ss: I am totally lost. S3: Oh yeah. I get it now. O: What did you discover? S3: I figured out my mistake. When I was . . . I should have been . . .

Stop and Think: Look back at Figure 5.2. What are you noticing about the student understanding and potential causes? How is the observer's thinking helping her make adjustments?

The observer determined that a number of students had simply forgotten how to solve algorithm problems using either of the strategies, but others were missing foundations. The teacher's adjustments—to provide individual feedback and to review a problem on the board—were not reaching all learners.

When we make decisions, adapt our evidence collection during an observation, and then share with the teacher our thinking and findings, we not only help the observed teachers see clearly what was happening, we are also modeling for the teacher high-quality and effective checks for understanding, use of language, and conversations with learners that support growth.

Observing for Good Struggle

> *"Knowledge rests not upon truth alone, but upon error also."* —Carl Gustav Jung

You might have noticed in Figure 5.2 that in the moment, the observer was wondering if students were engaged in *good struggle*, which can be difficult to discern (whether you are teaching or observing). It is important to be cautious of jumping to conclusions about students struggling, as "students often don't know that they don't know until they try it for themselves" (Frey et al., 2018, p. 46). We also know that learning from our mistakes is an essential part of our growth as humans. Students must be given the opportunity to have these experiences every day; it doesn't mean they aren't progressing or learning. Remember, level of challenge is one of our five focus areas and impacts engagement and learning. Notice in Danielson's framework, Indicator 3c, the attention to designing experiences that challenge students (Figure 5.3).

FIGURE 5.3: INDICATOR EXAMPLE FOR CHALLENGE

Proficient	Exemplary
The learning tasks and activities are fully aligned with the instructional outcomes and are designed to challenge student thinking, inviting students to make their thinking visible. This technique results in active intellectual engagement by most students, with important and challenging content and with teacher scaffolding to support that engagement. The groupings of students are suitable to the activities. The lesson has a clearly defined structure, and the pacing of the lesson is appropriate, providing most students the time needed to be intellectually engaged.	Virtually all students are intellectually engaged in challenging content through well-designed learning tasks and activities that require complex thinking by students. The teacher provides suitable scaffolding and challenges students to explain their thinking. There is evidence of some student initiation of inquiry and student contributions to the exploration of important content; students may serve as resources for one another. The lesson has a clearly defined structure, and the pacing of the lesson provides students the time needed not only to intellectually engage with and reflect upon their learning but also to consolidate their understanding.

Source: Danielson (2013).

Ensuring that students are working at the appropriate level of challenge is not easy. Teachers have been told to challenge students, to turn learning over, to "come down off the stage," and to increase learner independence, which we know students need. Without specific feedback from an observer about impact or their own deeper understanding of how students learn, teachers seeking to comply often forego necessary scaffolding, such as direct instruction or introductions to lessons, leaving students to struggle to frustration. The teacher then works incredibly hard for the rest of the lesson, which is what we observed in the algebra II lesson. Recently, we observed a feedback meeting between an elementary teacher and her principal. The teacher said, "Last time you told me to talk less, but now you are saying I should talk more. I am so confused."

Maybe you are this teacher or you have seen them—confused by messages conveyed through unclear feedback, which we know can diminish efficacy. These teachers work to reteach student by student, putting out fires, or interrupting the whole class for a mid-lesson stop. We want to help our algebra II teacher (and all teachers) see how choices are impacting the students' ability to be successful from the beginning of the lesson (and in lessons leading up to this one). Ideally, we can help them see how students can create notes and resources that will help them move forward when they are stuck so teachers can maximize instructional time and support them in different ways. On the flip side, think about our social studies teacher who thinks a task where students "create" paper banners is an appropriate challenge. If he had gone forward, it was going to be very easy for students. When tasks are too easy or too boring, there's no risk taking involved, discourse can fall flat, students won't see a need to reflect, and engagement decreases.

In the first six to seven minutes of all observations, strive to discern if the work is too hard for the students or if they are engaged in *productive struggle*. The more frequently you visit classrooms and as you get to know students, the easier this becomes. Frey et al. (2018, pp. 90–91) cite Kapur (2016) and chart his four learning events:

- **Unproductive failure** (unguided instruction that may lead to frustration)
- **Unproductive success** (rote memorization without conceptual understanding, completion of a task without understanding the purpose or relevance)
- **Productive success** (guided problem solving using prior knowledge, consolidation of learning). Think back to Chapter 2 and what we understand about the brain. This is an important part of learning.

- **Productive failure** (unsuccessful problem solving using prior knowledge followed by further instruction *that ultimately results in deep learning*). Watch for erasing and discoveries. This is where the magic happens.

It is important to note that Kapur does not see *productive failure* necessarily only as a description of an outcome or an event but as an entire approach. When we addressed a flipped gradual-release model as an optional progression in Chapter 2, we touched upon the idea of allowing students to struggle first before providing instruction. However, creating experiences in which students can achieve productive failure is reliant on a teacher's proficiency level in a plethora of necessary skills, such as effective assessment in the moment and scaffolding. Realize that achievement of deep learning and transfer through the successful execution of this type of approach is more complex than the few lines we have devoted to it here. For our purposes, we wanted to utilize the terms and concepts within these four events as descriptions of possible outcomes, to start you on the path of recognizing what each looks and sounds like.

Think through some of the lesson examples we shared throughout the book. In many of the cases described, the main issue was that students could not engage in productive failure or productive success, though the teachers were trying to create challenging experiences. When students do not have the prior learning to which they will make connections or tap into, they cannot operate within their zone of proximal development. "If the distance between what a learner currently knows and will need to know in order to resolve a problem is too great, chances are good that the learner will not be successful. In order to bridge this distance, teachers provide tools that will help students resolve problems" (Frey et al., 2018, p. 66).

Stop and Think: Consider a time when you were engaged in productive struggle. What did that look, sound, and feel like for you? What did you need to keep going and become successful? What did you learn from the struggle?

Based on what we know about how the brain works, unproductive failure can be a direct result of a lack of connection making. As lessons unfold, students will struggle to move from surface to deep learning without this step, so we can observe for whether this is happening or not and why. If needed, take time now to go back to Chapter 2 to revisit how teachers can impact learners' levels of thinking and learning and how our brains work.

Be attentive to all three goals we presented and the knowledge, skills, dispositions, and tools students and teachers need to meet those goals. As the lesson unfolds, observe how the teacher is providing students with the opportunities, the cognitive understandings and foundations, and learning experiences that will allow them to increase neural activity, engage in productive struggle, and transfer learning.

Adapting During an Observation

In our effort to support you in your ongoing evidence collection—without going too far into educational theory here—we took into account teaching moves aligned to cognitive constructivism, among other approaches, but also

- the lists from Tate and Fullan et al., and
- what Hattie, Fisher, and Frey offer as high effect size or identified as those practices that move students toward deeper learning and transfer.

We spent time breaking down what it is we might see students doing on any given day and then determined five aligned strategies (15–19) to help you adapt to what might be occurring. Remember, we could not possibly capture every classroom structure, task, or scenario, but we hope our list is broad enough to allow you to transfer the strategies regardless of what you see in your own observations. Included with each example, you will also find references to Chapter 2 learning, Strategies 1–14, and the five focus areas that impact engagement and learning.

The five adaptive strategies we have identified are as follows:

Strategy 15: Adapt based on what students are doing

Strategy 16: Adapt based on what students are writing

Strategy 17: Adapt based on what students are using (or not using)

Strategy 18: Adapt based on student conversations and group work

Strategy 19: Adapt based on teacher–student interactions

As you read on, you will find we provide short snippets of classroom examples for many scenarios. Each includes a quick note of the observer's thinking as he or she adapted evidence-collection strategies based on the learners. As you read, think about what the observer is learning and potential causal attributions for outcomes and how this is used to process strengths and next steps.

Adapting Based on Active Engagement

Ideally, during lessons we observe what students are *doing* as part of their learning, but that is a broad concept. All of our strategies are designed to help you adapt to those tasks, activities, and strategies that actively engage students. For this strategy, we incorporated products and performances of skills or understandings, in addition to process, not just completion (e.g., planning, organization, or research).

Strategy 15: Adapt based on what students are doing

One of the most important parts of this strategy lies in your ability to determine the depth of knowledge required to complete the tasks, products, or performances and an understanding as to where students are in the process of learning. In addition, if students are viewing, listening, or experiencing the product or performance, you want to be cognizant of the intended audience and purpose and the cognitive demand on the audience.

Creating a Performance or Presentation

Many observers ask us for help with observing those disciplines that are traditionally *performance based* (e.g., PE, career-technical courses, drama). Often, lessons occur in unique environments with unique equipment or tools. However, as all teachers increase levels of ownership, integration of authentic assessments, and the use of brain-compatible strategies, you will find more and more classrooms will begin to look and sound like those traditional performance-based classrooms (e.g., a makerspace). It is important to remember—and we remind these observers—that you would apply and adapt the same strategies you have encountered throughout the book, regardless of the environment, course, or discipline. However, it is just sometimes difficult to interrupt the learners in these settings or during tasks. You would still view, listen, and interact (when possible) and adjust evidence collection based on the learning context.

Acting Out Performances

Classroom Example 5.5

Subject: High School Mandarin II

Strategy	Evidence and Thinking
Listen	Ss are only speaking in Mandarin, T feedback and directions are in Mandarin, and students respond/adjust based on it. Classmates understand skits being performed, as they are laughing together at certain points.
Interact	O think aloud: I am wondering what unit this is and what the goals and criteria are, so I think I can chat with them between skits. O: What did your skits need to include? What are you learning through these skits? S1: They needed to include at least ten new vocabulary words from our unit, and we are working to keep a conversation going without switching to English. S2: We needed to use our research about the diets and habits of China to create 2- to 3-minute commercials about how to stay healthy. We started by talking about how there are now almost 5,000 Starbucks and McDonald's in China and the health crisis they are having. O think aloud: That student is helping me clearly see the broader context and relevance! (Strategy 13)

Observer's Analysis of Impact: Skits are common tasks in foreign-language courses, but this teacher has given students an opportunity to deepen and transfer their learning through her unit design and culminating task that

- helps to build their fluency or automaticity in the language, which will allow them to utilize those words in different contexts outside of this unit topic,
- combines the discipline goals of reading, writing, and speaking in the language,

- maintains a level of challenge for students through the overarching goal of fluency (working to not switch back to English), and
- integrates a current global issue, research, and problem solving, which results in an authentic product.

If the observer had not asked the students about the criteria and goals, she would not have known the level of challenge of the task. With this information and analysis, she can serve as a great think partner for this teacher.

Performing a Skill/Playing a Game

Classroom Example 5.6

Subject: Middle School PE

Strategy	Evidence and Thinking
View	Nearly all students are engaged in game/trying to play on 4 courts in a gym within a badminton unit. 3 of 4 groups have players swinging wildly—the birdie goes straight up or out of bounds repeatedly.
Interact	O think aloud: I wonder how long they have been in this unit and if they understand how to win the point (Strategy 12: Prior Learning). I think I can talk to them between points. O: How long have you been working on badminton? S: A few weeks. O: Where are you trying to hit the birdie? S: To get it over the net. O: How does the direction of the racquet head change where the birdie is going? S: I'm not sure. O think aloud: I need to talk to several other students to see what they understand about the various shots.

Observer's Analysis of Impact: One of the overarching goals of PE is to maximize instructional time for game play, which can build teamwork, and to get students moving. I know that in sports like volleyball, tennis, and badminton, the goal is not to just hit over the net but to try to ensure the other team is unable to return it. However, students were participating in game play or a task of low cognitive and metacognitive demand, not understanding this. I'm not looking for Olympic-level play but mindful, strategic play. Being that they were a "few weeks" into the unit, I was trying to figure out their basic understandings that might be influencing the students' lack of success. The teacher has the foundation, in that students are all willing to try and attempted to play the whole time I was there. I may want to work with the teacher on ongoing individual feedback and whole-group mid-game stops (for teaching points that can push thinking) and the design of the next unit.

Products or Projects

We know there are limitless types of projects or products students can create that allow them to demonstrate, learn, or transfer conceptual understanding. As an observer, you can walk in at any stage of the process. This provides rich opportunities to view, listen, and interact with students. But be discerning. It is always exciting to see students engaged in hands-on learning (or game play, like in PE), but they should ultimately be cognitively engaged in thinking critically and metacognitively about their work, assessing their progress and process, and self-regulating. In this respect, it is also important to remain aware of what you understand about the skills that experts in each field need to develop while you review products, come to understand process, and ask questions (Strategy 7: Discipline-Specific Expectations).

Working at Different Points of Different Projects

Classroom Example 5.7

Subject: High School Introduction to Metals II

Strategy	Evidence and Thinking
View	Students are spread out across the shop working on projects individually or in pairs. O think aloud: I notice the students are independently using the machines and equipment, and their projects show varied levels of complexity, so I want to find out more about why that is.
Interact	O: What are you making? S1: Bookends for my dad.

Strategy	Evidence and Thinking
	O think aloud: I want to know more about the goals and criteria for the project. O: What is it you want to show you know how to do? S1: I think that we are supposed to know how to use all of the equipment and machines. O: Are there certain requirements for your project or a list you are looking at? Like each project uses 1 or 2 of the machines? S1: No, we can create anything we want using whatever we want. O think aloud: I want to check to see if other students see this as the goal, but I need to time my questions so they can continue to use the machinery safely, Strategy 8: Purposefully Choose Your Evidence Collection Methods. S2: I am making an entrance sign showing that I know how to use this machine. O: What is this machine? How will you show that? S2: It is a CNC milling machine. [S explains what the machine does.] The teacher made us an example that I am using for help, but I have to show precision and how I am handling the cutter, that I know how to plan and then set up the machine. . . .

Observer's Analysis of Impact: The teacher has established high expectations and ensured students understand machine use and safety requirements. The freedom of choice allows students to work at their own pace and level, but my questions show there are varying levels of metacognitive and cognitive thinking.

I want to talk with the teacher about why certain students understood the criteria and goals. He is anxious to get them working, so he doesn't start each class with reminders, he just assumes students know, and some do. The teacher can reflect on ways he could communicate expectations but then push thinking and encourage reflection and goal setting as students select their next pieces based on his overarching expectations.

Researching as Part of the Process

Let's look at a fifth-grade social studies lesson in which students were researching, in partnerships, self-selected topics on colonial times.

Classroom Example 5.8

Fifth-Grade Social Studies

Strategy	Evidence and Thinking
View	Students have books out and are looking through them. O think aloud: I am wondering how they chose their topics and the books. What is the goal of the research? I want to ask questions to determine their process and what they understand about their topics.
Interact	Q1 to each O: What topic did you choose? S1: Jobs and weapons. S2: Farming. S3: The Pequot tribe. Q2 to each O: What are you trying to figure out or understand about this topic? S1: What jobs and weapons they had. What the settlers did. S2: What it's about, what animals they have. S3: Anything about this tribe. O: How did you choose your book? S4: Every book is about daily life, so that's what I chose.

Observer's Analysis of Impact: I am thinking about Strategy 10: Set High Expectations for Responses. The teacher had created opportunities for collaboration, choice, and student-driven learning, and all students were busy and respectful to their partners. She has the foundation. However, their responses point to surface levels of thinking; that is related to a lack of understanding about the purpose of the learning, research, or the project. But perhaps the purpose of the research is of a lower level, so I want to chat with her about where students are headed next.

Stop and Think: How did the observers collect evidence to understand teacher impact that will help them develop learner-focused feedback?

Strategy 16: Adapt based on what students are writing

Writing is very often part of the process to develop a product or performance, and students could be creating a written product. However, we wanted to separate this out as a different strategy. Students write all day long and engage in tasks like reflections, essays/blogs, notes, annotations, worksheet answers, and answers to problems, to name only a few. To adapt evidence collection, the observer in the algebra II example was using the students' written explanations and answers to the problems, and the observer in the fourth-grade reading lesson (Classroom Example 4.3) was using notes on stickies.

Student Notes

If you noticed, the observer in the last example saw students taking notes as they read. When students are writing, they are making their thinking visible and potentially using a strategy, so we want to be a part of it. We like to find out what they are thinking, if the note taking is helping them navigate complex text, and why they are recording that note. Let's go back to the fifth-grade social studies lesson.

Classroom Example 5.9

(Continuation of Classroom Example 5.8)

Subject: Fifth-Grade Social Studies

Strategy	Evidence and Thinking
View	7 to 10 Ss were taking notes while reading. O think aloud: I am wondering what they have learned about note taking and conducting research, and I want to see how they are taking notes.
Interact	O: What do you try to write down while reading? S1: Try to understand what it's about and write it down.

(Continued)

(Continued)

Strategy	Evidence and Thinking
	S2: Interesting notes.
	S3: I try reading and put what I could on my paper.
	S4: Information and then figure out what I need to put.
	O: What did you just write down?
	S1: I wrote down that they lived in their kitchens.
	O: Why did you write that? How does that connect to jobs and weapons?
	S1: Oh, it doesn't.

Observer's Analysis of Impact: The students were working independently, their books contain information related to their topics, and they were attempting to take notes. In thinking about Strategy 12: Prior Learning and Strategy 7: Disciplines, I see they are missing essentials in how historians investigate, using various sources to gather, synthesize, and organize information. If they were clearer on the goals for the project and had these foundations, they could learn how to take notes to arrive at conclusions as historians do. But maybe the teacher needs help aligning goals and projects to support discipline-specific literacy skills.

Recently, we heard a teacher remind students of good-note criteria in a sixth-grade classroom: "Notes should make sense to you and be useful in the assignment, fragmented, and easy to read and find information." Then, we observed to see how students were doing. The teacher had previously taught them note-taking minilessons and provided them with examples of her notes. We suggested a next step could be after this lesson, that they have a chance to reflect on the usefulness of their notes in completing the task. We were excited to meet a teacher working so diligently to teach students to note-make as middle and high school students often move through school with limited abilities and/or willingness to take notes or use them as resources.

Stop and Think: Take a few minutes to look through your instructional framework. Are there any expectations for the use of student resources? Are you seeing or teaching students how to create resources for themselves?

Mid-Lesson or End-of-Task/End-of-Lesson Reflections

We suggested that the sixth-grade teacher build in a reflection opportunity to help students evaluate the value and quality of their notes. Sometimes, teachers are providing students opportunities to write reflections. These are wonderful chances to view metacognition in action, one of the few times it can be highly observable. Figure 5.4 is a sample of one student's reflection sheet, completed at the end of a lesson.

FIGURE 5.4: REFLECTION SHEET

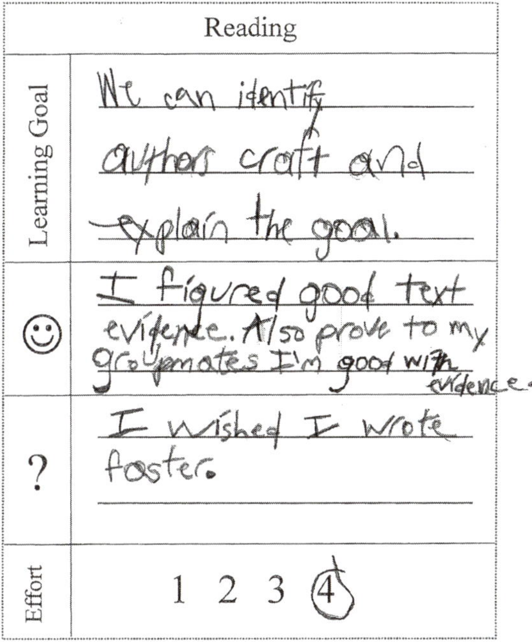

Reading	
Learning Goal	We can identify authors craft and explain the goal.
☺	I figured good text evidence. Also prove to my groupmates I'm good with evidence.
?	I wished I wrote faster.
Effort	1 2 3 (4)

Source: Adapted from material provided by Madilyn Da Ros.

Classroom Example 5.10

Subject: Fourth-Grade Reading

Strategy	Evidence and Thinking
View	In the last 4 minutes, all Ss are completing the reflection sheet. O think aloud: I can't get to all of them to review; I can use Strategy 8 and take pictures to review later. I think I can talk to 3 or 4 in that time and not slow them down.

(Continued)

(Continued)

Strategy	Evidence and Thinking	
Interact	O:	How did you determine your goal?
	S:	This is what our group was working on.
	O:	How would writing faster have helped you identify the author's craft?
	S:	It was taking me a long time to finish.
	O:	What does a 4 mean on effort?
	S:	I tried my best.
	O:	What will you do differently next time?
	S:	I have to use evidence in my answers, and I will write faster if I am the group's recorder.

Observer's Analysis of Impact: The teacher had taken the time to build in more in-depth reflection, her goal for the year. Based on student responses to my questions, she has clearly taken the time to explicitly teach each section of the reflection sheet before this lesson. She is working to develop assessment-capable learners in the classroom. The smiley (on the sheet) allowed them to think about what they did well that moved them toward the goal and the "?" is an opportunity for students to think about what is standing in the way of being successful or what is challenging them. After reviewing my pictures and thinking about my conversation with the students, I only see 1 or 2 who are struggling to make direct connections between the smiley and "?" back to the goal. We can have a good conversation about how to refine their ability to determine their own actionable strategies and steps to reach those and begin to move to setting personalized goals with some who are ready. I am reminded of this quote: *"Asking students about how the learning is proceeding in a class has several advantages. Students will give the teacher and [observer] powerful information that can help them set goals and monitor progress. The most effective goals are student-centered, so it only makes sense that students should be asked for their opinion about learning goals"* (Knight, 2018, p. 40).

Worksheets

Viewing items on their desks provides a plethora of information from which you can develop questions and adjust evidence collection. Start with the basics again. Do students know the directions, and can they read them? Remember to look for and question them about potentially challenging vocabulary to ensure they are set up for success (Strategy 14). Take a look at the two examples in Figure 5.5 from a fourth-grade math lesson. Each student was presented with a set of fraction unifix cubes, and they would be using these in the upcoming unit. They were to explore the cubes and complete the worksheet. Notice the differences and similarities in the level of thinking in the *writing*.

FIGURE 5.5: STUDENT WORKSHEETS

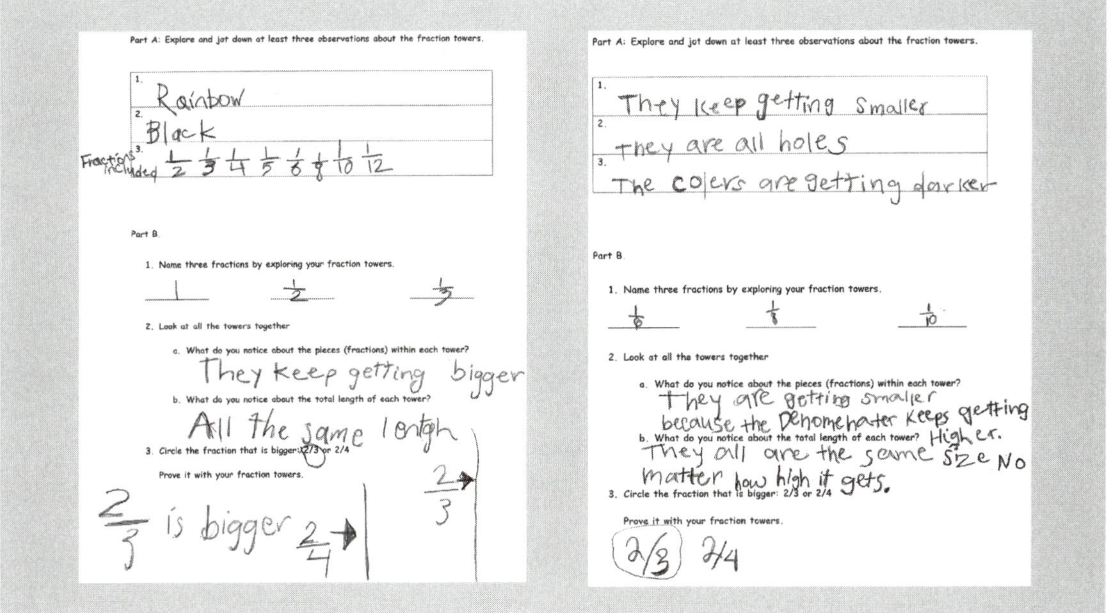

Part A: Explore and jot down at least three observations about the fraction towers.

1. Rainbow
2. Black
3. Fractions included 1/2 1/3 1/4 1/5 1/6 1/8 1/10 1/12

Part B.

1. Name three fractions by exploring your fraction towers.

1   1/2   1/3

2. Look at all the towers together

a. What do you notice about the pieces (fractions) within each tower?

They keep getting bigger

b. What do you notice about the total length of each tower?

All the same length

3. Circle the fraction that is bigger: 2/3 or 2/4

Prove it with your fraction towers.

2/3 is bigger 2/4   2/3

Part A: Explore and jot down at least three observations about the fraction towers.

1. They keep getting Smaller
2. they are all holes
3. The colers are getting darker

Part B

1. Name three fractions by exploring your fraction towers.

1/6   1/8   1/10

2. Look at all the towers together

a. What do you notice about the pieces (fractions) within each tower?

They are getting smaller because the Denomenater keeps getting higher.

b. What do you notice about the total length of each tower?

They all are the same size No matter how high it gets.

3. Circle the fraction that is bigger: 2/3 or 2/4

Prove it with your fraction towers.

2/3 2/4

Classroom Example: 5.11

Subject: Fourth-Grade Math

Strategy	Evidence and Thinking
View	All Ss are working, laying out cubes, taking them apart, sticking together, and completing the sheet questions. One is finished in 3 minutes.
Listen	T noticed Ss has finished [first example], looked at that student's sheet. T to S: Now, can you help Samuel?

(Continued)

(Continued)

Strategy	Evidence and Thinking
View	Ss turned to Samuel for 1 minute, then went back to playing with cubes. Observer think aloud: I definitely want to talk to that student to see why he was finished so quickly and how he is thinking about the cubes and fractions.
Interact	O to S1: I see you wrote down the colors and numbers that you saw. What else did you notice about the cubes? S1: That the cubes get smaller, but the numbers get bigger. O: Which numbers? S1: The denominators. O: Why do you think that is? S1: Because the parts are cut into smaller pieces, so there are more.

Observer's Analysis: The teacher built in time for exploration to promote "I wonder/I notice" thinking and to build comfort with a new learning tool. Investigation into a new manipulative also directly supports their development as mathematicians in Standard of Practice 3 (Strategy 7: Disciplines). Marcia Tate reminds me that worksheets don't grow dendrites (when students only rush to complete the sheet and aren't challenged). The teacher briefly explained the purpose but didn't make an explicit connection to the Math Standard of Practice (Strategy 13: Relevance/Context). Though she provided feedback, she focused on finishing the sheet. She missed opportunities to push student thinking (especially ones who have some conceptual understanding of fractions). The student who finished early and six others were only working at a surface level and, though this was an introduction, were capable of deeper learning. I know she has asked for help with differentiation, so we can look at these worksheets, both of our conversations with students, and the other work from the rest of the lesson to talk about how to support the varying levels of student understanding and need.

Adapting Based on Tools and Resources

You might have noticed the observers in our previous examples utilized what was immediately available or those things in front of students to adapt evidence-collection strategies to the context of the immediate learning.

Strategy 17: Adapt based on what students are using (or not using)

This strategy was one of the most challenging for us to process for you, as this level of adaptation involves pretty much anything that could be sitting on a student's desk! Like the others in this chapter, this is a very broad strategy, so consider that potential items in this category could be part of the task or a self-selected/teacher-designed resource, such as technology, tools, organizers, resources, or text/video. Remember, notes can fall into this category.

While you are observing, you might see students seek out or teachers recommend a tool for use. Ideally, learners know what is available for them to use and how to use it, and there is a willingness to use what is available. Tools can also be considered something that contains the criteria and allows students to self- and peer assess. Regardless of what they are using, ask them questions such as, "How is this helping you move forward?," "What are you shooting for (levels)/what are you trying to understand?," and "What do you still need to do to get there?"

Resources

As a second set of eyes in a classroom, we want to help a teacher determine whether the available resource is accessible and used, meaning that it is serving to move a student forward in thinking and learning.

Remember, though teachers work hard to make them available or design them, a tool is not useful if students can't pronounce or define words found within a resource or on items in front of them, and often, a teacher does not realize this. You might never have known this as an observer if you had not interacted with them about the resource. Consider how often you see lists available to students, especially in elementary grades, such as the one in Figure 5.6.

FIGURE 5.6: CHARACTER TRAIT LIST

Common Character Traits Vocabulary

active	generous	poor
adventurous	gentle	protective
artistic	grouchy	proud
athletic	happy	quiet
bold	honest	respectful
bossy	hostile	selfish
brave	humble	serious
charming	humorous	shy
cheery	independent	sloppy
considerate	intelligent	sly
courageous	lazy	studious
creative	mean	successful
curious	messy	thoughtful
daring	mischievous	trustworthy
energetic	neat	warm
entertaining	nervous	wild
fierce	nosy	wise
friendly	open	witty
fun	persistent	

Source: Adapted from Amber Polk, http://www.thepolkadottedteacher.com

Let's look at how an observer interacted with a first-grade student as he was getting started with a writing task. Students had just finished reading nonfiction texts about a self-selected person in history and were working to describe the person they chose.

Classroom Example 5.12

Subject: First-Grade Writing

Strategy	Evidence and Thinking
Listen	Before they went back to their seats, T gave students the trait list. T: You can use this to help you plan for your writing.

Strategy	Evidence and Thinking
View	10 or 11 (out of 21 Ss) students began looking at it. O think aloud: I wonder how this list will help students. Do the others not need it?
Interact	O: Does the word you will choose need to come from this list of traits? S: I think so. I am not sure. O: Can you read me some of the words? [O pointing purposefully thinking about Strategy 14 and understanding vocabulary] S: cur . . . [curious-not able to read], happy, gen . . . [not able to read generous], bold O: What does it mean when someone is bold? S: Mmm . . . I don't know. O think aloud: I wonder how many others are not able to use the list successfully and how many can. Is the teacher recognizing that? I think I want to watch and talk to more students but also follow her as she monitors and gives feedback.

Observer's Analysis of Impact: The teacher has provided a resource to help students in their thinking. Though many of the students were willing to use it and the list can be a valuable tool, it did not help them to identify their historical figure's traits or improve their word choices. The teacher wanted to get students writing, but she skipped some instruction on how to use the list. I think we can talk more about how to personalize supports or determine appropriateness of tools.

It is interesting how often this has occurred when we observe lessons at all grade levels. Similarly, in another first-grade writing lesson, a student asked us how to spell a word, so we asked her, "What do you do when you aren't sure how to spell something?" Her partner reminded her there was a list and got it for her. We were excited! One of the observers who saw this moved on. However, we stayed behind to see that the first student could not read the words on the list, nor locate her word on the list. (It wasn't there.)

In nonevaluative observations, we have often provided the proper pronunciation, spelling, and/or a quick tutorial so students can move on successfully or alerted the teacher that the resource is too challenging to use. But in either case, we need to help teachers see how to provide and create (and ultimately have students create) tools and resources that will advance thinking, learning, and ownership.

Organizers

Tools might take the form of organizers that can either be teacher assigned or student selected or designed. We observed a group of students using a required science organizer for a ninth-grade lesson (Figure 5.7).

FIGURE 5.7: SCIENCE ORGANIZER

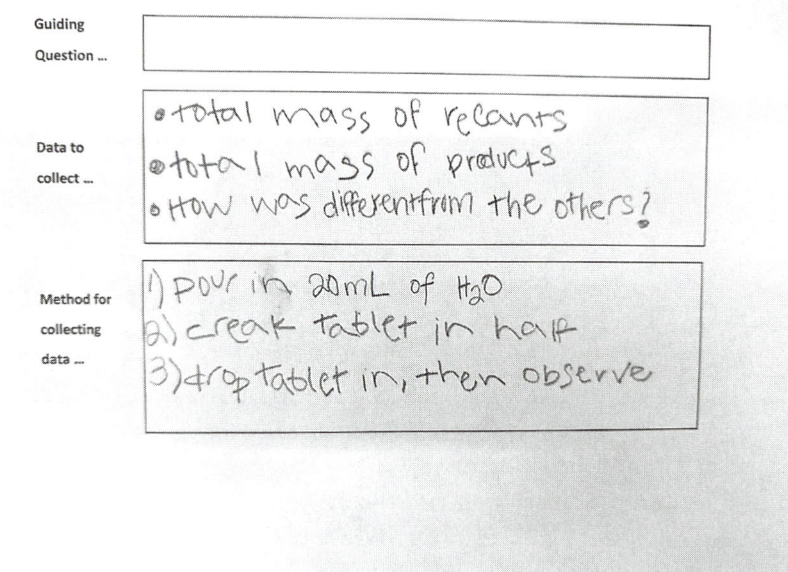

Guiding Question ...

Data to collect ...
- total mass of recants
- total mass of products
- How was different from the others?

Method for collecting data ...
1) pour in 20mL of H_2O
2) creak tablet in half
3) drop tablet in, then observe

Classroom Example 5.13

Subject: Ninth-Grade Science

Strategy	Evidence and Thinking
View	6 teams of 3 to 4 Ss had the organizer out and were working to complete it. (One per team) O think aloud: I am noticing that students in 3 groups are skipping the guiding question at the top. I wonder why and what they understand about the scientific practices (Strategy 7: Disciplines).

Strategy	Evidence and Thinking
Interact	O: I noticed you skipped the guiding question. Why did you skip it? S: We weren't sure what to put there. O think aloud: I wonder what unit they are in or phenomena they are investigating or how they were previously taught what a guiding question is (Strategy 12: Prior Learning). O: What is a guiding question? S1: We're not sure. O: Have you used this organizer before? S2: Yes, we have used it all year. O: Okay, let's back up and think about what you have learned. What is the purpose of a guiding question? S1: I think it tells us where we are going. O: Okay, it does in some ways. How do you develop or come up with a guiding question? S2: I'm pretty sure she taught us at the beginning of the year.

Observer's Analysis of Impact: The teacher is working to teach students to think like scientists. She wants them to work as groups to determine how they will move through the inquiry process to design an experiment that will allow them to collect the data they need (NGSS expectations, Strategy 7). However, this organizer is not helping three groups to do that. The groups who were skipping the question step are working on a surface level. They are only listing steps and supplies as if this is just a worksheet to complete, and they do not know what it is they are trying to uncover. This teacher has shared that she has been challenged by the transition of her students into more rigorous NGSS-aligned lessons, so I want to talk more about how we can support the transition into a new method of inquiry-driven teaching and learning.

Technology

Often, technology is the source of tools or resources for students. Remember our example from Chapter 1 and the students highlighting in the

Google Doc? The observers were excited to see students using technology, but they missed critical evidence of understanding. You may observe in many classrooms where technology plays a major part in the teaching and learning. This adds another layer for you as an observer because you are looking to determine not only if students understand the concepts being taught or applied but also if the tool is merely an add-on or is serving to enhance the teaching and learning. A few examples you may encounter include the following:

- A polling device that allows students to answer risk free if they don't know the answers and is a quick monitoring tool for the teacher.
- Google Classroom, which creates efficiencies for teachers and students to have all tools in one location, allows for differentiation and varied pace, and decreases need for teacher-led direction.
- Padlet or any interactive tool that allows students to create and share thinking in digital notes in real time as learning unfolds, such as during a debate or Socratic discussion.
- Digital storytelling tools or programs like iMovie that offer opportunities for choice and allow students to create products as learning or to demonstrate learning in varied ways. These tools can increase the level of thinking when products require synthesis and transfer and are intended for authentic audiences in authentic formats.

When technology enhances teaching and learning, it increases

- engagement beyond just being fun,
- organization and efficiency,
- opportunities for collaborative or interactive learning,
- capacity in research skills,
- real-world use of technology tools, and
- understanding of content or concepts.

Be cautious when recommending technology tools to teachers. Start with the impact on the teaching and learning instead of solely recommending the tool (say, Kahoot; this is just one fun tool available that increases engagement, allows all students to quickly answer questions risk free, and allows a teacher to quickly assess and make decisions).

Stop and Think: What could be a way technology might not enhance the teaching and learning? How would you determine this when observing?

We were watching a high school student look at his phone when students were supposed to be completing a task. Perhaps this is what you thought of for your example in the previous question. But remember, our goal is to determine what students are actually doing, not just what we think they are doing. In this technological age, we always *view* what the student is doing on the device and interact with them about it.

Students looking at images on a phone

Subject: Tenth-Grade Geometry

O: Whose notes are in the picture on your phone?

S: The teacher's.

O: Did you take your own, or did you want to use them this way?

S: I took a picture of hers only.

O: Is it helping you?

S: Not really.

Students looking at an iPad

Subject: AP World History

O: I noticed you are reading a digital version of the text. [Observer sees no annotations.] Do you know how to take notes on e-text?

S: No.

O: Do you want to take notes on this?

S: Yeah, that would help.

O: Would you rather do that digitally or have the text printed?

S: It would be easier to understand if this was printed.

O: Is your exam on the computer, or is it a paper test?

S: Paper.

These short interactions provide an informative window into the students' use of technology.

Adapting Based on Discourse

You have encountered classroom examples so far where the observer is adapting to what students are saying in response to his or her questions. This is critical to ensure you are engaging in an authentic conversation with the learners (Strategy 9: Engage in Conversations). However, students often are engaged in their own conversations when we are in the room. Therefore, it is often useful to listen first, view who is speaking, and then interact based on what you are hearing and seeing.

Strategy 18: Adapt based on student conversations and group work

For this strategy, we want you to think about what you are hearing students say to each other. We visited a middle school social studies lesson where students were discussing to determine a solution to their research on a global health crisis.

Classroom Example 5.14

Subject: Middle School Social Studies

Strategy	Evidence and Thinking	
View	Group 1 is only group not talking to each other and sharing information. They are all typing in their own docs. T prompts them twice to share.	
Listen	Group 2:	(Topic: HIV)
	S1 to S2:	We can't afford a cure. It is less expensive to provide treatment. We need to focus on that.
	S2 to S1:	I don't agree; we need to try to keep people from contracting it in the first place so they won't keep spreading it.
	Group 3:	(Topic: Malnutrition)
	S1 to S2:	We need to look at hospitals.
	S2 to S1:	Let's do the math . . . hospitals would cost . . .

Strategy	Evidence and Thinking
	Observer Think Aloud I can hear that they have a good handle on the details of their crisis. How deeply are they thinking about their problems and solutions? The teacher said they need to determine if they only have reactive solutions; do they know what that is?
Interact	O to Group 3 O: I hear you talking about facilities. How will those address the malnutrition issue? S1: People can go to the hospital for help. O: What happens there? S1: They are given milk. O: How does that help malnutrition? S2: The milk contains nutrients they need. O: Like here, if we got dehydrated and they give us fluids. But is this a reactive solution or proactive? S1/S2: I'm not sure. O: Is your idea something that prevents malnutrition or responds to the issue? S2: It is for when they are already malnourished . . . O think aloud: Group 1 is now talking, so I want to hear their discussion and engage them. Their topic is related to accessibility to quality health care. O: What do you understand about your crisis in India? What are the big issues that are contributing or need solutions? S1: There isn't enough health care for people. We are concerned that there is only one hospital for thirty thousand people. O: Is that different from here in the US . . . ? S2: Definitely [reading statistics]. O: What are you discovering about the causes of illnesses or diseases? S1: We know it's definitely connected to the water supply. O: How do you know that? [Student searches notes and cites statistics.] S2: Because . . .

Observer's Analysis of Impact: This teacher has built student capacity to work collaboratively and engage in discourse supported by research. Because the ELA and social studies teachers have partnered for this project, students have learned to synthesize various sources related to current global issues, which has created opportunities for students to think at deeper levels about complex problems and evaluate potential solutions. I want to talk to her about the students' uncertainty about proactive and reactive solutions and see if she addressed this after I left.

Strategy 19: Adapt based on teacher–student interactions

Teacher-to-student interactions can take on many forms while you are observing, such as teacher–student questions, teacher responses to student responses, teacher monitoring and feedback, and teacher adjustments. As you now have arrived at the last strategy of the book, let's pull several of the strategies together in a sequential fashion based on a fourth-grade writing lesson we saw so that you can see how to use Strategy 19 in the context of a lesson. The observer entered near the beginning of a minilesson and then remained for about ten more minutes to observe students applying the strategy. The learning objective was this: *I can preview nonfiction text by analyzing the text features to determine the subtopics I will learn*. They were previewing to determine book relevance and usefulness for research coming in the next few days. In this lesson, we encountered the following elements around which we needed to adapt: students using organizers, reading, writing, talking to each other and the teacher, and researching.

Classroom Example 5.15

Subject: Fourth-Grade Writing

Strategy	Evidence and Thinking
View and listen	• Arrived at 10:57. T was thinking aloud and modeling how to complete an organizer using a doc cam using the subheading to determine the subtopic: "It must be important. . . . It's making me think they're trying to make predictions. I am putting together ideas to figure out what subtopic I am learning about." • At 11:00, T turned the book page and included students. Turn-and-talk: "What is destruction?" [word from page] T: "You're already doing what I just modeled." [They were not.]

Strategy	Evidence and Thinking
	• Ss were not accurate in determining subtopic. "I saw wind in the text." "I saw blown away." Or were copying headings S: What is the question? T: Destruction caused by what? S: Path. [incorrect] • At 11:05, reviewed goals based on their research projects—to determine some subtopics in books they might use. "As you continue your research, you have to decide what areas you want to know more about." • At 11:08, Ss began working O think aloud to plan: Watch how they begin to complete the organizer; review the book choices; watch teacher move around the room to their group conversations; listen to teacher feedback and how she makes adjustments or mid-lesson shifts based on checks for understanding.
Interact	O: What is a subtopic? S1: It's this. [pointing to heading] O: I see you put "effects of the wind." How did you know that was the subtopic? S: Because they're trying to run away in the picture. O: How does that tell us that is about the effects of the wind? S: They are running from too much wind. O: How are you figuring out what the subtopic is? S2: I am putting the heading I see in that box. O think aloud: All students were working (half alone), but not all books had subheadings, so students could not apply the strategy, but they were still trying.
View and listen	Group 1: Floods: T stopped at all 3 students to give feedback, and I was erasing whole paper. S in Group 2: Erosion: Flipping rapidly through books without reading anything S in Group 3: Volcanos: Reading the whole book, not previewing 11:10—T stops. "I am realizing I want to add something. You can preview on your own or side by side." T monitoring a S: What are you thinking the subtopic will be?

(Continued)

(Continued)

Strategy	Evidence and Thinking
	11:17 T–stop #2. "It's tempting to take the heading and just copy it onto your paper as the subtopic . . . notice how Maria put it in her own words." The teacher was noticing the same things our observer was and was acting on it. The observer then moved around again to the groups to see if the adjustment changed outcomes. 11:20–7 students still had the copied subheading and did not change.

You will find a more detailed analysis in the next chapter, but notice the depth of the evidence collected by the observer, which surely serves to build on the teacher's existing strengths. The observer was noticing students were struggling before the end of the minilesson and adapted evidence collection to develop a clearer picture of who understood how to identify subtopics or preview a book or not and to what level. Then, the observer became a valuable second set of eyes by watching students after a teacher provided feedback and mid-lesson adjustments.

This is how we drive a culture of observation and feedback, one classroom visit at a time.

(You can review a high school lesson example—Resource 5.1: Observation Example: Pulling Strategies Together in the Resource Center, **resources.corwin.com/learnerfocusedfeedback**)

Give It a Try

Teachers

- Practice observing in your peers' classrooms with specific focus on when you should or could listen, view, and interact.
- Watch a video of one of your own lessons, and think about whether you needed to or did, in fact, shift your instruction or adapted a planned strategy or task. Ask yourself, Why? What did you notice about the learners?
- Practice asking students questions in your peers' classrooms based on Strategies 15–19, and share with the observed teacher the evidence you collected. Together, brainstorm possible causes for observed outcomes.

- In your own classroom, think about what each of the four learning events (Kapur, 2016) (under "Observing for Good Struggle" in this chapter) looks and sounds like. Work to design a lesson that will allow students to achieve productive struggle, and observe for potential look-fors.

Coaches

- Select one or two strategies at a time to practice. Reflect on the effectiveness and if these are allowing you to meet the goals for observation and feedback.
- Discuss with teachers you are supporting the evidence you are collecting, analyze potential impacts based on the five focus areas (Figure 2.8), and reflect together on how the teacher was causing or impacting the outcomes, narrowing to one focus area for coaching.
- Discuss if you are seeing one of the four learning events (Kapur, 2016), and note (possibly immediately pointing it out to a teacher) when you see productive struggle.

Supervisors

- Practice the new strategies using the big-picture lens (Figure 1.4) with a partner or team to share and compare evidence collection strategies and evidence collected.
- Create opportunities with your team to discuss concepts like productive struggle. Brainstorm professional-learning opportunities you can provide teachers for planning lessons and units that will promote this type of learning.
- Analyze potential teacher impacts based on the five focus areas (Figure 2.8)
    - Looking for trends
    - To practice narrowing to the highest leverage area
- Practice crafting feedback to help a teacher to see how he or she caused outcomes to occur.

What's Ahead

In this chapter, you have tackled some of the most challenging work for observers. You have successfully made your way through five chapters focused on the concept of observing not just for teaching but for impact on learners. Remember, the quality of your feedback is directly related to the quality of your evidence collection during classroom visits, and the nineteen strategies presented throughout this book take time to master. Each visit and conversation with a teacher will be different, but you now have added a significant number of foundational tools to your toolbox that will enable you to support all teachers in teaching and becoming assessment-capable learners. As you head into our final chapter, you will find suggestions for utilizing your refined skills to cultivate a culture of observation and feedback and a culture of learning for all.

6 How Do You Cultivate a Culture of Learning?

"The role of a creative leader is not to have all the ideas; it's to create a culture where everyone can have ideas and feel that they're valued."

—Ken Robinson

Congratulations! You've made it through five chapters and nineteen strategies focused on observing for impact! As our book has centered on the development of observation and evidence collection to assess student learning in our classrooms, we hope that you are working toward or are now able to do the following:

- Think more deeply about the outcomes we are seeking for our students (OECD Key Competencies, six Cs, our three goals)
- Recognize what "learning" means and how students learn (Chapter 2)
- Plan for interacting with students in order to observe for learning (Strategies 1–7)

- Modify and adjust evidence collection approaches at the beginning and as the lesson progresses (Strategies 8–19)
- Develop learner-focused feedback that supports observed teachers in understanding their impact based on what you have collected from learners (additional support lies ahead)

You are now on your way to becoming a Darkling beetle of the Namib Desert. This is a good thing; trust us. If you have ever stood in the middle of a classroom and listened to groups talk, you will know what we mean: This beetle adjusts to its surroundings to such a degree that it has learned to stand still to collect dew and ocean fog on its back. Then, it stands on a ridge facing into the wind, and the collection is turned to droplets it can drink—You can do this! You can take all of that evidence and turn it into high-quality, learner-focused feedback. Once you begin to collect more purposeful and comprehensive evidence from learners during your observations and create feedback that helps teachers see how they are impacting outcomes, you become a significant part of a culture of learning, driving a culture of observation and feedback. Every aspect of teaching and learning will be impacted by your shift.

It will take practice to become the darkling beetle, to understand when to move and when to stand still and how to turn moments into valuable evidence collection opportunities. As you learned in Chapters 3 through 5, preparing for and adapting during an observation requires varied skills that in many ways reflect those we are seeking for our students (and teachers). As observers, we must

- **metacognitively process** what we want to collect and how we want to collect it before and during an observation, and
- **remain flexible in our thinking**, purposefully adapting and processing throughout a lesson to collect evidence that will support a teacher's understanding of impact.

In this chapter, we will examine how to utilize your evidence and analysis to provide actionable feedback. This final step is necessary in ensuring the highest-quality feedback and setting you on a path for a sustainable culture of learning through a culture of observation and feedback.

Building a Culture of Learning

Recall from Chapter 1 that in a school with a strong **culture of learning**, the following are true:

✓ There is a firmly rooted *collective belief* that everyone has the ability to learn (Hattie & Zierer, 2018).

✓ A *growth mindset* (Dweck, 2006) permeates the school halls and walls.

✓ Staff's *perception of their current performance and understanding of their impact* is accurate.

✓ Staff and student *relationships* are based on a collaborative approach to learning.

✓ *Policies and procedures* are designed through the lens of supporting systems and structures that ensure learning for all.

These attributes are not easy to establish and sustain within any organization, let alone in schools. It takes patience to cultivate the type of collaboration necessary to realize these outcomes. Luckily, the darkling beetle's patience and perseverance give it a remarkable capacity to adapt to its surroundings and reach its goals.

Consider for a moment another friend from the animal kingdom who is adept at adaptation. Did you know that some fish have the ability to learn from each other, recognize other fish they've spent time with previously, understand how they fit within social hierarchies, and remember complex spatial maps of their surroundings? Marine biologists are now finding that many types of fish are demonstrating a "suite of complex cognitive abilities including the recognition of individual partners, the capacity to recall their previous actions, or the ability to make intentional investments under the expectation that [they] will entail a future reward" (Brandl & Bellwood, 2015). These fish leverage their individual abilities to work together toward common goals, such as optimizing food intake for the group. Maybe that's why we call them a school of fish—they apparently think and learn together. While our goals differ, educators can learn a thing of two from our fish friends—we are better together.

If we are to support an understanding of impact through learner-focused feedback, then we must shift from what Andy Hargreaves and Michael Fullan (2012) term a *culture of individualism* (p. 115), which pervades most of our school environments, to a **collaborative culture of learning**. We need to open classroom doors and engage in honest conversations with each other about what is happening for learners.

Districts/regions and schools must commit to building relationships so that there is a

- cultivation of a common, collective mindset about learning for all,

- creation of opportunities for teachers to develop honest and accurate perceptions of progress and performance, and
- feeding of each other's professional-learning needs toward the highest levels of practice by all on behalf of students.

Stop and Think: Are you existing in a culture of individualism? Why, or why not? Do the teachers in your building open the door to visitors and feedback? How did that come to be?

Developing Feedback About Impact

A culture of learning is driven by a culture of observation and feedback that feeds forward. Teachers must receive ongoing and high-quality feedback that

- goes beyond summarizing events to providing an analysis of effectiveness,
- allows teachers to accurately and clearly see how they are impacting learners, and
- leads to improved reflection, instructional practices, and student outcomes.

In other words, they need *learner-focused feedback*, in which the students *and* the teacher are the learners being supported.

For teachers to recognize how they are impacting students,

- clear, specific, and relevant student evidence must be collected and included in feedback to objectively support a claim about practice that is aligned to framework expectations (Remember from Chapter 1, RVL Standards 1.A, 1.B, and 1.E),
- they need to understand their areas of strength and growth and identify actionable next steps based on those (RVL 1.D and 1.F), and
- goals and next steps should be based on an analysis of causal attribution (RVL 1.C).

(Visit Resource 1.1: RVL Supervisory Continuum at **resources.corwin.com/learnerfocusedfeedback**)

Though we have discussed how to conduct a level of analysis of evidence in the classroom through Chapters 3–5, you will still need to continue that step at your desk after an observation. Even if you are planning to hold a collaborative conversation and may never provide written feedback, the practice of analyzing and organizing your thoughts prepares you for a highly impactful discussion—something we recommend after every visit.

Stop and Think: Consider how you have prepared in the past for a collaborative conversation after observing, or consider a conversation an observer had with you. Did it support your understanding of cause-and-effect relationships? Did it result in a change in practice or serve to improve outcomes? Why, or why not?

We chose to dedicate pages and pages to observation in this book because we know the quality of evidence collected directly influences the quality of the feedback. Therefore, before going on, we suggest that you conduct a review of your current skills and ability to develop actionable feedback that is learner focused (if you have not already). How close are you to becoming a darkling beetle? Do you know how to take all of that rich evidence and turn it into a meaningful learning experience for a teacher or colleague?

Tools you can use to self-assess include the following:

- The strategies from *Feedback to Feed Forward* listed in the front of the book
- Resource 6.1: Observation and Feedback Self-Assessment, available in the Resource Center, **resources.corwin.com/learnerfocusedfeedback**
- Resource 6.2: Feedback on Feedback Survey, available in the Resource Center, **resources.corwin.com/learnerfocusedfeedback**

Analyzing Impact

The first step after collecting comprehensive evidence is to sift through all of it, ask "Why?" questions, and begin to determine causal attributions. Let's look at the last lesson you encountered in Chapter 5, the fourth graders (Classroom Example 5.15) previewing text to identify subtopics, and examine what the observer is thinking about the teaching and learning. The observer knows that the teacher is working on strengthening her minilesson and assessing student readiness and used the Five Focus Areas to organize her thinking.

Progression: The teacher is using what she has learned from the workshop coach about the minilesson structure and use of time. She executed an "I do" step, but the way in which she modeled within that step caused them to struggle. Within the "we do," students didn't have a chance to practice the specific strategy.

Assessment: She built in the "we do" task, which is an opportunity for a quick check for understanding, but the prompt didn't quite give her all of the information she needed. This meant she was not sure about their readiness. By monitoring group to group and student to student, she noticed the misunderstandings.

Supports: She conferred with three students and checked in with quick support to two or three groups. The teacher's feedback allowed students to move forward. Though she noticed students were not on track and was willing to bring the whole group back for a shift/mid-lesson stop, it wasn't as effective, as it didn't change what students were doing.

I know there's great value in conferring and working with small groups after a minilesson. This teacher has a strength in immediately seeing learners' needs once she is monitoring. I think that addressing the fine points within a minilesson progression would be the high-leverage coaching area, and I will leverage our indicator about a progression advancing learning to support her in this work. This is in line with the teacher's goals, would allow more students to effectively practice or try out the new strategy before working on their own, and would allow her to use time more purposefully in supporting learners.

Let's review feedback the observer provided to this teacher. First, using a practice we promote, the observer left behind two stickies, one "glow" (or "wow") and one "I wonder."

I can see you are putting into practice what you have learned from Karrie! I listened in as you stopped at each student and group. You were clearly recognizing their needs and misunderstandings.	I wonder . . . what were you noticing as you were monitoring their organizers? Was there something you might have added or changed in your minilesson based on what you were noticing?

The observer then prepared the following:

Claim built from the instructional framework: While you have clearly been working on implementation of the workshop model and improving your minilesson to ensure student readiness for learning, I noticed the progression from your "I do" to the "you do" contributed to the student misconceptions during the independent work (which you noticed). A few subtle shifts could have set more students up for success, which would allow you to focus your conferring efforts.

Connect/Support: I talked to seven students who did not have a clear understanding of how to preview the text to identify subtopics, were confused about the difference between subtopic and heading, and were simply copying the heading onto the organizer. You noticed this, too, stopping them at 11:17. "I love seeing you go through your books . . . it is tempting to take the heading . . . let's look at Abby's . . . when she put it in her own words . . . " This last portion might have been an additional step needed in the modeling as well that was not included.(Before I left, I swept and saw none of the students had shifted.)

I asked students, "What do you think this page or section is about?," or while reading their organizer, "How does that show the 'effects of the wind'(which was the heading)? S: "They're trying to run away." (almost there) You conferred with three students in that time, swept the room visually, and checked in quickly with three other groups, which caused you to stop the lesson two times to make adjustments before the one at 11:17.

Beginning at 10:57, you modeled with a think aloud using a page of text to think about what the page was about ("It's making me think they're trying to make predictions . . . I'm learning how to predict a hurricane is coming . . . I think this because I saw a heading, a subheading, and 'coming storm'"). The modeling only lasted three minutes and did not include the next step of how to use the organizer and pull together the information gathered from multiple text features to determine a subtopic, which contributed to their misunderstandings.

Another cause lies in the *active engagement* portion. As you shifted to the "we do," though you were attempting to engage them, you included only four or five students through Q&A and had them only define a word (11:00: "What is destruction?") on the page prior to leaving the carpet and then said, "You're already doing what I just modeled." (But they were not.) Right after this, you asked, "What am I going to be learning about?," a question that can help you determine if they knew how to preview and identify the subtopic, but there were a variety of answers—correct and incorrect (S: "the path") (S: I saw wind in the text . . . I was thinking it might make me think it's about wind because it said "blown away").

The tasks at that point in the progression didn't give you the opportunity to see students try the strategy of previewing/ identifying subtopics. When you saw this at their desks, you recognized right away what was happening ("You don't need to read every word," and when you saw the book had no headings, "Are there other text features that can help . . . put all of that together?"). You gave effective feedback to shift individual students ("What are you thinking the subtopic will be?"). Your last line about pulling it together was probably the most important and the small piece also missing in the modeling.

Stop and Think: What did the observer need to do in the classroom to help this teacher understand causal attribution and impact on learners?

Because the observer took the time to analyze learner evidence, identify causal attribution, and align feedback to the teacher's goals, she not only has developed feedback that serves as a learning tool but also is setting herself up for an effective conversation. Her next step is to prepare reflective questions ahead of time. This level of preparation facilitates her ability to move between coaching approaches or stances as needed, which she thinks will be appropriate with this teacher (e.g., calibrating with evidence, then adapting reflective questions, then collaboratively thinking about the next lesson). (Remember, a more directive conversation is sometimes needed based on teacher skill and self-perception.)

Impacting Efficacy

This teacher had a clear picture of her learners as they worked independently but didn't quite know why they weren't successful and was frustrated with herself. Through the feedback, she recognized that the needed changes were subtle within her minilesson. She felt it was attainable and realistic to pay closer attention during planning and, in the moment, to her modeling and the students' opportunity to practice. She also realized that going forward, she needs to have a deeper understanding of the teaching point and expected new learning, or what she should be modeling. Through social persuasion and accurate causal attribution, a twenty-minute feedback conversation increased the teacher's belief in her own abilities and set her up for a mastery experience.

When this does not occur, though never intending to do so, observers can find themselves creating or perpetuating teacher self-disbelief, discomfort, and disillusionment—a path that is destructive to teacher well-being and a culture. Driving a culture of learning through observation and feedback requires an understanding of how observers can positively or negatively impact self-efficacy, mindframes, and collective efficacy. We know from Bandura (1994) that key diminishers of efficacy can include the following:

- Inaccurate understanding of expectations or vision
- Inaccurate understanding as to how long it will take to achieve expectations or next steps
- Faulty self-perception
- Inaccurate evaluation of performance

A lack of honest assessment can breed decreased motivation and performance and a defeated affect, leading to lower levels of self-efficacy over time. Aligning feedback to our six standards (RVL Supervisory Continuum) sets an observer on the path to sparking a cycle of growth, shift mindframes, increasing levels of efficacy, and avoiding diminishers. However, we also must remember that feedback is a collaborative process, or two-way street, that also requires giver *and* receiver dispositions and behaviors.

Feedback Dispositions

In Chapters 1 and 2, we introduced you to the idea of student and teacher skills, dispositions, and tools necessary to shift the ownership of learning in our classrooms. Your work in building a culture of observation and feedback can be broken down in a similar fashion. Throughout our two books, we have provided you the skills and tools necessary to successfully develop feedback that feeds forward or that is learner focused. However, we want to take a few minutes to discuss the dispositions both the provider and receiver need to possess for feedback to effect change and result in relationship building and collaborative problem solving.

Beginning with the terms *provider* and *receiver*, it is important for us to remember that when providing learner-focused feedback, we are seeking to become a facilitator of thinking and learning. "We want to develop learner [the receiver] expertise and ability to construct knowledge through self-analysis and then deconstruct the knowledge to gain more executive control." However, it is important to remember that many receivers "need time and support to develop the capacity to engage in this level of cognition" (Killion, 2019, p. 56). They may require a provider who offers directive support or who moves between coaching approaches when needed. At no point do we intend for receivers to become passive within the exchange.

Based on the work of Stone and Heen (2014), our experiences, and our feedback standards, we have created a tool (Figure 6.1) you can use either for assessment of the current status (to be addressed ahead) or as a list of expected provider and receiver *habits of mind*, so to speak.

FIGURE 6.1: PROVIDER AND RECEIVER DISPOSITIONS

Feedback Dispositions

Feedback is . . .	Provider Dispositions A willingness to . . .	Receiver Dispositions A willingness to . . .
Honest and accurate	• Be honest and candid • Dedicate time to understand the instructional framework and effective teaching and learning • Have conversations for growth, not ratings	• Recognize where you stand against expectations • Utilize the framework for reflection and growth • Look past a rating as a personal label
Specific and measured	• Improve data collection techniques • Move around the classroom during an observation to collect comprehensive evidence • Look at artifacts provided and listen to data shared by teacher	• Accept specific details and data • Understand how data can be used to promote growth vs. a "gotcha" • Be open to data the observer captured that you did not
Focused on impact	• Talk with students • Take time to analyze evidence after classroom visit	• Believe that you are the primary cause for learning in your classroom
Built on strengths for growth	• Identify teachers' strengths • *Hear*, not just listen • Build understanding of research-based strategies	• Continue learning (research-based teaching and learning) • Say "I don't know how" or "I don't understand"

Feedback is . . .	Provider Dispositions A willingness to . . .	Receiver Dispositions A willingness to . . .
	• Develop an understanding of programs, curriculum, disciplines, and student standards • Continue learning (research-based teaching and learning)	• Reflect on or hear areas of growth • Share challenges, misunderstandings, or needs (skills and feelings about feedback)
Objective	• Examine your own biases	• Trust the observer's intention
For learning	• Use feedback for learning within a cycle vs. isolated events • Commit to identifying or helping a teacher identify a specific high-leverage next step • *Hear* teacher ideas, don't just dictate your own	• See a "what's next" after each visit • Try an alternate strategy or next step • *Hear* and reflect, not just listen • Be an active participant, not a passive receiver

Source:

(Resource 6.2 has been created from Figure 6.1: Provider and Receiver Dispositions as a reproducible copy in the Resource Center, **resources .corwin.com/learnerfocusedfeedback**.)

> *"Here's our pitch; try the feedback out. Not because you know it is right or know it will help. But because it is possible it will help."*
> —(Stone & Heen, 2014)

Recently, we served as complementary evaluators (beginning in the spring) in an elementary school for teachers who did not know us. Before we began our observations, we met with the group and distributed this list, making a promise that, as providers, we would bring these dispositions to our work in their building. We shared our hope that they could bring the receiver dispositions or feel they could share where they were challenged. This was the start of building trust. After our work was completed (and with only thirty minutes to meet with each teacher), we asked them to complete Resource 6.3: Feedback on Feedback Survey, sharing their perceptions of our use of provider dispositions. This allowed us to reflect on our ability to align feedback to the RVL standards and utilize the twenty-one core skills and fifty strategies effectively. Responses from a five-point Likert showed highly favorable outcomes (Figures 6.2, 6.3, and 6.4).

Q1: ***To what extent was the feedback . . . honest and accurate (Observer demonstrated expertise in programs, effective instruction, and/or the CCT [Connecticut Common Core of Teaching] and was candid about observed outcomes)?***

FIGURE 6.2: TEACHER PERCEPTION: HONESTY AND ACCURACY

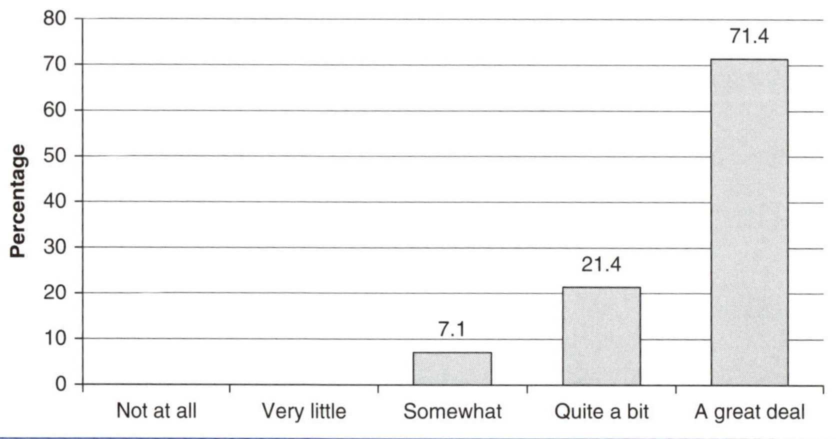

Q4: ***To what extent was the feedback . . . focused on teaching AND learning and your impact on your learners?***

FIGURE 6.3: TEACHER PERCEPTION: CONNECTED IMPACT ON LEARNERS

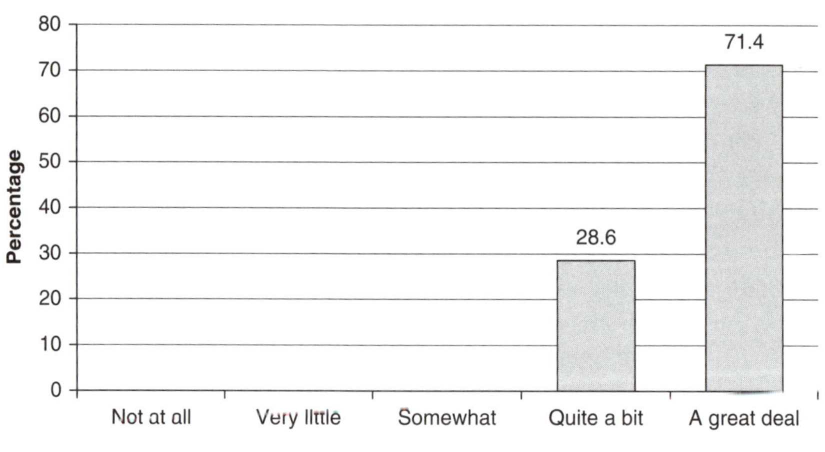

Q6: To what extent was the feedback . . . connected to your identified goals or challenge areas (your uploaded reflections when applicable), SLOs [Student Learning Objectives], and/or previous feedback?

FIGURE 6.4: TEACHER PERCEPTION: FEEDBACK AS A CYCLE

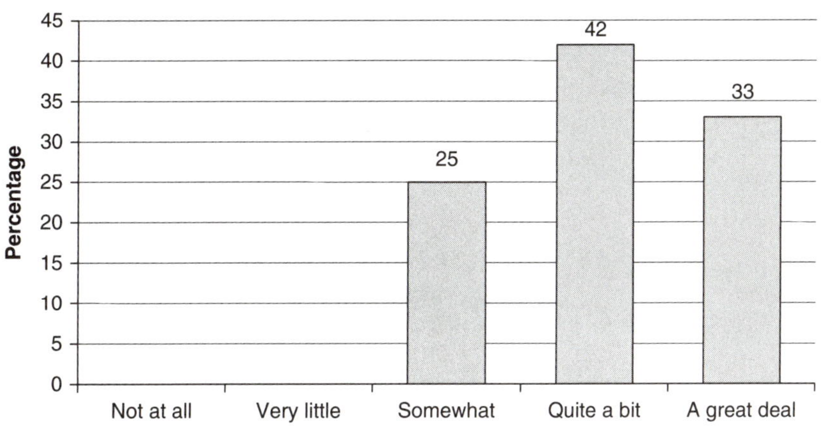

For any response categorized as "quite a bit" or "somewhat," we reflected. For Q6, we recognized we were relying on electronic resources to understand the teachers' strengths and identified areas of need ahead of the meetings. We were challenged by limited uploaded reflections, a single year-end meeting, and limited feedback provided from previous administrators throughout the year. For our purposes, we could have consistently inquired directly about ongoing professional learning and then made the connections in the conversations. We continue to strive for this to be 100 percent, as receivers should perceive feedback as a cycle versus an isolated event.

Building Trust

Stop and Think: Who is someone you trust, and what allows you to have that trust? How was it earned?

Sometimes, time is at the heart of building a trusting relationship. You need to see consistent behaviors or choices before you are won over. But Covey's title, *The Speed of Trust*, and the urgency of some situations we encounter in schools, remind us that we don't have long durations for change to take effect or shifts in culture to occur. We stepped into a situation at that school where we hoped and needed teachers to trust us within thirty days. We needed them to see our intent was not just about ratings or compliance in completing evaluations but to support them with impactful feedback for growth. We also wanted them to feel assured that we possessed the competence to be fair and accurate.

We recently encountered a "trust matrix" developed from Covey's work that resonated with us because it so clearly illustrates the important elements that contribute to trust building (or an inability to build trust) within organizations. In Figure 6.5, you can see that trust relies upon both character and competence, both of which must be not only communicated (e.g., "I will be transparent. I am credible.") but *demonstrated through actions*. As you look through the boxes, think about the interrelationship among all of the elements.

FIGURE 6.5: THE TRUST MATRIX

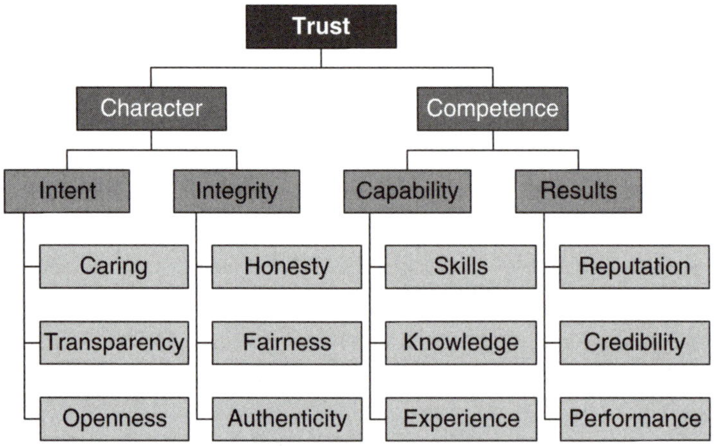

- Trust
  - Character
    - Intent
      - Caring
      - Transparency
      - Openness
    - Integrity
      - Honesty
      - Fairness
      - Authenticity
  - Competence
    - Capability
      - Skills
      - Knowledge
      - Experience
    - Results
      - Reputation
      - Credibility
      - Performance

Source: Barrett (2016).

When you look at this matrix and think about a logical progression, you might think trust must be in place initially in order to observe in classrooms or give or receive feedback. So we find ourselves in another chicken-or-egg dilemma; which comes first? We know the role of honesty is of critical importance, especially in feedback. However, for an observer to have the ability to be honest, he or she must understand with accuracy what occurred during the lesson and how the teacher impacted learners. This requires competence. The more competent, the more fair. The more honest and fair, the better your reputation and credibility. You get the picture.

We know these components all need to—and can be—built simultaneously when there is a commitment toward the dispositions and goals for feedback. Joe Jones and T. J. Vari (2019) remind us that we can be both candid *and* compassionate in our work in supporting teachers. Certainly, some feedback receivers who are still struggling with a fixed mindset, low efficacy, transient leadership, or memories of negative experiences with past observers will need to see more demonstration of the previously mentioned components than others. However, feedback that feeds forward can build trust.

We all have learned—or at least have heard the saying—that "honesty is the best policy." Think back to what you just read about factors that can decrease self-efficacy. Though it is difficult to be honest, we can show we care about a teacher by being courageous enough to be honest. (Think about how you value the friend who tells you *not* to buy that shirt.) Ultimately, if we are not honest, then we are allowing a teacher to continue on with an inaccurate perception of expectations or performance.

Stop and Think: Think back to the three feedback samples you read in Chapter 1 and the one in this chapter. Which are more accurate and honest?

It Takes Courage

We came across a blog that got our attention in the fall of 2018 titled "The Particular Agony of Teacher Observations" that included suggestions as to how to "survive observations." It further inspired us to work toward changing how teachers and leaders were experiencing observation and feedback.

In crafting a blog in response, we continued to ponder "How did we get here?" Many teachers we encounter have not visited a peer's classroom and have only experienced observation as a negative event through a flawed evaluation system not focused on growth. For as long as we can remember (and it still continues), when an observer entered a classroom, he or she found a seat in the back and watched as the lesson unfolded. Even just recently, a teacher pointed to a small table in the back that she made available for our visit to her third-grade classroom. We politely thanked her and mentioned that we probably would not need it. We know teachers are still receiving brief summaries of their actions, lists of evidence, or full scripts, all designated as "feedback."

> Imagine a world in which all observers have the skills to provide all observed teachers with feedback to feed forward. Could we daresay even that teachers and leaders would look forward to the visits and conversations? We can envision it because we have seen it. We have seen leaders [and teachers] providing impactful feedback based on a balance of evaluative and non-evaluative observations that are not only welcomed, but *sought out* by teachers. (Tepper & Flynn, 2018)

Stop and Think: Have you ever experienced or given feedback that you would describe as honest and courageous? How effective was that feedback?

As Confucius reminds us, "To know what is right and not do it is the worst cowardice." If you have come this far in your journey to improve feedback and are working to build your capacity to apply our strategies, you know that providing feedback that feeds forward is the right thing to do. The question now is, Do you have the courage to see it through? Those observers who are willing to be honest and who are equipped with the strategies and skills to provide evidence of learning (or a lack thereof) are those who will drive the learning in their schools. Schools must take mindful steps to build trust and thus a community of learners who seek feedback about performance and outcomes.

Making a Culture Shift

In Chapter 1, you encountered basic, immediate planning steps with *Strategy 1: Mindfully plan for effective observation and feedback*. These included the following:

- Building a shared understanding of effective teaching and learning
- Becoming transparent as observers
- Setting protocols and expectations for your classroom visits

While these actions are necessary for any school beginning to apply these strategies, the remainder of the chapter will take you further. We will provide guidance for the implementation of six steps that will support development of a sustainable culture of learning through observation and feedback. In following these steps, districts/regions and schools can ensure that the introduction of new practices in observation and feedback are tied to a greater vision and purpose. This may already be rooted within the school, district, or region or needs to be formed and reformed. Our steps provide straightforward activities that, when carried out, provide the clarity of the vision and action necessary to bring about change. This will allow schools to work toward establishing a new culture regardless of the challenges and obstacles they face.

We will provide you with a detailed description of each step ahead, but as a brief overview, the steps in Figure 6.6 are as follows:

FIGURE 6.6: STEPS TO SHIFT CULTURE

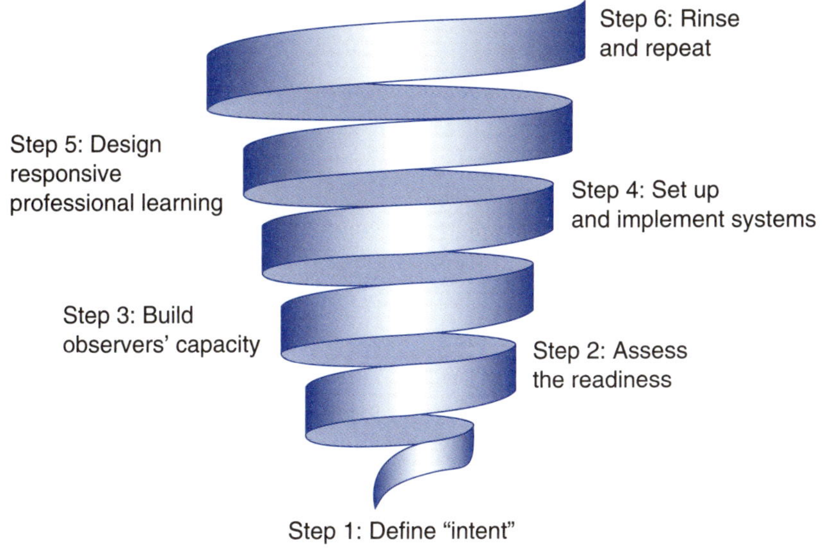

Developing a sustainable culture of learning through observation and feedback

> **Step 1:** Define *intent* and build toward a collective understanding of vision and purpose—student learning.
>
> **Step 2:** Assess the readiness to give and receive learner-focused feedback within the school or organization.
>
> **Step 3:** Build the capacity of all to give and receive learner-focused feedback.
>
> **Step 4:** Set up and implement the operational systems for schoolwide focus on impact and learners.
>
> **Step 5:** Design a systematic professional-learning model that is responsive.
>
> **Step 6:** Rinse and repeat.

We know it would be irresponsible of us to simply provide these steps and then send you on your merry way. Additionally, it would be foolish for us to believe we could comprehensively guide you through a change process of this magnitude in a single chapter. There will be hard decisions and commitments made as you prioritize learner-focused observation and feedback. How and where you spend your time will be greatly impacted by the systems and structures within your school.

Systems and Structures for Action

In *Feedback to Feed Forward,* we introduced school and district leaders to a cycle of planning and performance improvement (Figure 6.7), representing planned change that would be repeated annually. This cycle was originally created to support district or central-office leaders in understanding the overarching actions necessary to develop comprehensive professional learning for supervisors of teachers.

FIGURE 6.7: CYCLE OF PLANNING AND PERFORMANCE IMPROVEMENT

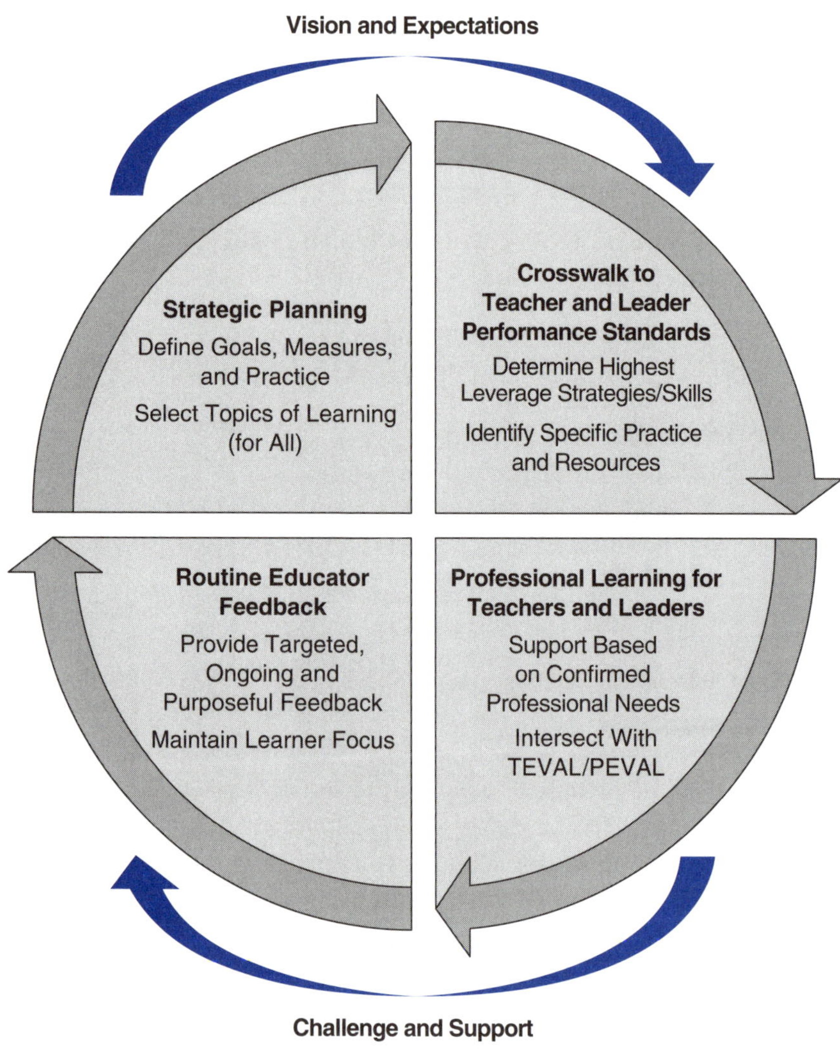

Source: ReVISION Learning Partnership, LLC.

First, this created a cycle for how their schools planned and supported the understanding of where they were headed, aligning the vision with expectations of performance (**strategic planning and performance standards**). Second, by implementing the cycle, their schools established greater clarity as to how they would support people along the way as levels of challenge increased (**professional learning and routine feedback**).

By taking action within the four identified focus areas, the schools and districts we highlighted were able to

- set a vision for the school,
- align the performance expectations with that vision,
- confirm the needs of teachers, and
- routinely observe and leverage feedback to continue to align the original vision with the ongoing implementation.

Without a collective understanding of where your team is headed, you cannot determine current performance (How am I going?) or outline the actions that will ensure you can close the gap between where you are and where you want to be (What's next?). In essence, this cycle allows your district, region, or school to own their own learning.

We know leaders of their own learning are continually adapting, learning from self- and external assessments, and setting aligned goals for growth. Using the same thinking, we can see how effective change is often the result of blurring planned and adaptive or iterative change (J. Wilson, 2018). This will be a critical understanding for success in shifting any culture. It is important for schools to create annual plans (strategic or school improvement plans) for our students and our schools. However, we also need to recognize that our teachers and administrators are living those plans day to day. Observation and feedback can become the vehicle through which you gain great insight into progress toward longer-term goals and to inform ongoing actions. The steps we provide ahead can be considered iterative, in that they act as "sprints" or "short bursts" within a larger, longer-term planning process.

Julie Wilson (2018) reminds us that this type of change

> is the land of "you don't know what you don't know." Iterative changing is required when the tasks and processes to implement the change are unknown. Iterative changing requires experimentation and the willingness to fail. . . . Iterative changing involves giving the work back to the people, knowing that it is up to the

> people who will implement the change to wrestle with the problem(s) they are trying to solve. This is a significant shift from the patriarchal or matriarchal model of school where the principal or superintendent will tell you what the problem is and, in many cases, provide the solution. (pp. 39–40)

Schools and districts/regions can set in motion the actions they believe will support the attainment of their stated strategic goals. However, as observation and feedback provide new understandings of impact, responsive adaptations can be made and new actions determined as necessary to achieve the anticipated change.

Stop and Think: Consider how your school, district, or region is applying the core areas of the cycle. Did their actions lead to improved performance? How often do you revisit your strategic plan? How could more frequent observation and feedback help?

The Six Steps

Currently, we are supporting schools in the early stages of implementation of our six steps, and we are collecting data on the benefits of this approach. This will allow us to draw conclusions and make adjustments to the model—a future publication for certain. Each step ahead includes its own set of aligned activities that will help to support a school in taking actions that will directly influence mindsets towards growth and change. Engaging in these requires a commitment to complete them with focus and determination and a willingness to embrace the unknown.

We are not proposing that this is the only pathway nor that our steps provide a cookie cutter solution for a school or district. Each step must be considered in the context of your current environment. Each of the actions outlined in the cycle of planning and performance, as well as the six steps, can be executed in a number of different ways, using a number of different approaches. The constant, however, is observation and feedback about the impact on learning.

Some staff will consider the observation and feedback intrusive or unnecessary, continuing to equate them only with evaluative measures versus formative assessment toward learning. Remember, many of these teachers have been part of past systems that included only two visits per year by an administrator focused only on rating against a rubric. Consistent, ongoing, and honest feedback from observers focused on growth demonstrates intent, transparency, and authenticity every day, leading to greater trust within a building or team.

Following each step, you will find we have included some recommended readings to further your understanding and thinking.

Step 1: Define Collective Intent

As you seek to create a culture of learning in a school through observation and feedback, the first step is to define what you are seeking to achieve. Your overarching intent should arise from the idea that we must generate school environments where the needs of your students are met. Learning must permeate all that you do and believe, and all members of the community must see themselves as learners. Chapter 2 laid the foundation for you to develop this vision based on what and how your students should learn.

During this step, schools collectively discuss often neglected *adaptive messages*, or the "Why?" behind the intent (Heifetz & Linsky, 2009). "Everyone involved needs to understand the purpose and rationale behind all of these [initiatives] to effectively shift mindsets from buy-in to ownership—and they also need to see the interconnectedness" (Tepper & Flynn, 2019, p. 198). When people understand the coherence among various actions, schools better control for initiative fatigue, a key impediment to collective efficacy.

Intent should be built upon three core components—*motive*, *agenda*, and *behavior*.

- Motive is your reason for engaging in the actions.
- Agenda is how you define what and how you will meet your motive.
- Behavior is the manifestation of these two in the actions taken. (Covey, 2006)

In order for people to trust and ultimately support a change, the intent behind that change must be made clear. As you apply this to observation and feedback, you need to arrive at a common belief and communicate directly for (and with) people these three elements. For example,

- the *motive* of observation and feedback is driven by an urgency to see our students succeed,
- our *agenda* is to define learner-focused feedback and outline how observation and feedback will be leveraged to promote improvements in student learning and to ensure that teachers receive the support they need to understand their impact, and,
- the *behaviors* associated with observation and feedback will be
    - carried out using strategies that ensure trained observers visit classrooms frequently,

- focused on student learning, and
- utilized by teachers to grow professionally and improve impact on students.

Without understanding the intent, teachers can create their own perceptions that will directly influence attitudes and beliefs about actions and interactions. "The main reason why declaring intent increases trust is that it 'signals your behavior'—it lets people know what to look for so that they can recognize, understand, and acknowledge it when they see it" (Covey, 2006, p. 88). When schools are able to include teachers in defining and communicating intent, there is clarity about all behaviors associated with the initiative.

As the *motive, agenda, and behaviors* are defined to help your team understand the intent, it is essential you never stray from your universal message of the "why?"—improved student learning. However, collaboratively agreeing to an intent is only half the battle. Everyone's actions must also *demonstrate* the dispositions (Figure 6.1) and intent over time, which will lead to mutual accountability and trust among all team members. Some examples could include

- administrators visiting classrooms without determining ratings,
- instructional leaders/coaches supporting teachers in their individual identified goals, and/or
- teachers being given the tools to privately videotape their own lessons and offered the option to delete once viewed (a first step) and/or share findings with their coach or in a PLC.

Stop and Think: What has been the big "why?" in your school, district, or region behind observation and feedback? How well has that been communicated to staff? Does your school already incorporate any strategies that demonstrate an overarching intent?

A Few Recommended Readings

10 Mindframes for Visible Learning: Teaching for Success (2018), John Hattie and Klaus Zierer

Human Side of Changing Education: How to Lead Change With Clarity, Conviction, and Courage (2018), Julie Wilson

Speed of Trust: The One Thing That Changes Everything (2006), Steven Covey

Step 2: Assess Readiness

There is more than enough research and literature on the change process and cycles of change within schools to understand and adequately prepare for potential reactions when working to shift the culture. We know from Stone and Heen (2014) that not all people are ready for feedback or to take ownership of their own learning. This can be related to a fixed mindset, a lack of will to change, and/or a lack of skills to meet the new expectations. Shifting a culture requires that you uncover whether these issues exist and examine *all* team members' readiness for the change. Earlier in the chapter, we offered you potential self-assessment tools that can be utilized to assess readiness that included the following:

- The strategies from *Feedback to Feed Forward* listed in the front of the book
- *Feedback to Feed Forward* Self-Assessment (Resource 6.1)
- The Feedback on Feedback Survey (Resource 6.2)
- Feedback Provider and Receiver Dispositions (Resource 6.3)

At North Branford Intermediate School in North Branford, Connecticut, a think tank of teachers, coaches, and administrators recently reviewed the Provider and Receiver Dispositions (Figure 6.1). Through an honest dialogue and exchange, teachers were able to share where they felt there were gaps in their feedback provider's actions or willingness and reflect on their own challenges with specific receiver dispositions. Similarly, coaches and leaders were honest about their personal challenges as providers. We have never once shared these in our training without hearing from someone admitting they need to personally work on one or more.

Additional resources exist to support a school, district, and/or region in assessing the levels of readiness to effect change. We would encourage you to review any and all of these as you prepare to take the steps toward a culture of learning through observation and feedback.

- Max Landsberg (1996/2015), in the *Tao of Coaching*, presents the skill–will matrix to provide a method for analyzing readiness through the lens of the best methods of supervising and coaching.
- Julie Wilson (2018), in her book *The Human Side of Change*, provides an Organizational Change Capacity Questionnaire, used to determine the capacity of a school to carry out change.
- Lyn Sharratt (2019), in her book *Clarity*, provides useful aligned resources for the 14 Parameters of system and school improvement (which were identified with Michael Fullan through their previous research).

- John Hattie and Klaus Zierer offer *ten mindframes* necessary for teachers and leaders who willingly and routinely examine their impact on students—a list we have also converted to anonymous online polls that we immediately make visible to whole teams

A number of different approaches are available for schools to complete internal or external audits of instructional practice to determine breadth and scope of need. We have provided this service through multiday visits, conducting broader sweeps and deep analyses of teaching and learning to build an understanding of readiness, identify trends, and set priorities.

As the great Bob Marley said, "I know now. I am willing and able. I throw my cards on your table." As we prepare for change, we need to all be singing these lines.

A Few Recommended Readings

Beyond the books mentioned in the preceding text . . .

Leadership for Learning: How to Help Teachers Succeed (2008), Carl D. Glickman

Professional Capital: Transforming Teaching in Every School (2012), Andy Hargreaves and Michael Fullan

Step 3: Build Capacity to Give and Receive Learner-Focused Feedback

Ideally, after working through Step 2, you will possess a comprehensive assessment of your team's readiness to give and receive feedback. We know as feedback quality improves, most receivers' levels of trust, ability to reflect, and willingness to try new strategies will increase. However, the primary commitment you must make for Step 3 is to ensure that the necessary training is built upon your initial assessments and identified areas of strength and growth. We have already suggested several tools you can use simultaneously as readiness assessments, to establish expectations, *and* to build capacity for all learners' to receive feedback in a positive and productive way. These include Stone and Heen's (2014) truth, relationship, and identity triggers; Hattie and Zierer's (2018) mindframes, and our provider and receiver dispositions.

We know that with the shift in evaluation and supervision, there was a lack of training to ensure observers provided accurate and honest learner-focused feedback about impact. Anyone who will be observing in classrooms should participate in professional learning toward this end. Training should provide direct instruction, modeling and thinking aloud, and opportunities to apply and reflect. This learning should be grounded in our six standards, twenty-one core skills, and thirty-one strategies from *Feedback to Feed Forward*. It should begin with building a common understanding of the expectations for teaching and learning, what those look and sound like in a classroom, and how to observe them. You cannot jump to coaching for, say, difficult conversations without spending time on identifying if learning is occurring and to what level, why, and how you know. You will find once observers build capacity for RVL 1.A, B, and C (Resource 1.1 RVL Supervisory Continuum) that they become more skilled in promoting reflection and objectively identifying areas of growth and strength and next steps grounded in evidence and your instructional framework (RVL 1.D, E, and F). For those who are ready, the next nineteen strategies outlined in this book serve to refine skill sets even further.

In multiple districts where we work, observers (administrators, coaches, teachers) are placed into small learning communities of six or so members and engage in full- and half-day embedded sessions with a facilitator. This group engages in a prebrief or preexamination of classroom expectations, along with explicit skill building for observers based on need, before going into a classroom together to observe a lesson. The participants self-reflect but share as a group conclusions about process and evidence collection strategies before and while discussing the lesson together. They use the indicators and expectations from their instructional framework to guide the process, with a central focus on identifying causal attribution (debrief). As a result, the debriefs become safe environments for discussion of teaching and learning, allowing each participant to learn not only about highly effective observer practice but also about quality classroom practice. Ongoing self-reflection and goal setting is an integral part of the process to inform future sessions (related to Step 5).

What is clear based on the complexity of the work is that training for observation practice is never a one-and-done process. As you have come to see, mastering our standards, skills, and strategies takes practice. We have seen the best results in those schools that continued with job-embedded training for evidence collection and analysis skills. "Even after high-quality initial training is in place, a school system may find as many as 40 percent of trainees still need additional support" (MET Project, 2015, p. 14). Videoed lessons offer a powerful tool and time-efficient method for observer reflection and growth. However, there is truly nothing like the real thing—observing live learners—when it comes to building the capacity to observe for impact.

Stop and Think: What training have the observers in your school, district, or region received to support high-quality observation?

Many schools provide opportunities for rounds or for teachers to visit other classrooms. Though there is great value in these (leaders are visible, and teachers in other classrooms may pick up a new strategy or idea), to maximize these opportunities, we need to ensure that all observers become highly attentive to impact on learners. It is important to remember that you cannot simply drop people into classrooms and expect them to effectively observe. (We would not have written two 250-page books on the subject if it were so.) This assumption has been the biggest mistake policy makers and thought leaders have made in the past decade about training for observation and feedback. It's time to get it right!

A Few Recommended Readings

Seeing It Clearly: Improving Observer Training for Better Feedback and Better Teaching (2015), MET Study

Feedback to Feed Forward: 31 Strategies to Lead Learning (2018), Amy Tepper and Patrick Flynn

Thanks for the Feedback (2014), Doug Stone and Sheila Heen

Step 4: Set Up and Implement the Operational Systems That Focus on Impact

> "Be pervasive (system minded) or stand aside." (Fullan, Quinn, & McEachen, 2018, p. 9)

Step 4 is designed to help you think through technical information—to consider all of your operational systems, policies, and structures and determine what needs to be created, amended, or removed to ensure that you can build a culture of learning through observation and feedback. You will begin this step by asking, "What current systems, policies, and structures are promoting *and also standing in the way* of the change we are envisioning?" Our goal is to help you proactively plan so that your implementation is not derailed by unexpected challenges or obstacles. We know that some policies, structures, and systems exist at the district level, which, until changed, will challenge schools. Leaders and teachers need to find ways together to go beyond the policy when possible. Simultaneously, district and policy leaders need to push for those substantive changes that would directly affect schools' ability to have more ownership and become more efficient and effective.

Know that we could not possibly address all of the potential systems here, as each school and district or community is different. To promote your thinking, however, we provide a few common areas that can influence your success in Figure 6.8. With each, you will find one or two aligned suggestions. You will also find that these are clearly interdependent.

FIGURE 6.8: AREAS FOR ANALYSIS OF OPERATIONS

Operational Category	Suggestion
Classroom schedules	• Adjust schedules so teachers are able to visit each other's classrooms and have ample time to collaborate. (Consider how this can also be supported by substitutes or leaders covering.)
Budget	• When possible, ensure funds are allocated for substitute coverage, coaches, or additional administrators. • Identify any current need for outside consultants or experts, or determine if there is internal capacity to support the work.
Evaluation policies	• Move away from a requirement of two formal forty-five-minute evaluations per year to more frequent unannounced visits (up to ten per year of shorter duration) that might include video and additional observers. • Simplify record keeping and number of indicators on an instructional framework that must be addressed.
Instructional practice	• Develop structures for teachers to recognize a need for or build upon vertical and cross-discipline alignment. • Concentrate on Tier 1 instructional practice; add to teachers', counselors', and psychologists' SEL toolboxes to support learners in the classroom (freeing up leaders who become frequent responders/interventionists).
Professional-learning design (Step 5)	• Develop a blended and responsive model (including, workshops, job-embedded learning, supplemented eLearning). • Organize and facilitate PLC or data team models so that the focus is on student learning and impact.
Time management/ leader schedules	• Identify what is an "emergency" or a leader-only crisis, and create effective behavior/response teams within schools. • Create a system to block time on schedules for classroom visits or leaders'/coaches' work with PLCs/data teams that is untouched but for emergencies.

During planning and implementation of change, the issue of time always rises to the surface in discussions, and in Chapter 1 of *Feedback to Feed Forward*, we addressed the challenge instructional leaders face in efforts to effectively lead learning. We all have heard or lamented, "There's not enough time," or "It takes too long." Conflicting priorities, policies (even the most well meaning), and the lack of cohesive structures are creating this reality. Without question, significant change in organizations can take five to seven years, and the day-to-day life of a school administrator is reactive and full, to say the least. Changes to systems and structures can have a powerful effect as they offer immediate space for people to engage in the practice that is being built through Step 3. These changes cause the gaps that are revealed through a readiness analysis in

Step 2 to become less daunting and create a greater sense of hope that we can achieve our vision and meet our intent outlined in Step 1.

We also know how hard school and district staff members are working, and initiative fatigue can sometimes lead people to simply comply with existing policy, as opposed to challenging the status quo. In these moments, challenge yourself. Ask yourself and the group our leading question over and over: "What is the most effective way for us to reach our goal of a culture of learning?" Make this question a mantra, an idea that is repeated frequently to support your focus and attention back on your students first.

Once you have begun to identify efficient and effective—as well as inefficient and ineffective—systems that are within your scope to maximize, manage, address, or work around, it is time to determine how, when, and who will implement changes across a district/region and/or school. Get observers out into classrooms, build capacity of PLCs, design responsive professional learning (Step 5), and demonstrate the intent to shift toward a culture of learning through a culture of observation and feedback. Without adequate attention to the structures and systems that need to be in place, the establishment of intent and all the readiness in the world will not lead to action and change.

A Few Recommended Readings

Deep Learning: Engage the World, Change the World (2018), Michael Fullan et al.

Schools That Learn (Updated and Revised): A Fifth Discipline Fieldbook for Educators, Parents, and Everyone Who Cares About Education (2012), Peter Senge et al.

Step 5: Design Systematic and Responsive Professional Learning

In the same way we desire to create spiraling learning for our students to achieve deep learning and transfer, responsive professionals should be spiraling as well, allowing teachers to transfer their learning about instruction—our Step 5. It should be informed by teacher voice and ongoing data collection.

We would propose that the most impactful data, evidence of causal attributions of student outcomes, is best collected through routine observations being conducted by teachers, coaches, and administrators. Observation and feedback can reveal professional gaps for teachers, as well as identify exemplary practice within a building, leading to ongoing, focused conversations about teaching and learning and more direct opportunities for application in the classroom.

In most schools, overarching professional learning topics are selected or plans are set each year to support teachers and administrators toward achievement of district, region, or school goals.

But that does not mean the learning design is necessarily responsive. Observation and feedback allow districts, regions, and schools to ask themselves several critical questions:

- "What trends/individual practices and outcomes are we seeing in day-to-day teaching and learning that can inform professional learning?"
- "What causal relationships between teaching and learning are we discovering?"
- "What are teachers asking for as a result of observations and feedback discussions?"

Informed, real-world, responsive professional learning is based on the answers to these questions.

To determine if your professional learning is responsive, ask yourself if it meets the following criteria:

- Allows for teacher voice, collaboration, and choice or pathways for learning
- Promotes self-monitoring and self-regulation and individual ownership of learning
- Is personalized based on ongoing data collected and feedback cycles
- Promotes teachers supporting teachers and taps into the strengths of everyone on staff (resulting in staff members leading sessions, EdCamps, model lessons, videotaping of exemplary practice, development of resource banks for e-learning, lesson studies, and lab classrooms)
- Drives the capacity of teams so professional-learning communities (PLCs) and data teams truly become communities of professional learning

Two structures that align well to observation and feedback cycles and include collaborative inquiry are PLCs and data teams. When either are effectively facilitated so the focus is on learners and a continuous search for causal attributions, they result in an understanding of the impact practice is having on students. Additionally, when the focus of a data team is informed by ongoing observation and feedback, the opportunity to effect instruction is high. Collaboratively, teachers identify effective strategies with their colleagues for implementation in the classroom and then are able to design their lesson studies, observations, artifact and data reviews, and feedback to support implementation and analysis of the impact on learners. This leads to significant shifts, a continuation of effective practices, and/or slight adjustments that lead to deeper learning for the teachers *and* the students. Any time, anywhere, professional learning becomes a reality when a whole community is thinking and talking about impact on learners.

High-quality, responsive professional learning not only meets the criteria listed previously but also integrates social persuasion (learner-focused feedback) and ensures routine exposure to both mastery and vicarious experiences (Bandura's sources of self-efficacy). These serve to generate positive emotional and physiological states and a deep sense of individual and collective efficacy. Teachers experience less fear or anxiety and feel successful, heard, and empowered—leading to improved results for students.

Stop and Think: How has professional learning been responsive to your needs as an educator? If it has not, why not?

A Few Recommended Readings

Personalized PD: Flipping Your Professional Development (2015), Jason Bretzmann

Standards for Professional Learning (2015), Learning Forward

Step 6: Rinse and Repeat

Though "rinse and repeat" is a recommended step on a shampoo bottle (or an option on your playlist), we are not suggesting that when you reach Step 5, you always execute the exact same steps again in the same way. We reminded you in Step 3 that learning for our students *and* our teachers should be iterative and spiraling. It is never-ending and grows in depth and complexity.

Consider the following scenario: In one of our schools, we supported planned professional learning and began implementation of formative assessments because they discovered that teachers were not making data-driven decisions to support all learners (e.g., flexible grouping, differentiation, lesson designs). However, early on, through observations of classroom practices and discussions at department meetings (trying to understand, "Why are teachers not able to effectively measure student understanding at critical points in a lesson?"), it was uncovered that a large portion of the staff struggled to identify clear learning targets and criteria that were, in fact, measurable. This created the need for the school to rinse and repeat the steps with this new discovery. Connecting back to the ultimate goal of student learning, the school assessed its readiness to address learning targets and criteria, examining current levels of teacher capacity and designing new and responsive professional learning to support the change.

A word of caution: No matter how often we say there is no quick solution or cookie cutter approach to change, we still watch as schools limit their investment in these steps to a single year (or even less). Schools must consistently and collaboratively do the following:

1. Revisit their intentions, and communicate these openly.
2. Visualize their expected and desired outcomes in the clearest terms by establishing their vision of teaching and learning.
3. Explore the current teaching and learning through observation, providing ongoing rich feedback that supports new levels of learning.
4. Respond by ensuring that those areas of greatest professional need are supported as they become evident through the ongoing observations, PLCs, and data teams.

If schools are to successfully shift to a culture of learning through observation and feedback, then they must be willing to relentlessly focus their attention on the impact on learners or causal attributions, day to day, month to month, and year after year.

Final Thoughts

> *"Nothing in the world is worth having or worth doing unless it means effort, pain, difficulty. . . . I have never in my life envied a human being who led an easy life. I have envied a great many people who led difficult lives and led them well."* —Theodore Roosevelt

We know that what has been outlined throughout our book is challenging and complex work, but the results of your efforts will be realized in classrooms every day. You are on your way, now equipped with our strategies, to challenge yourself and observe for impact and provide learner-focused feedback. Each day, you can take one step forward, taking actions that lead to the change you wish to see for your students. Identify what you believe, and be willing to learn and grow as you contribute to a change in your school community in pursuit of those beliefs.

> We believe that every student deserves the opportunity to thrive inside a culture of learning that cultivates motivation and the confidence to learn.
>
> We believe that every school and classroom environment can and should be set up to provide students with the knowledge, skills, dispositions, and tools they need to truly own their own learning.
>
> We believe all teachers deserve the feedback they need to learn and grow as professionals, building their own knowledge, skills, dispositions, and tools to ensure that all students have access to high-quality teaching in the classroom.

These goals can become a reality in every school.

We ended our first book with a quote from Batman . . . *"It's not who I am underneath, but what I do that defines me."* As he takes actions to provide hope to Gotham, Commissioner Gordon reminds Batman, *"You're going to make a difference. A lot of times it won't be huge, it won't be visible even. But it will matter just the same."*

We cannot bring the shift in our classrooms and school communities until we make a shift within ourselves. Your actions will matter. Where minds and doors are open, you can create a culture of learning through observation and feedback.

Strategies List

Chapter 1

Strategy 1 • Mindfully plan for effective observation and feedback

Chapter 2

Strategy 2 • Define *learning*

Strategy 3 • Create goals for all learners

Strategy 4 • Understand how learners learn

Strategy 5 • Understand how teachers create outcomes

Chapter 3

Strategy 6 • Plan evidence collection based on your framework

Strategy 7 • Plan evidence collection based on discipline-specific expectations

Chapter 4

Strategy 8 • Purposefully choose your evidence collection methods

Strategy 9 • Engage in conversations through questions

Strategy 10 • Set high expectations for responses

Strategy 11 • Use what you know about the timing of your arrival

Strategy 12 • Interact to determine prior learning

Strategy 13 • Interact to determine relevance and context

Strategy 14 • Interact to determine understanding of essential vocabulary

Chapter 5

Strategy 15 • Adapt based on what students are doing

Strategy 16 • Adapt based on what students are writing

Strategy 17 • Adapt based on what students are using (or not using)

Strategy 18 • Adapt based on student conversations and group work

Strategy 19 • Adapt based on teacher–student interactions

List of Figures

Chapter 1

Figure 1.1 • Pathways to Professional Growth

Figure 1.2 • RVL Core Skills Overview

Figure 1.3 • Foundational Strategies FF 7–9

Figure 1.4 • Big-Picture Goal

Figure 1.5 • Foundational Strategies FF 10–13

Figure 1.6 • Foundational Strategies FF 14–16

Figure 1.7 • Skills, Dispositions, and Tools for Teachers

Figure 1.8 • The Magic

Chapter 2

Figure 2.1 • Learning Preassessment

Figure 2.2 • Learning Brainstorm

Figure 2.3 • Challenging Phrases Indicator Examples

Figure 2.4 • The Taxonomy Table

Figure 2.5 • Teacher and Student Look-Fors

Figure 2.6 • Brain Functions and Teaching

Figure 2.7 • If–Then Relationships

Figure 2.8 • Five Focus Areas

Chapter 3

Figure 3.1 • Environment Indicator Example

Figure 3.2 • Evidence Collection Preparation: Expectations

Figure 3.3 • Focus Area Questions
Figure 3.4 • Progression of Student Responses
Figure 3.5 • Discipline Literacy Indicator Example
Figure 3.6 • Deep Learning and Disciplinary Literacy
Figure 3.7 • Social Studies Discipline-Specific Considerations
Figure 3.8 • Evidence Collection Preparation: Disciplines
Figure 3.9 • Evidence Collection Preparation: Standards

Chapter 4

Figure 4.1 • Listening and Viewing Basics
Figure 4.2 • Listening and Viewing Example
Figure 4.3 • Observer Thinking: Introduction
Figure 4.4 • Observer Thinking: Independent Work
Figure 4.5 • Evidence Collection Based on Expectations
Figure 4.6 • Adapted Questions for Context
Figure 4.7 • Nonevaluative Adapted Questions
Figure 4.8 • Questions for Vocabulary Understanding
Figure 4.9 • Follow-Up Questions

Chapter 5

Figure 5.1 • Deep-Learning Integration
Figure 5.2 • Ongoing Thinking Aligned to Focus Areas
Figure 5.3 • Indicator Example for Challenge
Figure 5.4 • Reflection Sheet
Figure 5.5 • Student Worksheets
Figure 5.6 • Character Trait List
Figure 5.7 • Science Organizer

Chapter 6

Figure 6.1 • Provider and Receiver Dispositions

Figure 6.2 • Teacher Perception: Honesty and Accuracy

Figure 6.3 • Teacher Perception: Connected Impact on Learners

Figure 6.4 • Teacher Perception: Feedback as a Cycle

Figure 6.5 • The Trust Matrix

Figure 6.6 • Steps to Shift Culture

Figure 6.7 • Cycle of Planning and Performance Improvement

Figure 6.8 • Areas for Analysis of Operations

References

Anderson, L. (Ed.), Krathwohl, D. (Ed.), Airasian, P., Cruikshank, K., Mayer, R., Pintrich, P., . . . Wittrock, M. (2001). *A taxonomy for learning, teaching, and assessing: A revision of Bloom's Taxonomy of Educational Objectives* (Complete edition). New York, NY: Longman.

Antonetti, J., & Garver, J. (2015). *17,000 classroom visits can't be wrong: Strategies that engage students, promote active learning and boost achievement.* Alexandria, VA: Association for Supervision and Curriculum.

Atherton, J. S. (2013, December 31). Learning and teaching. *Creative Education, 4*(12B). Retrieved from https://www.economicsnetwork.ac.uk/archive/atherton_learning/deepsurf

Bandura, A. (1991). Social cognitive theory of self-regulation. *Organizational Behavior and Human Decision Processes, 50*(2), 248–287.

Bandura, A. (1994). Self-efficacy. In V. S. Ramachaudran (Ed.), *Encyclopedia of human behavior* (Vol. 4, pp. 71–81). New York, NY: Academic Press. (Reprinted in H. Friedman [Ed.], *Encyclopedia of mental health*. San Diego, CA: Academic Press, 1998). Retrieved from https://www.uky.edu/~eushe2/Bandura/BanEncy.html

Barrett, R. (2016). *An exercise for building trust in your team.* Retrieved from https://www.linkedin.com/pulse/exercise-building-trust-your-team-richard-barrett

Berger, R., Rugen, L., & Woodfin, L. (2014). *Leaders of their own learning: Transforming schools through student-engaged assessment.* San Francisco, CA: John Wiley & Sons, Inc.

Biggs, J. B. (1987). *Student approaches to learning and studying.* Hawthorn, Victoria: Australian Council for Educational Research.

Biggs, J. B., & Collis, K. (1982). *Evaluating the quality of learning: The SOLO taxonomy.* New York, NY: Academic Press.

Brandl, S., & Bellwood, D. (2015). *Coordinated vigilance provides evidence for direct reciprocity in coral reef fishes.* Retrieved from https://www.nature.com/articles/srep14556#article-info

Caine, R., Caine, G., McClintic, C., & Klimek, K. (2015). *12 brain/mind learning principles in action: Developing executive functions of the human brain.* Thousand Oaks, CA: Corwin.

Calkins, L., Ehrenworth, M., & Pessah, L. (2018). *Leading well: Building schoolwide excellence in reading and writing.* Portsmouth, NH: Heinemann.

Common Core State Standards Initiative (CCSSI). (2018). *Standards for Mathematical Practices.* Retrieved from http://www.corestandards.org/Math/Practice

Connecticut State Department of Education (CSDE). (2017). *The Connecticut Common Core of Teaching (CCT) rubric for effective teaching* [online pdf]. Retrieved from https://portal.ct.gov/-/media/SDE/Evaluation-and-Support/CCTRubricForEffectiveTeaching2017.pdf?la=en

Cossett Lent, R. (2016). *This is disciplinary literacy: Reading, writing, thinking, doing . . . content area by content area*. Thousand Oaks, CA: Corwin.

Costa, A. L., & Kallick, B. (2009). *Habits of mind across the curriculum*. Alexandria, VA: Association of Curriculum and Supervision.

Covey, S. (2006). *The speed of trust: The one thing that changes everything*. New York, NY: Free Press.

Danielson, C. (2016). *Talk about teaching! Leading professional conversations*. Thousand Oaks, CA: Corwin.

The Danielson Group. (2013). *The framework*. Retrieved from https://www.danielsongroup.org/framework

DeWitt, P. (2017). *Collaborative leadership: Six influences that matter most*. Thousand Oaks, CA: Corwin.

Donahoo, J. (2017). *Collective efficacy: How educators' beliefs impact student learning*. Thousand Oaks, CA: Corwin.

Dweck, C. (2006). *Mindset: The new psychology of success*. New York, NY: Random House.

Entwistle, N., & Ramsden, P. (1982). *Understanding student learning*. London, England: Social Science Research Council.

Erickson, H. L. (2007). *Concept-based curriculum and instruction for the thinking classroom*. Thousand Oaks, CA: Corwin.

Fisher, D., & Frey, N. (2013). *Better learning through structured teaching: A framework for the gradual release of responsibility* (2nd ed). Alexandria, VA: Association for Supervision and Curriculum Development.

Flavell, J. (1979). Metacognition and cognitive monitoring. *American Psychologist, 34*(10), 906–911.

Frey, N., Fisher, D., & Smith, D. (2019). *All learning is social and emotional: Helping students develop essential skills for the classroom and beyond*. Alexandria, VA: Association for Supervision and Curriculum Development.

Frey, N., Hattie, J., & Fisher, D. (2018). *Developing assessment-capable visible learners grades K–12*. Thousand Oaks, CA: Corwin.

Fullan, M., Quinn, J., & McEachen, J. (2018). *Deep learning: Engage the world, change the world*. Thousand Oaks, CA: Corwin.

Gabriel, R. E., & Woulfin, S. L. (2017). *Making teacher evaluation work: Guide for literacy teachers and leaders*. Portsmouth, NH: Heinemann.

Goddard, R. D., Hoy, W. K., & Hoy, A. W. (2004). Collective efficacy beliefs: Theoretical developments, empirical evidence, and future directions. *Educational Researcher, 33*(3), 3–13.

Great Schools Partnership. (2013). Retrieved from https://www.edglossary.org/school-culture

Hargreaves, A., & Fullan, M. (2012). *Professional capital: Transforming teaching in every school*. New York, NY: Teachers College Press.

Haring, N. G., Lovitt, T. C., Eaton, M. D., & Hansen, C. L. (1978). *The fourth R: Research in the classroom*. Columbus, OH: Charles E. Merrill Publishing Co.

Hattie, J. (2012). *Visible learning for teachers: Maximizing impact on learning*. New York, NY: Routledge.

Hattie, J. (2017). Visible learning plus 250+ influences on student achievement. Retrieved from https://visible-learning.org/wp-content/uploads/2018/03/VLPLUS-252-Influences-Hattie-ranking-DEC-2017.pdf

Hattie, J. A. C., & Donaghue, G. M. (2016, August 10). Learning strategies: A synthesis and conceptual model. *NPJ: Science of Learning*. Retrieved from https://www

.mcrprimaryitealumni.co.uk/wp-content/uploads/2016/08/HattieLearning-strategies-a-synthesis-and-conceptual-model.pdf

Hattie, J., & Zierer, K. (2018). *10 mindframes for visible learning: Teaching for success.* New York, NY: Routledge.

Heifetz, R., & Linsky, M. (2009). *The practice of adaptive leadership: Tools and tactics for changing your organization and the world.* Boston, MA: Cambridge Leadership Associates.

Jensen, E. (2005). *Teaching with the brain in mind* (2nd ed.). Alexandria, VA: ASCD.

Jones, J., & Vari, T. J. (2019). *Candid and compassionate feedback: Transforming everyday practice in schools.* New York, NY: Routledge.

Kapur, M. (2016). Examining productive failure, productive success, unproductive failure, and unproductive success in learning. *Educational Psychologist, 51*(2), 289–299.

Killion, J. (2019). *The feedback process: Transforming feedback for professional learning* (2nd ed.). Oxford, OH: Learning Forward.

Knight, J. (2018). *The impact cycle: What instructional coaches should do to foster powerful improvements in teaching.* Thousand Oaks, CA: Corwin.

Landsberg, M. (2015). *The tao of coaching: Boost your effectiveness at work by inspiring and developing those around you.* London, England: Profile Books. (Original work published 1996)

Learning Science International (LSI). (2017). *Learning map, scales and evidences for the Marzano focused teacher evaluation model.* Retrieved from https://www.schenevuscsd.org/Downloads/Marzano%20Focused%20Teacher%20Evaluation%20Rubric.pdf

Lupien, S. J., Gillin, C. J., & Hauger, R. L. (1999). Working memory is more sensitive than declarative memory to the acute effects of corticosteroids: A dose-response study in humans. *Behavioral Neuroscience, 113*(3), 420–430.

Marshall, K., & Marshall, D. (2017, December). Mini-observations: A keystone habit. *School Administrator,* 26–29.

Martinez, M. (2006). What is metacognition? *Phi Delta Kappan, 87*(9), 696–699.

Marton, F., & Säljö, R. (1976). On qualitative differences in learning: I—Outcome and process. *British Journal of Educational Psychology, 46,* 4–11.

Maslow, A. H. (1943). A theory of human motivation. *Psychological Review, 50*(4), 370–396.

McCaffrey, T. (2016, June 6). *Rethinking the gradual release model.* Retrieved from https://www.nctm.org/Publications/Mathematics-Teaching-in-Middle-School/Blog/Rethinking-the-Gradual-Release-of-Responsibility-Model

MET Project. (2015). *Seeing it clearly: Improving observer training for better feedback and better teaching.* Bill and Melinda Gates Foundation. Retrieved from http://k12education.gatesfoundation.org/resource/seeing-it-clearly-improving-observer-training-for-better-feedback-and-better-teaching

Miller, D. C. (2007). Essentials of school neuropsychological assessment. Hoboken, NJ: Wiley.

Moss, C., & Brookhart, S. (2015). *Formative classroom walkthroughs: How principals and teachers collaborate to raise student achievement.* Alexandria, VA: ASCD.

Next Generation Science Standards. (NGSS). (2019). Retrieved from https://www.nextgenscience.org

Nuthall, G. (2007). *The hidden lives of learners.* Wellington, New Zealand: NZCER Press.

OECD. (2018). *The future of education and skills: Education 2030.* Retrieved from https://www.oecd.org/education/2030/E2030%20Position%20Paper%20(05.04.2018).pdf

Park, S., Takahashi, S., & White, T. (2014). *Learning teaching (LT) program: Developing an effective teacher feedback system: 90-day cycle report.* Stanford, CA: Carnegie Foundation for the Advancement of Teaching. Retrieved from https://www.carnegiefoundation.org/wp-content/uploads/2013/08/CF_Feedback_90DC_2014.pdf

Pearson, P. D., & Gallagher, M. (1983, October). The instruction of reading comprehension. *Contemporary Educational Psychology, 8*(3), 317–344.

Quaglia, R., & Corso, M. (2014). *Student voice: The instrument of change.* Thousand Oaks, CA: Corwin.

Quaglia Institute for Student Aspirations (QISA). (2013). Retrieved from https://www.qisa.org

Ramsden, P. (2003). *Learning to teach in higher education* (4th ed.). New York, NY: Routledge.

Ritchhart, R., & Church, M. (2011). *Making thinking visible: How to promote engagement, understanding, and independence for all learners.* San Francisco, CA: Jossey Bass.

Shanahan, C., Shanahan, T., & Misischia, C. (2011, December 8). Analysis of expert readers in three disciplines: History, mathematics, and chemistry. *Journal of Literacy Research, 43*(4), 393–429. Retrieved from http://journals.sagepub.com/doi/pdf/10.1177/1086296X11424071

Shanahan, T., & Shanahan, C. (2008). Teaching disciplinary literacy to adolescents: Rethinking content area literacy. *Harvard Educational Review, 78*(1) 40–59. Retrieved from http://www.eoc.sc.gov/Information%20for%20Educators/Everything%20You%20Wanted%20to%20Know%20About%20Reading/Teaching%20Disciplinary%20Literacy%20Shanahan%202008%20copy.pdf

Silver, D. (2012). *Fall down 7 times, get up 8: Teaching kids to succeed.* Thousand Oaks, CA: Corwin.

Silver, D., & Stafford, D. (2017). *Teaching kids to thrive: Teaching kids the other essential skills for success.* Thousand Oaks, CA: Corwin.

Sousa, D. (2017). *How the brain learns* (5th ed.). Thousand Oaks, CA: Corwin.

Sousa, D., & Tomlinson, C. (2018). *Differentiation and the brain: How neuroscience supports the learner-friendly classroom (use brain-based learning and neuroeducation to differentiate instruction)* (2nd ed.). Bloomington, IN: Solution Tree.

Sprenger, M. (2018). *How to teach so students remember* (2nd ed.). Alexandria, VA: ASCD.

Stanford History Education Group. (2018). Retrieved from https://sheg.stanford.edu/history-lessons

Stern, J., Ferraro, K., & Mohnkern, J. (2017). *Tools for teaching conceptual understanding: Designing lessons and assessments for deep learning—Secondary.* Thousand Oaks, CA: Corwin.

Stone, D., & Heen, S. (2014). *Thanks for the feedback: The science of receiving feedback well.* New York, NY: Penguin Books.

Tate, M. (2016). *Worksheets don't grow dendrites: 20 instructional strategies that engage the brain* (2nd ed.). Thousand Oaks, CA: Corwin.

Tepper, A., & Flynn, P. (2018). Leading the learning through courageous observations [Web log post]. Retrieved from https://corwin-connect.com/2018/10/leading-the-learning-through-courageous-observations

Tepper, A., & Flynn, P. (2019). *Feedback to feed forward: 31 strategies to lead learning.* Thousand Oaks, CA: Corwin.

Vygotsky, L. (1978). *Mind and society.* Cambridge, MA: Harvard University Press.

Webb, N. (1997). *Criteria for alignment of expectations and assessments in mathematics and science education*. Madison: Wisconsin Center for Education Research University of Wisconsin–Madison.

Wilson, D., & Conyers, M (2011). *Thinking for results: Strategies for increasing student achievement by as much as 30 percent* (4th ed.). Orlando, FL: BrainSMART.

Wilson, D., & Conyers, M. (2016). *Teaching students to drive their brains: Metacognitive strategies, activities, and lesson ideas*. Alexandria, VA: ASCD.

Wilson, J. (2018). *The human side of changing: How to lead change with clarity, conviction, and courage*. Thousand Oaks, CA: Corwin.

Wilson, J., & Clarke, D. (2011). Towards the modelling of mathematical metacognition. *Mathematics Education Research Journal, 16*(2), 25–48.

Wolfe, P. (2010). *Brain matters: Translating research into classroom practice* (2nd ed.). Alexandria, VA: ASCD.

Zimmerman, B. (1989). A social cognitive view of self-regulated academic learning. *Journal of Educational Psychology, 81*, 329–339.

Zygouris-Coe, V. (2015). *Teaching discipline-specific literacies in grades 6–12: Preparing students for college, career, and workforce demands*. New York, NY: Routledge.

Index

Figures are indicated by f following the page number.

Action steps, feedback, 5, 13f, 15, 21, 117, 146, 153, 162, 182
Activators, teachers as, 54
Adaptation on arrival to classroom
  analysis of feedback example, 137–138
  basics of, 99–102
  expectations of students and, 130–131
  foundational understandings and, 120–130, 125–127f, 129–130f
  learning goals and, 96–99, 117–120, 118–119f
  metacognition and, 102–107, 103–104f, 180
  observation goals and, 96–99
  overview, 95–96, 130–131
  role-specific suggestions for, 131–132
  steps to take when entering, 100–102
  time management and, 107–111
  timing of entry and, 111–117, 114f, 116f
Adaptation as lesson unfolds
  active engagement and, 153–158
  causal attribution and impact, 145–149, 146–147f
  discourse and, 172–176
  good struggle and, 149–152, 149f
  look-fors, 140–141
  observation for learning, 138–145, 139f
  overview, 133–138, 152–153
  reflection and, 161–164, 161f, 163f
  role-specific suggestions for, 176–177
  student notes and, 159–160
  tools and resources and, 165–172, 166f, 168f
Adaptation phase of learning, 38. *See also* Deep learning; Transfer
Adaptive messages, 199
Affect of students, 101
Agenda, motive, and behavior, 199–200
Assessment, 64, 78, 87, 90, 101, 140, 147, 184
Assessment-capable teachers, 18–20
Assessment-capable visible learners, 18, 46–47
Assumptions, 42–43, 106
Attention, 57–58

Backward design, 139–140
Bandura, Albert, 4, 5, 7, 187
Basic literacy, 83
Battelle for Kids, 139, 139f
Beetle analogy, 180
Behavior, motive, and agenda, 199–200
Bellwood, D., 181
Bias, 105–106
Big picture, 16, 16f, 71, 100, 114, 138
Bloom's Taxonomy, 39, 39f
Brain function, 48–53, 50–51f, 80
Brandl, S., 181
Brookhart, S., 34, 60, 76, 82

Capacity building, 37, 202–204
Causal attribution
  determination of, 61–63f, 61–64
  importance of, 4–5
  observation for, 145–149, 146–147f
  self-efficacy and, 60, 61
CCSS (Common Core State Standards), 144
Challenge level, 62, 149–152, 149f

Change process. *See* Culture of learning, steps to create
Character, learning goals and, 45–46
Clarke, D., 45
Classroom environment, 64, 73–74, 73f, 75f
Classroom visits. *See* Observation
Coaching, 65, 72, 177, 184, 188, 201, 203
Cognitive engagement, 57. *See also* Engagement
Cognitive flexibility, 53–54, 135, 180
Collaborative culture of learning, 3, 20, 181–182
Collective belief, 6–7
Collective teacher efficacy, 6–7, 61
Comfort zones, getting out of, 24, 24f
Common Core State Standards (CCSS), 144
Conceptual thinking, 38–43, 39f, 63
Confucius, 194
Connections, and learning, 38, 46, 48–52, 55
Content expertise, 121–124
Context of learning, 124–128, 125–127f
Continuous improvement cycle, 56–57, 56f
Conyers, M., 43, 44, 54, 58, 64, 135
Corso, M., 57, 124
Cossett Lent, R., 86
Costa, A. L., 43
Courage, 193–194
Covey, S., 191–192, 192f, 200
Critical thinking. *See* Deep learning
Critical understandings, 31–32, 31f
Cultivators, teachers as, 54
Culture of individualism, 181
Culture of learning
  belief in, 209–210
  building of, 3–7, 4f
  collaborative culture of learning, 181–182
  elements of, 3, 180–181
  feedback about impact and, 182–191, 188–191f
  trust building and, 23, 191–194, 192f
Culture of learning, steps to create
  capacity building, 202–204
  collective intent and, 199–200
  cycle of planning and performance management, 196–198, 196f
  iterative nature of, 208–209
  operational systems and, 204–206, 205f
  overview, 194–195, 195f, 198–199
  professional learning and, 206–208
  readiness assessment, 200–202
Culture of observation and feedback, 3, 8–12
Curriculum, 41, 81–82
Cycle of continuous improvement, 56–57, 56f
Cycle of planning and performance management, 196–198, 196f

Danielson, Charlotte, 42, 55
Darcy, Jesse, 67
Darkling beetle analogy, 180
Data, quantitative and qualitative, 13f, 14, 15, 67, 136
Data teams, 207–208
Deep learning
  brain development and, 49
  cautions for observers about, 41–43
  defined, 37, 38, 140
  discipline-specific literacy, 86, 86f
  observation for, 139–140, 139f
  surface learning compared, 38–43, 39f
Deep Learning: Engage the World, Change the World (Fullan et al.), 37
DiCorpo, Alisha, 55–56
Differentiation, difficulty with, 5
Digital storytelling, 170
Discipline-specific literacy, 82–90, 85–87f, 89f
Dispositions, observation and, 43–44
Dispositions, skills, and tools, 19f, 47f, 187, 188–189f
Donaghue, G. M., 53

Edison, Thomas, 30
Emotion, 58–59
Emotional and physiological states, 4
Engagement, 57, 150
  impact on, and learning, 56–64, 74, 76
  observing for, 16, 76, 91, 94, 102, 103, 105, 107, 149f, 153, 170. *See also* Struggle

related to feedback, 12, 13f, 14, 97. *See also* RVL 1.C
Entertainment versus engagement, 57
Erickson, Lynn,, 41, 49
Evaluation, not just, 72, 81, 106, 192, 193, 202, 205f
Evidence. *See also* Data, quantitative and qualitative
Evidence collection
discipline-specific literacy and, 88–89, 89f
essentials of, 15–18, 16–17f
mapping strategy for, 100–101
reasons for, 12
relevance of, 96–97, 135
See also Adaptation on arrival to classroom; Planning for evidence collection
Evidence Collection 2.0, 102
Expectations
aligning the vision with, 197
building a common understanding of, 22, 203
for observation, 23, 68, 72–79f, 81–82, 84–90, 102, 108, 113, 114f, 116f, 188f, 120, 125, 128
for students, 19f, 23, 47f, 52
for teaching and learning, 15, 22, 25, 32. *See also* Instructional frameworks
inaccurate understanding of, 187
Explanations, 113

Feedback
about impact, 182–191, 188–191f
focus on student understanding, 11–12
importance of, 26
ineffectiveness of, 5
preparation for, 183–186
Feedback on Feedback Survey, 189
Feedback to Feed Forward (Tepper & Flynn)
advanced stages of learning and, 38
capacity building and, 14
cycle of planning and performance management, 196–198, 196f
directive feedback and, 11
engagement and, 57–60
evidence collection and, 15
readiness for change and, 201
reasons for, 1–2
understanding purposes of, 199
Feeding forward, defined, 1–2
Ferraro, K., 38, 42, 43, 63, 143
FF Strategies, 15–18, 16–17f, 70
Fish analogy, 181
Fisher, Dianna, 39, 113
Fisher, Douglas, 38, 53, 62, 63, 64, 124, 139, 140–141, 149, 151
Flavell, J., 45
Flynn, Patrick, 193. *See also Feedback to Feed Forward* (Tepper & Flynn)
Focus area questions, 76, 77–79f, 79–81, 81f
Follow-up questions, 130
Formative assessment, 64
Frey, Nancy, 38, 53, 62, 63, 64, 113, 124, 139, 140–141, 149, 151
Fullan, Michael, 37, 38, 46, 53, 140, 181, 204

Goals. *See* Learning goals; Observation goals
Good struggle, 149–152, 149f
Google Classroom, 170
Gradual-release model, 62, 62–63f, 111–112
Graphic organizers, 75, 75f
Great Schools Partnership, 3
Grit, 45–46

Habits, observation and, 43–44
Habits of mind, 74, 188, 188–189f
Hargreaves, Andy, 181
Hattie, John, 6, 38, 53, 54, 62, 63, 64, 124, 139, 140–141, 149, 151, 202
Hawking, Stephen, 96
Heen, S., 189
History, 87–88, 87f
Honesty, 193
The Human Side of Change (Wilson), 201

If-then relationships, 56–57, 56f
Impact
adaptation as lesson unfolds, 145–149, 146–147f
analysis of, 183–186
culture of learning and feedback, 182–191, 188–191f

observation for, 9–10
recognizing, 54–60, 56f
See also Causal attribution, *specific strategies*
Independent work, arrival during, 114–117, 116f
Instruction, 52, 61–63f, 61–64, 82
Instructional frameworks, 33–34, 34f, 72–75, 73f
Interactive synergy, 49
Intermediate literacy, 83
Interruptions, 105, 108
Introductions, arrival during, 113–114, 114f
Iterative nature of change and learning, 63, 143–144, 197–198, 208–209

Jensen, Eric, 42, 48, 54, 58, 59, 124

Kahoot, 170
Kallick, B., 43
Kapur, M., 150–151
Killion, J., 188

Labels, 42–43
Landsberg, Max, 201
Leaders leading learning, 20–25, 24f
Leading own learning
progression and, 63
scaffolding and, 150
student-owned learning and, 46–47
for teachers, 18–20, 19f
teaching skills for, 64
Learned helplessness, 60
Learning
brain function and, 48–53, 50–51f
character and, 45–46
context of, 124–128, 125–127f
critical understandings for, 31–32, 31f
focus on, 29–30
identifying, 53–54
as iterative, 143–144, 197–198
levels of, 39
observation for, 10–12, 138–145, 139f
prior learning and, 120–124, 151
recognizing impact on, 54–60, 56f
role-specific suggestions for, 64–66
self-regulation and self-monitoring and, 44–45
student experience of activities and, 15
surface learning, 38–43, 39f
understanding concept of, 32–35, 33–34f
See also Culture of learning; Deep learning; Learning goals
Learning communities, 203
Learning goals
character and, 45–46
conceptual thinking, 38–43, 39f
connection between, 37
creation of, 36–37
metacognition, 37, 43–44
overview, 35–36
planning for evidence collection and, 81–82
student-owned learning and, 46–47
Learning progressions, 111–112
Learning targets, 101
Learning to Teach in Higher Education (Ramsden), 32
Level of challenge, 62
Listening and viewing, 103–104f, 103–107
Literacy levels, 83
Long-term memory, 51f
Look-fors, 47f

Maris, Roger, 67
Marley, Bob, 202
Marshall, D., 8
Marshall, K., 8
Martinez, M., 43
Marton, Ference, 34–35
Maslow's Hierarchy of Needs, 54–55
Mastery experiences, 4
McEachen, Joanne, 37, 38, 46, 53, 140, 204
Memorization, 41–42
Metacognition
adaptability and, 102–107, 103–104f, 180
defined, 43
learning goals and, 37, 43–44
observation for, 141–142
MET Project, 203
Mindframes for visible learning, 6–7, 202
Misichia, C., 83
Mistakes, 149, 151
Mohnkern, J., 38, 42, 43, 63, 143

Moss, C., 34, 60, 76, 82
Motivation, 60, 62, 64
Motive, agenda, and behavior, 199–200

Next Generation Science Standards (NGSS), 90–91, 92f
Notes, use of, 106, 159–160
Novelty, 59
Nuthall, G., 10, 15

Objectivity, 106
Observation
  analysis of feedback example, 136–138
  for causal attribution, 145–149, 146–147f
  culture of observation and feedback and, 3, 8–12
  dispositions and, 43–44
  disruptions, least amount of, 108
  for impact, 9–10
  for learning, 10–12, 138–145, 139f
  for student affect, 101
  of learning versus teaching, 9–10
  protocols and expectations for, 23–25, 24f
  skills of, 13–18, 13f, 16–17f
  teaching during, 106–107
  transparency with, 22–23
  of whom and how often, 25
  See also Adaptation as lesson unfolds; Adaptation on arrival to classroom; Observation goals; Planning for evidence collection
Observation goals
  adaptability and, 96–99, 117–120, 118–119f
  planning for evidence collection and, 81–82
  relevant evidence and, 96–97, 135
Observer thinking, 116f, 154f, 155f, 156–157f, 158f, 159f, 161-162f, 164f, 166–167f, 168–169f, 172–173f
Okakura, Kakuzo, 134
Olearczyk, Gina, 30
Operational systems, 204–206, 205f
Organisation for Economic Co-operation and Development (OECD), 36–37
Organizers, 168–169, 168f

Padlet, 170
"The Particular Agony of Teacher Observations" blog, 193
Partnership for 21st Century Learning, 139, 139f
Performances, 153–156
Perseverance, 45–46, 74
Personalized learning, 127. *See also* Context of learning
Physiological needs, 54–55
Planning for evidence collection
  analysis of feedback example, 137
  disciplines and, 82–90, 85–87f, 89f
  expectations and, 72–75, 73f, 75f
  interaction with learners and, 75–81, 77–79f, 81f
  learning goals and, 81–82
  overview, 67–69
  preobservation planning meetings, 69–70
  role-specific suggestions for, 92–93
  standards and, 90–91, 92f
  tool preparation, 70–72
PLCs (professional learning communities), 6, 207–208
Praise sandwiches, 146
Preobservation planning meetings, 69–70
Presentations, 153–156
Prior learning, 120–124, 151
Productive failure, 151
Productive struggle, 149–152, 149f
Productive success, 150
Products, 156–157
Professional learning, 202–203, 206–208
Professional learning communities (PLCs), 207–208
Progression, 62–63, 62–63f
Projects, 156–157

Quaglia, R., 57, 124
Questions
  focus area questions, 76, 77–79f, 79–81, 81f
  follow-up questions, 130
  purposes of, 108–109
Quinn, Joanne, 37, 38, 46, 53, 140, 204
Quizzes, arrival during, 117

Ramsden, Paul, 32, 35
Reading skills, 83
Recall, 41–42
Reflection, students,161–164, 161f, 163f
Reflection, teachers, 12, 13f, 14, 15, 19, 97, 186
Relevance and content determination, 124–128, 125–127f
Relevance of evidence, 96–97
Research, 21, 158
Resilience, 45–46
Resources, 165–167, 166f
ReVISION Learning Partnerships (RVL), 14
ReVISION Learning Supervisory Continuum Domain 1, 14–15, 182, 187, 203
Robinson, Ken, 179
Roosevelt, Theodore, 209
RVL 1.A, 14, 182, 203
RVL 1.B, 14, 182, 203
RVL 1.C, 14, 182, 203
RVL 1.D, 14, 182, 203
RVL 1.E, 14, 182, 203
RVL 1.F, 14, 182, 203
RVL Core Skills, 13, 13f

Safety needs, 54–55
Säljö, Roger, 34–35
Scaffolding, 19f, 47f, 64, 101, 109, 122, 123–124, 128, 150
School culture, 3. *See also* Culture of learning
Selective attention, 58
Self-assessment, 183, 201
Self-belief, 3–6, 4f
Self-efficacy
- belief versus, 7
- causal attribution and, 60, 61
- defined, 4
- feedback and, 186–187
- leading own learning and, 46–47
- overview, 4–6, 4f

Self-evaluation, 44
Self-monitoring, 19f, 37–38, 44–45, 47f, 53, 57, 80, 109, 207
Self-regulation, 36, 37–38, 44–45, 57, 80, 109, 142–143, 207
Sensory memory, 50f
Shanahan, Cynthia, 83–84, 86, 88
Shanahan, Timothy, 83–84, 86, 88
Shared understandings, 22
Sharratt, L., 201
Short-term (working) memory, 50–51f
Silver, Debbie, 42, 45, 60
Six Global Competencies/six Cs, 37, 38, 140
Skills, dispositions, and tools, 19f, 47f, 187, 188–189f
Social-emotional learning, 46
Social persuasion, 4
Social studies, 87–88, 87f
Socrates, 1
SOLO taxonomy, 36–37
Sousa, D., 49
The Speed of Trust (Covey), 191–192, 192f
Standards, planning for evidence collection and, 90–91, 92f
Standards of effective observation and feedback, 14–15, 182
Stanford History Education Group, 88
Stern, J., 38, 42, 43, 63, 143
Stewart, Elizabeth, 95
Stone, D., 189
Strategies
- FF Strategies, 15–18, 16–17f, 70
- mapping strategy, 100–101
- purposes of, 2
- *See also specific strategies*

Strategy 1 (mindful planning), 21–25, 24f, 69. *See also* Planning for evidence collection
Strategy 2 (define learning), 34–35
Strategy 3 (create learning goals), 36–37. *See also* Learning goals
Strategy 4 (understand how learners learn), 48–49
Strategy 5 (understand how teachers create outcomes), 54
Strategy 6 (planning for evidence collection), 73–75, 73f, 75f. *See also* Planning for evidence collection
Strategy 7 (plan evidence collection based on discipline), 84, 156–157, 160, 164, 169
Strategy 8 (purposeful choice of methods), 103

Strategy 9 (conversations through questions), 108–109, 172. *See also* Strategy 13 (relevance and content determination); Strategy 14 (vocabulary understanding determination)
Strategy 10 (high expectations for responses), 109–111, 158
Strategy 11 (timing of arrival), 111–117, 114f, 116f
Strategy 12 (prior learning determinations), 120–124, 160
Strategy 13 (relevance and content determination), 124–128, 125–127f, 144–145, 164
Strategy 14 (vocabulary understanding determination), 128–130, 129–130f
Strategy 15 (adaptation based on what students are doing), 153–158
Strategy 16 (adaptation based on student writing), 159–160
Strategy 17 (adaptation based on tools and resources), 165–172, 166f, 168f
Strategy 18 (adaptation based on student conversations), 172–174
Strategy 19 (adaptation based on teacher-student interactions), 174–176
Stress, 54–55
Struggle, 149–152, 149f
Student achievement, 4, 6
Supports, 63–64
Surface learning, 38–43, 39f

Tao of Coaching (Landsberg), 201
Task expectations, 101–102
Tate, Marcia, 52, 59
Teachers
  as activators and cultivators, 54
  adaptation by, 135
  collective teacher efficacy, 6–7, 61
  as learners, 18–20, 19f
  skills, dispositions, and tools for, 19f
Technology, 169–172
Telling versus explaining, 113
Templates, 71–72
Tenacity, 45–46
Tepper, Amy, 193. *See also Feedback to Feed Forward* (Tepper & Flynn)
Thinking, observation and, 43–44
Time management, 107–111
Tomlinson, C., 49
Tools, skills, and dispositions, 19f, 47f, 187, 188–189f
Tools and resources, 165–172, 166f, 168f
Tools for Teaching Conceptual Understanding (Stern et al.), 38
Tranberg, Chris, 134
Transfer, 38, 39, 40, 42, 49, 54, 86, 90, 125, 140, 152, 154, 170. *See also* Deep learning
Transformative competencies, 36
Transparency, 22–23
Trust, 23, 191–194, 192f
Trust matrix, 192, 192f

Unproductive failure, 150, 151
Unproductive success, 150

Vicarious experiences, 4
Viewing and listening, 103–104f, 103–107
Vocabulary understanding, 83–84, 85f, 128–130, 129–130f

Willingness, 60
Wilson, D., 43, 44, 54, 58, 64, 135
Wilson, J., 45
Wilson, Julie, 197–198, 201
Wolfe, P., 58, 120–124
Working (short-term) memory, 50–51f
Working backwards, 87–88
Worksheets, 162–164, 163f
Worksheets Don't Grow Dendrites (Tate), 52

Zierer, Klaus, 6, 202
Zimmerman, B., 37, 44
Zone of proximal development, 62, 64, 151
Zygouris-Coe, V., 88, 89, 90